Unlocking the Bible Story flows from the pen of a pastor who understands how important it is to encourage God's people to read and discover the power of the Bible. Colin Smith has written a practical tool to facilitate the wonderful adventure of reading and understanding the Bible. **I recommend that every pastor and church consider deepening their Bible knowledge by utilizing this tool** that has produced incredible results in the church Pastor Smith leads.

WILLIAM HAMEL
PRESIDENT, EVANGELICAL FREE CHURCH OF AMERICA

"... touches the deepest concerns of our hearts."

Colin Smith's *Unlocking the Bible Story* is a significant work. In fact, I'm convinced it will make a lasting contribution to God's people regardless of age or ethnicity.

DR. GREGORY L. WAYBRIGHT
PRESIDENT, TRINITY INTERNATIONAL UNIVERSITY

At first glance the Bible appears to many people as a puzzle, with parts that are not easily assembled. Here is **a simplified explanation for understanding and learning to love the Scriptures.** My colleague Colin Smith capably serves up a pleasing and satisfying literary meal that merits thoughtful consumption in our day of biblical starvation.

HOWARD G. HENDRICKS
DISTINGUISHED PROFESSOR
CHAIRMAN, CENTER FOR CHRISTIAN LEADERSHIP
DALLAS THEOLOGICAL SEMINARY

Unlocking the Bible Story explores the mountain peaks of Scripture, helping us trace the Bible's story line from beginning to end. I promise, it does unlock the Bible, showing us the unity of God's revelation. Best of all, it shows that Christ is the central theme, as the biblical narrative moves from one event to another. Excellent for those who want to "get into" the Bible.

ERWIN W. LUTZER
SENIOR PASTOR, MOODY CHURCH

"Excellent for those who want to 'get into' the Bible."

This is a satisfying and insightful overview of Scripture that tells "the old, old story" in a fascinating way. Even seasoned Bible students will find their eyes opened and their hearts warmed as they read it.

WARREN WIERSBE
AUTHOR AND CONFERENCE SPEAKER

Unlocking the Bible Story
Volume 3

Colin S. Smith

Moody Press
Chicago

Library of Congress Cataloging-in-Publication Data

Smith, Colin S., 1958–
Unlocking the Bible Story/by Colin S. Smith
p.cm.
ISBN 0-8024-6543-9
1. Bible—Criticism, interpretation, etc. I. Title.
BS511.3.S65. 2002
221.6—dc21 2001056268

ISBN: 0-8024-6545-5

1 3 5 7 9 10 8 6 4 2

Printed in the United States of America

For Andrew and David,

with the prayer that your lives
will be for the glory of God.

Contents

INTRODUCTION

At last! Two thousand years after God promised to bless the nations of the world through a descendant of Abraham, Jesus Christ was born.

So it is with a sense of anticipation that we open the pages of the New Testament to discover how God will deliver His people from evil and bring us into a relationship with Himself in which we know His presence and His blessing. This volume will take you to the heart of the Bible story.

The four Gospels introduce Jesus, recording His life, teaching, miracles, death, and resurrection. Matthew, Mark, Luke, and John will show us how Jesus offers Himself as the one in whom we may find forgiveness of sins, reconciliation with God, and the power to live a new life.

When a story is reported in many newspapers, we would expect to find considerable repetition of the central facts, and some information that would be unique to one source. That is precisely what we find in the four gospels. They are all drawn from eyewitness accounts of the life of Jesus, and together bear witness to the central facts of His life, death, and resurrection. But each of the Gospels makes a unique contribution to the story.

Think of a picture printed in one color, and then reproduced in two, three, and four colors. With each additional color, there is a new richness in the image. The one-color print would be sufficient to convey the image, but the four-color print brings out its full splendor. In the four gospels God gives us a full-color portrait of His Son, Jesus Christ.

In our journey through Matthew and Mark, I have chosen to focus on some central themes in the teaching of Jesus. We will discover how He fulfills God's promises, calls us to repentance, offers us entrance to heaven, invites us to follow Him, reveals His authority, warns about the dangers of hell, and demonstrates His almighty power.

In our journey through Luke's gospel, we focus on the main events in the life of Jesus: His birth, temptation, transfiguration, crucifixion, resurrection, and ascension into heaven.

In John's gospel we pick up the great promise of the second coming of Jesus and discover why the Gospels were written. But our central focus from the fourth gospel is the awesome mystery of the Trinity, that God is Father, Son, and Holy Spirit. This truth is of central importance to the Christian faith, and I have chosen to focus on Jesus' clearest and most remarkable statements about the Father, the Son, and the Spirit in John chapters 14, 5, and 16.

Coming to the book of Acts, we will discover the significance of Pentecost for us today, and then trace the marvelous story of how the gospel spread from the Jews to the rest of the world.

This third volume takes us through the greatest story ever told, and it is my privilege to invite you on this journey of discovery.

1

Fulfillment

MATTHEW 1

Who is Jesus

and why did

He come?

1 Fulfillment

MATTHEW 1

DISCOVER

God's "To Do list" and how it was done.

LEARN

why Christ cannot be ranked alongside Moses or Mohammed.

WORSHIP

as you see how Jesus answers the questions raised by the Old Testament.

HOW do you organize your day? Do you work to a tight schedule, or do you just take things as they come? At the start of most days, I write a "To Do list." It gives direction and helps with setting priorities. Not that everything on my To Do list gets done! The reality is that a fair amount gets rolled onto the next day. What's really discouraging is when the list is longer at the end of the day than it was at the beginning.

Some things on the To Do list are pretty simple: Make a call, write a letter, or follow through on a decision. Other things are more extensive: Write an essay or prepare a presentation. When the list is complete, it's time to stop planning and start working.

The real joy of a To Do list comes later in the day, when you draw a heavy line through each item and mark it "Done." There's nothing quite like the satisfaction of knowing that everything you planned to do is complete.

God's "To Do List"

In volumes 1 and 2 of *Unlocking the Bible Story*, we discovered God's amazing promises. God told the prophets what He would do. You can think of the prophets as announcing God's "To Do list."

Of course, God's To Do list does not arise from obligations that are laid on Him. Nobody can tell God what to do. God's To Do list arises from commitments that He has made freely and voluntarily. God has promised to do certain things, and because God is always faithful to His word, these things must be done. By the end of the Old Testament story, it's quite a list.

The New Testament opens by reminding us of the people to whom God made His greatest promises. Matthew arranged the genealogy of Jesus in three groups of fourteen generations, beginning with Abraham, David, and the exile, respectively. In this way, he focused readers on three points during the Old Testament genealogy where God's greatest promises were made. Matthew wanted us to know that the coming of Jesus was the fulfillment of all that God had promised to do.

> *A record of the genealogy of Jesus Christ the son of David, the son of Abraham.* (MATTHEW 1:1)

Jesus is introduced as "the son of Abraham." Two thousand years before Jesus was born, God promised that His blessing would flow through Abraham to every nation. "I will bless you . . . and all peoples on earth will be blessed through you" (Genesis 12:2–3).

Abraham wondered how this could be since he had no children. But God stepped in and caused Abraham and Sarah to have a child in their old age. The birth of Isaac was a miracle, but God's blessing did not come to the world through him. So the promise to Abraham remained on God's To Do list.

Jesus is also introduced as "the son of David." God had spoken to David about a descendant who would build a house for God's name. God promised to establish that Son's throne and kingdom forever. Then God added, "I will be his father, and he will be my son" (2 Samuel 7:13–14).

David's son Solomon built a magnificent temple for the glory of God. But Solomon did not fulfill God's promise. His temple was eventually destroyed, and his kingdom certainly did not last forever. So this whole business of building a permanent house and establishing a throne was added to God's To Do list.

Matthew's third focal point in the genealogy is the Exile.

> *There were fourteen generations in all from Abraham to David, fourteen from David to the exile to Babylon, and fourteen from the exile to the Christ.* (V. 17)

Some of God's greatest promises in the Old Testament are associated with the Exile. When His people faced their darkest hour, God promised that He would make a new covenant and give His people a new heart (see Jeremiah 31 and Ezekiel

36). He promised to create a community of people who would live according to His Law, not out of obligation but because of an inner desire. These promises were made about six hundred years before the time of Jesus, and during those centuries they remained on God's To Do list.

Despite all that God had done for His people through the Old Testament story, God's greatest promises were still unfulfilled. God's blessing was still to come to the nations, the kingdom that would never end was still to be established, and the hearts of the people were still to be renewed. By the end of the Old Testament story, there was a long list of things to be done.

GETTING GOD'S TO DO LIST DONE

Matthew then tells us how the birth of Jesus Christ came about (in verses 18 and following). Mary was found to be with child through the Holy Spirit. Joseph did not know what to make of this until one night God spoke to him through a dream. He saw an angel, who told him not to be afraid. He was to call Mary's child Jesus because this child would "save his people from their sins" (v. 21). Then Matthew tells us,

> *All this took place* to fulfill *what the Lord had said through the prophet*. (V. 22, EMPHASIS ADDED)

In other words, when Jesus Christ came into the world, the things God had said He would do were done.

As you read through the Gospels, you find the same point repeated again and again. We are told about how Joseph took Mary and the child to Egypt when Herod was searching for the child with the intent of destroying Him. Matthew explains that this "fulfilled what the Lord had said through the prophet: 'Out of Egypt I called my son'" (Matthew 2:15). It was as if the event had been on God's To Do list, and now it was done.

Then the young family moved to a town called Nazareth. Matthew explains that this "fulfilled what was said through the prophets: 'He will be called a Nazarene'"(v. 23). Done!

At the beginning of His ministry, Jesus moved from Nazareth to Capernaum, which is in the area of Zebulun and Naphtali. Matthew reminds us that this was "to fulfill what was said through the prophet Isaiah" (Matthew 4:14). Done!

"This happened that the Scripture might be fulfilled."

Luke tells us about the first public event in the ministry of Jesus. He came into the synagogue and read from the prophet Isaiah. "The Spirit of the Lord is on me, because he has anointed me to preach good news to the poor. He has sent me to proclaim freedom for the prisoners and recovery of sight for the blind, to release the oppressed, to proclaim the year of the Lord's favor." Then Jesus rolled up the scroll, returned it to the attendant, and took His seat. Everyone in the synagogue stared intently; then Jesus announced, "Today this scripture is *fulfilled* in your hearing" (Luke 4:18–19, 21, emphasis added).

"What God has promised is now being done—by Me!" He had declared. No wonder the people were astonished at His teaching!

The theme of God's promises being fulfilled runs throughout the Gospels. The detail is staggering. Even the enemies of Jesus, who had every interest in showing that He did not fulfill the prophecies of the Old Testament, found themselves playing their part in demonstrating that He did!

When Judas betrayed Jesus, the chief priests gave him thirty pieces of silver, which he used to buy a field. Matthew reminds us that this fulfilled what God had spoken by Jeremiah the prophet (Matthew 27:9).

When Jesus was on the cross, the soldiers took His clothes and divided them between them. But Christ had a seamless robe, and they decided to draw lots and give it to the winner. John wrote that "this happened that the scripture might be fulfilled which said, 'They divided my garments among them and cast lots for my clothing'" (John 19:24).

Later, the soldiers came to break the legs of the three who were being crucified. They did this to hasten the process. They broke the legs of the two thieves who were crucified with Jesus, but when they came to Jesus, they found that He was already dead. So they did not break His legs but instead thrust a spear into His side. Again, John noted that, "These things happened so that the scripture would be fulfilled: 'Not one of his bones will be broken,' and, as another scripture says, 'They will look on the one they have pierced'" (19:36–37).

The Portrait on a Different Wall

This theme of fulfillment is important for those who question whether Jesus really is the Savior God had promised from the beginning of time. Jesus Himself was in no doubt about it. "Do not think that I have come to abolish the Law or the Prophets; I have not come to abolish them but to fulfill them" (Matthew 5:17).

If you want to know who Jesus is, you need to understand that He is altogether different from the Old Testament prophets, or indeed from any other religious leader who has ever lived.

A friend of mine recently attended a seminar on religious education in which he was told that Judaism stops with Moses, Christianity stops with Jesus, and Islam stops with Mohammed. The assumption was that Moses, Jesus, and Mohammed could be compared, as if their portraits belonged together on the same wall.

Many people see Jesus as another great figure in the line of religious history. They see Abraham, Isaac, Jacob, David, Jesus, Paul, and others continuing into contemporary times as belonging to a "class" of great religious teachers. As people view this "gallery," they draw different personal conclusions about who is the greatest.

But Jesus cannot be placed alongside the prophets, or alongside any other religious teacher. The prophets announced God's promises. Every time they spoke, God's To Do list became longer! If Jesus were another prophet, He would be limited to announcing more things that God would one day do. His coming would contribute nothing to getting them done.

Of course, there have always been people who thought of Jesus as one of the prophets (see Matthew 16:14), but Jesus made it clear that we must not understand Him in this way. "I have come to fulfill the prophets," He said. Jesus did not come to make God's To Do list longer. He came so that God's To Do list would be done!

God . . . has fulfilled His promises through Jesus Christ.

Opponents of Christianity like to suggest that it is a new religion invented by a man called Jesus who lived a mere two thousand years ago. But the Bible story goes back to the beginning of time. It tells us what God has said He would do, and it tells us that He has fulfilled His promises through Jesus Christ.

This is the uniqueness of Jesus Christ. The prophets announced God's promises of blessing for all nations, a kingdom that will never end, and a new heart for God's people, but only Jesus Christ was able to fulfill them. His portrait belongs alone on a different wall.

Getting Our To Do List Done

Once we understand the uniqueness of Jesus, we will be able to grasp what He has done more clearly. When Jesus announced what would be accomplished through His ministry, He made it clear that He came to fulfill not only the Prophets but also the Law.

> *"Do not think that I have come to abolish the Law or the Prophets; I have not come to abolish them but to fulfill them. I tell you the truth, until heaven and earth disappear, not the smallest letter, not the least stroke of a pen, will by any means disappear from the Law until everything is accomplished."* (MATTHEW 5:17–18)

If the prophets represent God's To Do list, then the Law—all the commands given to Moses, including the Ten Commandments—represents our To Do list. In the Law, God tells us what He requires us to do. Jesus makes it clear that He did not come to abolish the Law. The Law of God will stand until heaven and earth disappear, and that hasn't happened yet!

So it would be a grave mistake to think that God was concerned about the Law and righteousness in the Old Testament, but that somehow He changed His focus and switched to grace and forgiveness in the New Testament. The whole Bible is one story. God has always been gracious and forgiving, and His Law stands forever.

The Law of God is still our To Do list. But Jesus says that He has come to "fulfill the Law." In other words, He came to move the Law from the To Do list to the Done list. He does this in three ways: in His life, by His death, and through His people.

BRINGING THE LAW TO LIFE

The Law is not an arbitrary set of moral rules but a written description of God's character and glory. As we saw in volume 1 of *Unlocking the Bible Story*, the reason we should not lie is that God is truth. The reason we should not commit adultery is that God is faithful. The reason we should not murder is that life is the gift of God.

The Law tells us what God is like and describes His calling for our lives. Jesus came to live the life that God has put on your To Do list. He lifted the words of God's Law off the page and expressed them fully in His perfect life. That is why Jesus could say, "Anyone who has seen me has seen the Father" (John 14:9).

"The Son is the radiance of God's glory and the exact representation of his being," the Scripture says. This is why Paul wrote that we see "the light of the knowledge of the glory of God in the face of Christ" (Hebrews 1:3; 2 Corinthians 4:6).

In the Law, God told us how we are to live in this world. He said, in essence, "This is your To Do list." Consider the long list of names at the beginning of Matthew's gospel. Not one of them fulfilled the Law of God. But when Jesus came, it was done.

Paying Off Some Old Debts

The Law does more than tell us the kind of life God requires. It also announces the consequences of sin. This is why the Bible talks about the curse of the Law. The soul that sins will die.

Throughout the Old Testament story, God repeatedly postponed this condemnation. When Adam disobeyed in the garden, God was gracious to him, and although he was excluded from Paradise, his life continued. Abraham told lies about his wife, but he remained a friend of God. David committed adultery, and yet he remained on Israel's throne. Isaiah confessed to being a man of unclean lips, but he was still used as a prophet. None of them came under the condemnation of God announced in the Law.

Why? The reason cannot be that their sin didn't matter, because the whole point of the Law is that it does. "The soul who sins will die" (Ezekiel 18:4 NASB). And Christ says that God's Law will stand even when heaven and earth pass away (Matthew 24:35).

The answer is that throughout the Old Testament God held back the condemnation of the Law. He put off the Day of Judgment. He didn't cancel it, but He did postpone it. God said, in effect, "We will deal with that later." He put the whole matter of dealing with the consequences of human sin on His To Do list.

The windows in our shopping malls are regularly filled with advertisements enticing us to buy. Often you will see a poster saying, "Nothing to pay until January of next year." It sounds wonderful—Why, it's virtually free!—and it is, until the letter arrives in January of next year announcing that the time for payment has come. The payment was not canceled; it was only postponed. At some point the bill has to be paid.

Throughout the Old Testament, the sacrifices reminded God's people that there would come a time when something had to be done. But the consequences of sin remained like an accumulating debt that one day would have to be paid.

Then Jesus came. "I have come to fulfill the Law," He said. That meant not only that He would fulfill everything the Law required in His life, but also that He would bear the condemnation of the Law in His death.

This is why He had to go to the cross. God's time for dealing with the consequences of sin had come. On the cross, Jesus bore the consequences of human sin in His own body (see 1 Peter 2:24).

> All that remained "to do" . . . has been accomplished fully . . . by Jesus Christ.

The judgment and condemnation described in God's Law were poured out on Him, and when He had absorbed it fully, He cried out in a loud voice, "It is finished!" At that moment, dealing with sin was struck off God's To Do list because, for all His people, it was done.

Done!

This is why we do not offer sacrifices. The communion service is not a new sacrifice, as if our sin still needed to be dealt with, but a reminder that through the death of Jesus, it is done. This is why we do not need a temple but have direct access to God by the Spirit through faith in Jesus Christ. It's done!

All that remained "to do" throughout the entire period of the Old Testament has been accomplished fully and finally by Jesus Christ. In the words of Jonathan Edwards:

> Though millions of sacrifices had been offered, yet nothing was done to purchase redemption before Christ's incarnation. . . . But as soon as Christ was incarnate, the purchase began. And the whole time of Christ's humiliation, till the morning that he rose from the dead, was taken up in this purchase. Then the purchase was entirely and completely finished. As nothing was done before Christ's incarnation, so nothing was done after his resurrection to purchase redemption for men. Nor will there ever be any thing more done to all eternity.[1]

A New Desire and a New Direction

As we follow the Bible story, we will discover still another way in which Jesus fulfills the Law. The apostle Paul wrote:

> *What the law was powerless to do in that it was weakened by the sinful nature, God did by sending his own Son in the likeness of sinful man to be a sin offering. And so he condemned sin in sinful man, in order that the righteous requirements of the law might be fully met in us, who do not live according to the sinful nature but according to the Spirit.* (Romans 8:3–4)

Jesus came to bring you into a new life in which you will begin to fulfill the Law of God. He died to bring you out of condemnation, and He lives to lead you into a righteous life.

Over the years, I have noticed a pattern in the things that get pushed to the bottom of my To Do lists. They are the things I don't like and the things I feel I can't do. That is exactly our problem when it comes to the Law of God. By nature, we don't like it, and we can't do it, so our first instinct is to leave it on the list of good intentions for another day.

Jesus came to save us from that. He came to make you the person God always intended you to be. He will do that by giving you a hunger and thirst for righteousness and with that new desire, the power of the Holy Spirit so that your life may move in the direction of the Law of God.

When I was fourteen, our family went for a vacation in the town of Torquay in England. The accommodation was poor, the beaches were crowded, and it was one of those vacations that just didn't work out well. I remember traveling home in the backseat of the car. None of us was happy, and at one point I remember saying a very foolish thing. "Dad," I said, "I don't ever want to go to that town again."

My mother pointed out that this was the sort of thing that one might regret saying. She was right. Six years later, I met a girl from that town. I fell in love with her and married her. At the age of twenty, I said to my mother, "I want to go to Torquay." I've enjoyed going there ever since!

When God's Spirit begins to work in your life, you will have a new hunger and a thirst for righteousness. You will begin to own the Law of God as your To Do list. You may be a long way from doing it fully, but you will discover a new desire to grow in it. Jesus said, "Blessed are those who hunger and thirst for righteousness" (Matthew 5:6). They have come to want what God wants for them, and their desire will be satisfied.

Jesus died to save us from the condemnation of the Law. He lives to lead us into new lives in which we fulfill the Law by the power of the Holy Spirit. Christ accepts us as we are, but He never leaves us as we are. It is the purpose of God to make us righteous so that we will reflect His glory in a life that fulfills the Law of God.

If you roll the story of the Bible forward to the end, you learn that on the last day Christ will stand before the Father and say, "Here am I, and the children God has given me" (Hebrews 2:13). We shall not only see Christ, but we will be like Him. The day is coming when God will take you off His To Do list. He will look at you and He will say, "Done!"

UNLOCKED

Jesus cannot be compared to the Old Testament prophets or the prophets of any other religion. The prophets announced what God required and what God would do. Jesus came to fulfill what God requires, and to accomplish what God said He would do. He fulfills both the Law and the Prophets by delivering what God promised through them. All that God had placed on His "To Do list" is done through Jesus Christ.

Christ fulfills the Law in three ways: (1) by living a life that perfectly reflected everything that God requires of us in His Law; (2) by absorbing the condemnation of the Law for our sin through His death on the cross; and (3) by making it possible for us to live a new life in line with the Law of God by the power of the Holy Spirit. He came to demonstrate the Law to us. He died to fulfill the Law for us, and He lives to fulfill the Law in us.

PAUSE FOR PRAYER

Almighty Father,

Thank You for every one of Your promises, and for the knowledge that every one of them will be fulfilled. Thank You for sending Jesus Christ so that in Him everything You promised would be done.

Thank You for the life of Jesus in which all that You are is perfectly expressed. Thank You for the death of Jesus, in which the condemnation of my sin is fully absorbed.

Help me by the power of Your Spirit to grow in the new life that is Your purpose for me. Strengthen my desire to live according to Your Law, and for Your glory, as I look forward to the day when Your work in me will be done, through Jesus Christ. Amen.

Note

1. Jonathan Edwards, *A History of the Work of Redemption*, vol. 1 of *The Works of Jonathan Edwards* (Edinburgh, Scotland: Banner of Truth, 1974), 572.

2

Repentance

MATTHEW 3

What does it

mean to repent?

2 Repentance

MATTHEW 3

DISCOVER
the secret of real and lasting change.

LEARN
why repentance continues throughout the Christian life.

WORSHIP
because Jesus has opened the kingdom of heaven.

ON March 16, 1978, a supertanker called the *Amoco Cadiz* ran aground off the coast of Brittany, France, and lost its entire load of nearly a quarter of a million tons of crude oil into the Atlantic Ocean. Oil was swept onto more than 130 beaches, and some of them were covered with oil up to a foot deep.

The damage was incredible. Over 30,000 seabirds died; 230,000 tons of crabs, lobsters, and other fish perished. That, plus the destruction of rich oyster and seaweed beds, devastated the fishing economies of the local communities.[1]

When a disaster like this happens, there are multiple problems. In the months that followed, there were legal proceedings. There was a price to pay; in this case, a judge in Chicago awarded damages of $85.2 million to the affected French towns. But there was also a problem of pollution on the beaches. A clean-up operation had to be mounted to restore what had been so dreadfully damaged.

The story of the *Amoco Cadiz* can help us to understand the multiple effects of the great disaster of sin and the different dimensions of God's clean-up operation that the Bible calls salvation. Most Christians understand that there is a penalty to pay for sin, and that Jesus paid this for us in His death on the cross. But salvation also involves a clean-up operation to deal with the damage caused by sin in our lives.

Think about the beauty of a line of sandy beaches. Think about crystal clear water supporting the life of fish, plants, and birds. Now picture crude oil pouring from a stricken vessel. That's what sin does. It pollutes and destroys.

When Christ came to save us, He had to pay the penalty for our sins by His death on the cross. But that is not enough—He must also deal with the effects of sin within us. Salvation involves restoring the beauty that has been devastated by sin.

This is where we ended the first chapter. Jesus came to demonstrate the Law to us and to bear the condemnation of the Law for us. But there is a third dimension that is often forgotten: He came so that the Law should be fulfilled in us, and if God's Law is going to be fulfilled in our lives, it's going to mean change. Big change!

TIME FOR A CHANGE

When the angel announced the birth of Jesus, he did not say, "You shall call his name Jesus, because he will *forgive* his people for their sins." He said, "You are to give him the name Jesus, because he will *save* his people from their sins" (Matthew 1:21, emphasis added).

To "save" people from their sins means to bring them out of their sins. It means delivering them from every dimension of this disaster. If Christ delivered us from the condemnation of sin without delivering us from its power in our lives, it would be like paying the fine for the *Amoco Cadiz* but doing nothing to clean up the beaches. That would be ridiculous. Anyone who thinks that salvation is forgiveness without change is completely mistaken. Salvation is much more than forgiveness and a free ticket to heaven. Christ came to make you the person God wants you to be.

One of the greatest errors among Christian people has been to divide the Bible as if we had one book in which God's interest was in issuing commandments and calling people to a holy life, and another alternative book in which God's interest was in issuing free tickets to heaven.

That would be a complete misunderstanding of the Bible. It has always been God's purpose to deliver His people from sin *and* lead us into a holy life. The whole Bible is one story. God's grace is written all over the Old Testament, and His call to a holy life is written all over the New. That call was central to the message of John the Baptist and Jesus.

ECCENTRIC PREACHER DRAWS A CROWD

By any standards John the Baptist must have been an eccentric kind of a preacher. His personal style was rather strange. "John's clothes were made of camel's hair, and he had a leather belt around his waist. His food was locusts and wild honey" (Matthew 3:4).

His choice of avenue was also rather strange. We find him preaching in the desert. I guess that would solve some parking problems on Sunday mornings, but you wouldn't expect to find much of a congregation in such a desolate place!

The remarkable thing is that people came out to hear him. "People went out to him from Jerusalem and all Judea and the whole region of the Jordan" (3:5).

Clearly some kind of spiritual awakening happened during John's ministry, and people were willing to travel to be part of it. They were tired of the placid words they heard from other preachers of the day. They were hungry for truth, and they knew that when they heard John speak, they were hearing the Word of God.

Jesus said that people went into the desert to hear John because he was a prophet (see Matthew 11:7–9). There was a certain courage and integrity in John the Baptist that was powerfully attractive. He was absolutely fearless. He gave the same message to the king as he did to the people in the desert. John told Herod that he had to repent. Herod didn't like the message, and he ordered John imprisoned and later had him beheaded. Jesus commended John as the greatest of the prophets.

John's message was very simple: "Repent, for the kingdom of heaven is near" (3:2). What God has promised since the beginning of time is about to happen. "So you need to change!" John was saying.

When Jesus began to preach, His message was exactly the same, "Repent, for the kingdom of heaven is near" (Matthew 4:17). Peter preached the same message on the Day of Pentecost, "Repent and be baptized, every one of you, in the name of Jesus Christ for the forgiveness of your sins. And you will receive the gift of the Holy Spirit" (Acts 2:38). The apostle Paul also proclaimed the same truth. "I have declared to both Jews and Greeks that they must turn to God in repentance and have faith in our Lord Jesus" (Acts 20:21).

Repentance is fundamental to the gospel. It is the first thing that Jesus Christ says, and if we do not understand this, we will not be able to enter into anything else.

An Open Door of Opportunity

"Repent, for the kingdom of heaven is near." (*Matthew 3:2*)

The message of John and Jesus gives us the most marvelous motivation for repentance. Throughout human history, heaven had been closed to men and women. The cherubim and the flaming sword barred the way into the Garden of Eden, where Adam and Eve had known the blessing and presence of God.

Access to heaven had been cut off for Abraham, Isaac, Jacob, David, and the prophets. God was gracious to them and made great promises to them, but when they died, they joined a long line of people waiting for God's promise to be fulfilled.

Now, at last, God was about to open up access to heaven through the coming of Jesus Christ. In effect, John was saying, "The promise men have longed for throughout history is about to be fulfilled. This is a moment of golden opportunity, and if you want to grasp it, you are going to have to change. Repent, for the kingdom of heaven is near."

Living in a New Kingdom

Notice that John described heaven as a kingdom. A kingdom is a place under the rule of a king. If you want to be in the kingdom of heaven, you have to submit yourself to the rule of the King of heaven.

For thirty-eight years of my life, I was not subject to the laws of the United States of America, for the simple reason that I was living in Great Britain. I was outside the laws of America and I was outside its blessings.

Then, in 1996, I was invited to come to the United States and serve as senior pastor of the Arlington Heights Evangelical Free Church in Illinois. When I came, I was immediately released from an old set of laws I used to be subject to in Great Britain, and I became subject to a whole new set of laws in America.

I have to admit that some of the new laws are difficult for me, like driving at incredibly low speeds on open roads. But I have found from experience that if I am stopped by a police officer, it simply will not do for me to say I am operating under the laws of Her Majesty, the queen! The officer would properly point out that if I want to operate by another set of laws, I had better go back to the place where those laws hold sway.

Many Christians are confused at this point. They have the idea that as long as they believe certain things about Jesus Christ, all is well. That is exactly the error that James addressed when he pointed out that "even the demons believe" in God, and they tremble when they think about Him (James 2:19)!

The blessings of the kingdom of heaven are available to all who will receive them. The borders of heaven have been thrown open. Immigration to this kingdom is open to all who will come from north, south, east, or west. But if you would come to the kingdom where Christ reigns, you must place yourself under His authority, and John was saying, "That means you will have to change. Repent, for the kingdom of heaven is near. You cannot have the benefits of the kingdom if you will not bow to the King."

A Change of Direction

The word *repent* means "change." Repentance is a change of mind that results in a change of behavior.

Jesus illustrated the meaning of repentance through a story He told about a man who had two sons (see Matthew 21:28–32). The father told the first to go and work in the field. The son refused, but later he changed his mind and went. The father also told the second son to go and work in the field. He agreed to go, but then he changed his mind and stayed at home. Both of them repented; they changed their minds and their behavior (though only the first changed for the good).

Jesus explained that this was what was happening when John the Baptist preached. People who had resisted God's commandments changed their minds and did what they had previously refused to do. There was a fundamental change in their response to the commandments of God.

The Power of Confession

It is important to notice that this change did not remain a private matter in the mind of the individual. "Confessing their sins, they were baptized by [John] in the Jordan River" (Matthew 3:6).

This does not mean that the people confessed all of their sins publicly. That would clearly be inappropriate. A good rule is that confession should normally be at the level of the people who are affected by an offense. If I have sinned in my thoughts, I should confess to God alone. If I have sinned in words or actions against one person, I should also confess to him. If my actions have affected many people, then many need to know about my repentance.

These people were moving out of denial, which in some cases had been going on for many years. John's ministry brought them to the place where they were ready to say, "I am a person who needs to be forgiven," and that's where change begins.

Matthew tells us that the Pharisees and Sadducees came to look at what was happening in this spiritual revival, but they did not feel the need to be forgiven or to be baptized. They never discovered repentance, and they went home unchanged.

This must have caused great sadness for John. He warned them about their smugness and complacency. "Do not think you can say to yourselves, 'We have

Abraham as our father'" (v. 9). Relying on your heritage while you refuse to repent is a sure formula for spiritual disaster.

It worries me when people speak about how they have tried to live a good life. Not that I don't think it's true; I am sure it is. It worries me because words like these often come from a mind that has never seen the need for Jesus Christ.

Repentance begins when we get out of the denial that causes us to think of ourselves as fundamentally "OK" and come to the place of saying, "I am a person who needs to be forgiven. I am therefore a person who needs Jesus Christ, and the forgiveness that flows from His cross." It's strange that many people who have been in church for years find that the hardest thing to say.

Here's What You Can Do Now

Repentance goes beyond our thoughts and beyond our words to a change in our behavior. John was clear about this:

> *"Produce fruit in keeping with repentance."* (v. 8)

Fruit is visible, and repentance will show up in a visible change in what you do. Luke gives us some additional information about the response to John's preaching. As the crowd listened to his message, they were clearly moved by what they heard and wanted to know what they should do (Luke 3:10).

They probably thought that he would tell them some things they could change when they got home. But John stunned them with a call to immediate action. The crowd was in the desert. Some of them would be cold and some would be hungry, so John called on the others to share their clothing and food (v. 11). In effect, he said, "Here's what you can do. Some of you over here have two coats. Find someone without a coat and give him one of yours. Others have a large picnic hamper. Find someone who has no food and share your meal with him or her."

This was on-the-spot teaching and discipleship. The whole thing was so alive, so dynamic. Repentance is not an intention to lead a new life in the future; it begins now, as you step out in obedience to God in your immediate situation.

Repentance is also specific. Tax collectors asked John what they should do, and John told them, "Don't collect any more than you are required to." Soldiers asked him what they should do, and he told them, "Don't extort money and don't accuse people falsely—be content with your pay" (vv. 12–14).

The application to specific cases was different, but the principle was the same: Do what you have to do to bring your life into line with the commandments of God. That's repentance. It comes from a change of mind about your response to God, and it works through different patterns of behavior.

DON'T EVER STOP CHANGING

Repentance should never be limited to a onetime event. Many Christians see repentance as an initial act, which is completed at the beginning of the Christian life, a kind of gateway that we pass through and then leave behind. God's call to repent is immediate and specific; but it is also continuing.

Many Christians know that Martin Luther nailed ninety-five theses to the door of the cathedral at Wittenberg, Germany, but not so many know what those theses said. The first of the Ninety-five Theses made that simple point. When Jesus Christ said that we should repent, He called us to an entire lifetime of repentance.

Theologian and Bible expositor James Packer helps us to understand this when he writes, "Repentance means turning from as much as you know of your sin to give as much as you know of yourself to as much as you know of your God. . . . As our knowledge grows at these three points so our practice of repentance has to be enlarged."[2] Grow in the Christian life, and you will see things in yourself that you never saw before. God is gracious and He will show us our sins slowly. If He showed them all at once, we would be devastated.

The Christian life is a journey of discovery. As we come to know more about God, we will discover more about ourselves, and our repentance will become deeper, touching areas that were hidden from us before.

THE MINISTRY OF MATCHMAKING

John's message led people to the point where they saw the need for change and had a desire for it. But he could not give them the power they needed to follow through. When John was faced with an audience of people who knew that they needed to change, he told them that they should go to Christ.

> *"I baptize you with water for repentance. But after me will come one who is more powerful than I, whose sandals I am not fit to carry."* (v. 11)

John was a great leader because he knew the limitations of his own ministry. "I can baptize you with water. I can help you express your desire to live a new and different life," he was saying. "I can counsel you, I can encourage you, but I cannot give you the power to change. What I can tell you is that someone is coming after me, and He will give you that power."

When Jesus began to preach, John identified Him as "the Lamb of God, who takes away the sin of the world" (John 1:29). And of course, when he did that, those who had been following John left him and became followers of Jesus, which is exactly what he wanted them to do. So this great preacher ended up with no personal following, but his ministry was the means of many coming to Christ. John did what God had called him to do, and then he cleared the stage. He did not draw people to himself; he told them to go to Jesus.

My wife, Karen, and I have friends in England who have been happily married for twenty years and have three delightful children. They represent our one successful attempt at matchmaking. I was speaking at a youth leader's conference, and we persuaded the two of them to join us for the weekend.

She had an eye on him but he, lacking confidence, found that hard to believe. So we seized this ministry opportunity. She was saying to Karen, "I really like him, but I don't think he is interested." He said to me, "I really like her, but I don't think I have a chance."

"Ask her for a date," I said confidently. "Tell her what you feel. I can tell you on good authority that if you do, you will get a good response."

Finally it happened. I have no idea what he said to her, but it obviously met with an enthusiastic response. Frankly the precise words he used didn't actually matter all that much. The important thing was that he made it clear he wanted her in his life, and that was exactly what she felt about him.

I can tell you . . . Christ will welcome you.

After that, we faded from the picture. That's the ministry of John the Baptist. He knew that the only way to a new life was to go personally and directly to Christ and ask Him for it.

I've spoken to people who are rather like my friend when it comes to approaching Christ. They say that they wouldn't know what to say in a prayer.

The precise words that you use are not important. There is no formula. Tell Him you are a sinner. Tell Him what your sins are. Tell Him you need to be forgiven. Tell Him that you need His power if you are to change. Pursue Him as you would pursue a lover.

I can tell you on good authority that Christ will welcome you. He promised, "Whoever comes to me I will never drive away" (John 6:37; see also Matthew 11:28). He also said, "Ask and it will be given to you; seek and you will find; knock and the door will be opened to you" (Matthew 7:7). God will meet with you.

Talking to a pastor, counselor, or Christian friend can be helpful, but it can never be a substitute. They may encourage you, they may answer your questions, they may even tell you what will happen if you go to Christ, but at the end of the day you have to make that move, and nobody else can do it for you.

Drenched in the Life of God

John the Baptist told the people what would happen if they came to Christ.

> *"He will baptize you with the Holy Spirit."* (v. 11)

The word *baptize* means to dip, plunge, or immerse. The Holy Spirit is, of course, the Spirit of God, so when John said, "He will baptize you with the Holy Spirit," he was saying that Jesus will drench you in the life of God.

This baptism [is] like fire. . . . It purifies and it destroys.

If you go to Christ, there will be a divine invasion of your life. The Holy Spirit of God will take up residence in you. He will be poured out in you. Like water saturating, there is no place that He will not go.

John also described this baptism as being like fire. Fire does two things. It purifies and it destroys. Our God is a consuming fire, and when Jesus pours out the Spirit, the rubbish in our lives gets burned up.

Try to picture John and Jesus standing some distance apart with their followers around them. John baptizes with water. Jesus baptizes with the Holy Spirit. John is able to help people express their desire for a new life. Jesus gives them the power to live a new life. John cannot give the Spirit. Jesus can.

Now read the following testimony. It's the sort of thing one hears in church quite often. Read carefully, and ask yourself whether there is anything in what this person says to indicate that he or she has received what Christ offers:

"I was brought up in a Christian family and attended church since I was very young. When I was about sixteen years old, some of my friends were going to a Christian camp and I decided to go along and see what was happening.

"As I listened to the speaker—he was great—I began to realize that there was a lot wrong with my life. I really wanted to change, so I prayed a prayer of commitment to God. Since then things have been different. It hasn't always been easy, but today I am being baptized to show that I want to live a life that is pleasing to God and then to be with Him in heaven."

There is nothing distinctively Christian about that testimony. This person has said nothing about Christ and nothing about the Holy Spirit.

This person is in exactly the same position as those who gathered around John.

"Brought up in a Christian family" (religious background).

"Went to camp and heard a great speaker" (sounds rather like hearing John in the desert).

"Began to realize there was a lot wrong with my life and wanted to change" (just like John's audience).

"Today I'm being baptized to show that I want to live a life that is pleasing to God." (That's what the people who were baptized by John would have said.)

This person is standing with John. He or she hasn't experienced anything more than John has to offer. He is confessing that he needs to change and wants to change, but nothing more.

There are many people like this in churches today. They have a religious background and have made some kind of commitment, but they have never sensed their great need of Christ and never come to Him. As a result, they have never experienced the life of God invading their soul. They think they have what the Bible offers, but they have missed its heart. They are living in the world of the Old Testament, and Jesus came to deliver us from that. John would say to them, "Go to Christ, and He will baptize you with the Holy Spirit."

UNLOCKED

Repentance is a change of mind that results in a change of behavior. It is motivated by the fact that God has opened up the borders of heaven and extended an open invitation to all who would like to live under His blessing and rule. Heaven is a kingdom, so entering it means becoming subject to the laws of the King.

God's Spirit is able to break the power of sin in our lives and lead us in a new direction that is pleasing to God. God gives us His Spirit when we come to Jesus Christ in repentance and faith.

PAUSE FOR PRAYER

Gracious Father,

My great desire is to live under Your authority as a citizen of Your kingdom.

Help me by the power of Your Spirit to grow in that new life. Show me hidden sins that I had not seen before. Deliver me from the blindness that keeps me from seeing the truth about myself. Show me more of Your glory so that I may worship You more fully, through Jesus Christ my Lord. Amen.

Notes

1. "Historic Environmental Events: *Amoco Cadiz* Oil Spill Disaster," on the Internet at www.lexisnexis.com/academic/3cis/cist/eanet/history.htm. Accessed on 10 May 2002.
2. J. I. Packer, *Keep in Step with the Spirit* (Old Tappan, N.J.: Revell, 1984), 104.

3

Kingdom

MATTHEW 13

If Christ's kingdom has come, why is there so much evil in the world?

3 Kingdom

MATTHEW 13

DISCOVER

the mystery of God's kingdom.

LEARN

the secret of patience in serving Christ.

WORSHIP

because the full value of what God has done for you in Christ has not yet been revealed.

IT'S time to pause and ask some honest questions. That's what John the Baptist did when things didn't make sense.

Remember, John had announced that the kingdom of heaven was at hand. He had told his audience that Christ would baptize with the Holy Spirit and fire. He had the highest expectations as he anticipated the coming of Jesus; and when Jesus began His ministry, John identified Him as "the Lamb of God, who takes away the sin of the world."

John must have wondered what would happen next. No doubt he lay on his bed at night thinking about the privilege of actually being alive at the very time when all that God had promised was about to be fulfilled. No doubt many of the promises ran through his mind, promises such as men will turn "their swords into plowshares and their spears into pruning hooks," and they will not "train for war anymore. . . . Sorrow and sighing will flee away. . . .The earth will be filled with the knowledge of the glory of the LORD, as the waters cover the sea" (Isaiah 2:4; 51:11; Habakkuk 2:14). John must have wondered what the morning would bring.

FAITH HAS ITS QUESTIONS

But then something happened that must have shaken John to the core. He was arrested and thrown into prison, and when that happened, the man who had preached with such great faith found himself surrounded with doubts and questions.

If Jesus really is the Christ, then why is this happening to me? As John languished in jail, he began to wonder if he had gotten it all wrong.

So he sent messengers to Jesus with this question: "Are you the one who was to come, or should we expect someone else?" (Matthew 11:3).

You can see the point of his question. If God was fulfilling His promise through the coming of Jesus, then He was doing it in a pretty strange way.

We have similar questions today. If God's promises are true, what are we to make of the war, violence, corruption, and greed that are rife in the world? As we look at the church, what are we to make of the compromise, sin, confusion, and complacency that are so prevalent? When I look at my own life, how am I to make sense of the ongoing battle with indwelling sin and the struggle to live a godly life?

If God is doing everything that He promised through the coming of Jesus, then He seems to be doing it in a pretty strange way. There is a mystery to this kingdom.

We need to understand this mystery or we will drown in confusion, discouragement, and even despair. And we can understand it, for Jesus Himself declared, "To you it has been granted to know the mysteries of the kingdom of heaven" (Matthew 13:11 NASB).

The Parable of the Sower ... and the Bomber

He told them many things in parables, saying: "A farmer went out to sow his seed." (Matthew 13:3)

Jesus told a story about a farmer who tossed seed on different kinds of ground. The story is so familiar that we may be in danger of missing the point. So here's my alternative parable that may help us to see the power of Jesus' story more clearly. It's called the parable of the bomber.

> A certain bomber went out to drop his bombs. He flew over an evil city with many kinds of buildings. Some of the buildings were of wooden construction, so when the bombs hit them they were immediately flattened. Other buildings were built from concrete reinforced by steel. They looked as if nothing would move them, but when the bombs hit them, they crumbled like powder too. In fact, everywhere the bombs were scattered the buildings were completely destroyed.

> After the bomber had finished his work, he flew over the city to take photographs. No matter where the bombs fell, the effect was exactly the same. Bomb craters covered the ground like bubble wrap. Rubble was strewn everywhere. Enemy activity was reduced to zero. The bomber's mission was accomplished.
>
> Afterward, the disciples asked, "What is the meaning of the parable of the bomber?"
>
> And He said to them, "The bombs are the ministry of the Word of God. The buildings are the evils of the world, the flesh, and the devil. Some evils are deeply entrenched, and strongly reinforced. But wherever the Word of God comes, evil is reduced to nothing!"

I sometimes wish that Jesus had given us the parable of the bomber. But He didn't! He gave the parable of the sower, because God works by sowing seeds, not by dropping bombs.

Christ is telling us that the will of God gets done in people's lives not by earth-shattering explosions but by the quiet teaching of the Word of God. It will be like a gardener sowing seed. The seed will not grow everywhere, but where it is received, it will produce an abundant harvest.

THE POWER OF PATIENCE

I have to admit that there are times when I find this frustrating. I wish that we could send a team of missionaries to an unreached people group and know for sure that when the Word was preached, the culture would be transformed, the darkness dispelled, the corruption ended, and faith in Christ born so that the whole community would become worshipers of Jesus. But God works by sowing seeds, not by dropping bombs.

When I think about America, I wish we could see our culture transformed. I wish that abortion was unneeded and unwanted now. I wish that divorce would end and families would be happy and secure. I wish that we would be delivered from the postmodern delusion that truth is whatever an individual happens to think. I wish that we would all know the living and true God and fall before Him in worship. But God works by sowing seeds, not by dropping bombs.

The problem with sowing seed is that it takes patience. It's not a very spectacular work, and things don't look very different when you are finished sowing than they did when you started. It's just the same old plowed field. The bomber can look at the immediate effects of his work, but the sower can't.

If you teach Sunday school for an hour on Sunday morning, or pray with your children at home, or share an encouragement with a neighbor, you will sometimes wonder if your work makes any difference. Remember that you are sowing seed.

Jesus made it clear that a great deal of the seed is unproductive. Some fall on the path or among thorns or in rocky places and nothing of lasting value comes from it. But the Word of God is living seed. It has life in it! And where that Word takes root, there will be a harvest. So keep sowing God's truth.

HARVEST IS COMING

As John languished in prison, he must have wondered why God was not bringing in the harvest. No doubt he was thinking about that winnowing fork that would separate the wheat from the chaff (see Matthew 3:12), and hoped that Christ would wield it soon and separate John from Herod!

That day of justice will come, but before God harvests His field, it has to be sown. Jesus makes it clear to the disciples that this is their ministry. When the seed is grown, God will announce the harvest, and then Christ will separate the wheat from the chaff, gathering the one into His barns and casting the other into the fire.

So be encouraged! Keep receiving the Word with faith and obedience. Keep believing His Word and hiding it in your heart. Keep asking Him to give you strength to do what He says. You will change and you will grow.

There may be times when you feel discouraged in ministry and feel like giving up. You dreamed of making an impact, but the work has been tougher and the progress has been slower than you thought. Keep sowing the Word. Keep watering it with your prayers. Keep putting it out there, and God will bring a harvest.

Recently, I spoke with a friend in England. She has been praying for her son who has been rebelling against the Lord for fifteen years. I have prayed for the lad many times, and so I was interested to know what was happening. "How is it with your son?" I asked.

God has called us to plant seeds, not to drop bombs.

She told me that they had talked the previous week, and he had said, "Just give me time." Time! This is after fifteen years! I could feel my own frustration and disappointment rising. But then his mother said, "I'm just continuing to trust in God and look for what He will do."

Here was a woman who understood what it means to sow seeds, and not to drop bombs. That's what ministry is like in this world.

I have found this truth liberating. I cannot change the world; only God can do that. God has called us to plant seeds, not to drop bombs. Sowing takes humility and faithfulness, but it is something that with His help we can do. When we look at the great tides of opposition to the gospel in our own culture and other cultures, we may often feel overwhelmed. That's why it is important to grasp that God has called us to plant the living seed of God's Word, knowing that God will make it grow.

SABOTAGE IN THE FIELD

> *"The kingdom of heaven is like a man who sowed good seed in his field. But while everyone was sleeping, his enemy came and sowed weeds among the wheat, and went away."* *(MATTHEW 13:24–25)*

Jesus told a second story to help us understand the mystery of the kingdom. In this story, the seed that is sown is people, and the field is the world (v. 38). Jesus is telling us that God plants His people in the world.

But Christ speaks about another sower who comes into the field at night. He is an enemy who wants to sabotage the work of the gardener, so he sows weeds in the gardener's field.

The following morning nobody knows what has happened. In fact, for a long time it is difficult to distinguish the wheat from the weeds. But when the wheat sprouts, and the heads form, it becomes obvious that an enemy has been at work in the field. At this point, the gardener's servants want to pull out the weeds. But the gardener refuses. "Let both grow together until the harvest" (v. 30). Then the whole field will be cut down, and the wheat will be separated from the weeds.

If you are going to grasp the mystery of the kingdom, you need to know that there are two sowers, and they are sowing different kinds of seed. God is sowing His people in the world and bringing a great harvest, but the Enemy is also at work, sowing his weeds; and Jesus is saying, "Let both grow together until the harvest."

We live in the tension of a world where two kinds of seed are growing. The work of two sowers is in evidence. Christ has come, and God is doing what He promised. But the Enemy is still at work, and his weeds are also growing. God has determined that this is how it will be until the harvest.

Even the weeds play their part in God's purpose.

Have you ever wondered why God does not pull up the weeds now? Sometimes we wish that He would and wonder why He does not. After all, God is able to stop the work of the Enemy and to bring his weed-sowing activity to nothing, so why does He not do that now?

Jesus' parable reminds us that even the weeds play their part in God's purpose. How can you love your enemies if there are no enemies to love? How can we reconcile our differences if there are no differences to reconcile? How can we overcome our fears if there are no fears to overcome? How can we know the comfort of God if we have never shed tears?

The greatest battles of our lives are the struggles in which Christ makes us the people He wants us to be. Christ tolerates the world, the flesh, and the devil because they are useful to Him. They are the anvils on which kingdom character is painfully hammered out within us. They are the heat in which gold is refined, the obstacles on which we climb, the pressure in which we demonstrate that we truly love Christ.

BURIED TREASURE

> *"The kingdom of heaven is like treasure hidden in a field. When a man found it, he hid it again, and then in his joy went and sold all he had and bought that field. Again, the kingdom of heaven is like a merchant looking for fine pearls. When he found one of great value, he went away and sold everything he had and bought it."* (vv. 44–46)

Jesus used a third picture to help us understand the mystery of the kingdom. What God is doing is like treasure buried in a field. That is very different from treasure on display. God's kingdom is not like the crown jewels on display in London for everybody to come in and admire. His kingdom is like treasure that is hidden in a field, and that means that many people pass it by without ever knowing they are missing something of infinite value.

Jesus spoke about a man who finds this treasure. Perhaps he is hired to plow the field, and suddenly his plow hits something hard. He almost falls over it, so he gets down and digs around in the dirt wondering what it is. Then he realizes that he has just stumbled on buried treasure.

What should he do? Jesus said that he will cover it up and then sell everything he has to buy the field. Notice Christ said the man will do it with joy.

People who sell all that they have usually do so because they are bankrupt. It is the most miserable thing. So folks in the market must have wondered why this man, who was selling everything, wore a grin from ear to ear! He couldn't stop smiling, because he knew that he had stumbled on the opportunity of a lifetime.

Of course, the marvelous thing was that even after he had signed the papers to buy the field, he still did not know the full value of what he had found. But he knew it was worth more than anything and everything else in his life.

The priceless treasure of Christ's kingdom is ours, but the day is still to come when it will be dug up and each piece laid down and its true value fully known. Right now, the full glory of what we have in Jesus Christ is hidden from view. But when He comes again, the treasure chest will be opened, and we will gasp as we see for the first time the full value of what He has done for us.

The parable of the buried treasure reminds us that although God's kingdom has already come, there is also a sense in which it is still future. That creates a tension, and understanding that tension is one of the most important keys to the Christian life.

Tension and Balance

The tension runs through many of Jesus' statements about the kingdom. When He cast out demons, Christ announced this as evidence that "the kingdom of God has come upon you" (Matthew 12:28), but at the Last Supper He spoke about how He would not drink of the cup again until He drank it in the kingdom of God.

Luke explained that Jesus told the parable of the talents because people thought that the kingdom of God was going to appear at once (Luke 19:11). Jesus' story made it clear that there would be a long interval between the time when the master gave talents to his servants and the time when he would give them their reward.

God's kingdom is both a present reality through the coming of Jesus and a future hope that awaits His return. It *has* come, but we are to pray that it *will* come.

So we live in this tension of knowing God and yet struggling with many mysteries: of growing in holiness and yet battling with sin; of praying for healing and yet living with suffering; of rejoicing in the growth of the church and yet weeping over its shortcomings; of being thankful for God's grace in the world and yet longing for the day when Christ shall come and sin will be no more.

Many of the questions we struggle with boil down to the difficulties of living with this tension. Why did God not heal my friend's cancer? How could that scandal have happened in the church? Why is it so difficult to live the Christian life?

These questions are all asking how we can believe that God's kingdom has come when our world is so troubled, and that was precisely the question John the Baptist was struggling with when he sent messengers to Jesus. John needed to know if he had been right in identifying Jesus as the Christ. If God's kingdom had come, why was he in prison?

God's kingdom has come, and it is advancing.

Jesus sent messengers back to John with this message: "Go back and report to John what you hear and see: The blind receive sight, the lame walk, those who have leprosy are cured, the deaf hear, the dead are raised, and the good news is preached to the poor. Blessed is the man who does not fall away on account of me" (Matthew 11:4–6).

Jesus was saying, "God is at work, John. Sure, the weeds are still growing, but don't let that cause you to stumble. God hasn't pulled up that old weed Herod yet, but don't lose faith because of that. The weeds will grow with the wheat until the harvest. Then Christ will burn the weeds, and gather the wheat into His barns." That is the way that God has chosen to build His kingdom, and Jesus said, "Blessed is the man who does not fall away on account of me."

It's not easy to live in the tension between what God has done and what He will do when Christ returns. This is where many people stumble. What we have in Jesus Christ now is more valuable than any of us can fully grasp, but it is only a foretaste of what is to come.

When Christ returns in glory, sin will be no more; sickness will be gone, and the church will be everything Christ calls her to be. Until that time, God calls us to sow the seed of His truth, knowing that He will make it grow even in a field where the enemy is planting many weeds.

God's kingdom has come, and it is advancing. Those who belong to Christ will face many difficult circumstances, and live with many unanswered questions, but belonging to this kingdom is like owning a field with buried treasure, and one day we will discover its full value.

UNLOCKED

God has chosen to grow His kingdom slowly by planting the living seed of His Word in the lives of people. He calls us to sow that seed patiently and persistently and promises that although it will not grow everywhere, there will be an abundant harvest.

Christ reminds us that an enemy is also at work, planting weeds in God's field. God has chosen to allow the weeds to remain until Christ returns. We live with the tension of knowing that God's kingdom has come, and yet we are waiting and longing for its coming.

What we have now is only a foretaste of what is to come. Like a man who has come into possession of buried treasure, we are truly rich in Christ, but only when Christ returns will we discover the full value of our treasure.

PAUSE FOR PRAYER

Gracious Father,

Help me to see where You are at work in my life, in the church, and in the world, and to rejoice in all that I see You doing. Help me to be patient, as I groan over the effects of sin, disease, and evil and long for Your coming. Make me faithful in sowing the seed of Your Word, and keep my eyes focused on the day that is coming when Christ will come, and faith will be turned to sight, and sin will be no more.

Help me to grow where You have planted me, and to live for Your glory. Through Jesus Christ my Lord I pray. Amen.

4

Disciples

MATTHEW 28

How can we

make disciples?

4 Disciples

MATTHEW 28

DISCOVER

why the first disciples immediately followed Jesus.

LEARN

why the world hates Christ and His followers.

WORSHIP

as you see the glory of Jesus.

THROUGHOUT the church there is a new interest in discipleship. Many are tired of shallow decisions to "believe in Jesus" that do not bear fruit in lives that are significantly different from the world. There is a new awareness that Christ did not call us to log decisions but to make disciples.

It is all too easy to slip into an unbalanced and unbiblical presentation of the gospel that makes it sound like a low-cost insurance policy providing protection against eternal disasters for the one low price of believing in Jesus: "All you have to do is say the prayer, raise your hand, sign on the dotted line, and heaven is yours."

The gospel has too often been reduced to something like the "Get out of jail free" card in a game of Monopoly. In this version of Monopoly, the player receives a "Get out of hell free" card if he lands on the "church" square and follows the instructions. The result is seen in "Christians" who are little different from the world, show no obvious submission to the King, and are *dangerously* certain about everlasting life.

Jesus undermines such complacent confidence. The first word of His preaching was "Repent" (Matthew 4:17), and He didn't mean "Say sorry." He meant "Turn around and move in a different direction."

In the Sermon on the Mount, He said, "Not everyone who says to me, 'Lord, Lord,' will enter the kingdom of heaven, but only he who does the will of my Father who is in heaven" (Matthew 7:21). Then He spoke about seed that falls into the shallow soil and springs up quickly but then, when the pressure comes, withers away; and seed that falls among thorns and is quickly choked by worry or wealth (Matthew 13:20–22).

True faith is like a tree laden with the fruit of obedience. That's why Paul wrote about the obedience that comes from faith (Romans 1:5). Faith is the means by which our lives are joined to Christ so that His life begins to flow into us and through us so that we will bear fruit. Where there is no fruit of obedience, there is no spiritual life.

When we listen to the Gospels seriously, it is clear that Jesus is calling people to a different kind of life. The first call of the gospel is not to believe in Jesus, but to follow Him. If we settle for something less than this, we miss authentic Christianity. So we must discover what it means to be a disciple.

Walking the Wards

The word *disciple* was in common use at the time of Jesus. It literally meant "to go somewhere with someone."[1] Disciples were rather like junior doctors following a consultant on his rounds through a hospital. The way young doctors learn is by observing and then by participating in what the consultant is doing. They walk the wards of the hospital.

When Jesus called the first disciples, He said, "Come, follow me" (Matthew 4:19). He was inviting them to a personal loyalty in which their lives would be bound up with His. When Christ appointed the Twelve, His first priority was that "they might be with him" (Mark 3:14). A disciple of Jesus is first and foremost a person marked by a distinctive loyalty to Christ. He or she is one of Christ's people. But why should we follow Jesus?

The Secretary on the Second Floor

Imagine that you are a secretary working on the second floor of a large multinational corporation in the city. You have a pile of work beside you, and you are rushing to meet several deadlines.

As you are hacking away on your keyboard, a stranger walks into the office. You have never seen him before. He wanders around the desks like he owns the place, and your colleagues are getting a bit annoyed.

Then he arrives at your desk. He stops, waiting for you to look up from your screen, and when you do, he says, "Follow me."

I want to suggest to you that there is not the slightest likelihood that you are going to get up, leave your computer, and follow him. In fact, your most likely reaction is going to be to call security. You are going to say, "Excuse me, but who do you think you are?"

But let's rerun that scene, with one additional piece of information. The stranger walks into the office. You have never seen him before. But as he enters, the receptionist scribbles a note on a piece of paper, which is quickly passed from one secretary to another and eventually comes to you. The note says, "It's the CEO!" He has never visited the second floor before; in fact this is the first time he has ever been in the building. It is, after all, a multinational company. But the receptionist is quite sure it's him, and nobody doubts that she is telling the truth.

It doesn't bother you now that he walks around like he owns the place because, of course, you know that he does! And when he stops at your desk and says, "Follow me," you get up and you leave your computer because you recognize his authority and you know that whatever he wants you to do is a higher priority than anything you were doing before.

The Compelling Christ

It must have been something like that with the first disciples. John the Baptist had identified Jesus as the Lamb of God who takes away the sin of the world, and when Christ came to the first disciples, they recognized His authority. There was something about Him that they found irresistibly compelling, and when He said, "Follow me," they followed Him.

John gives us the key to discipleship at the beginning of his gospel, when he writes, "We have seen his glory, the glory of the One and Only, who came from the Father, full of grace and truth" (John 1:14).

They followed Jesus because they saw His glory. Of course, they did not know or understand everything about Him at the beginning, but John (like the receptionist) had identified Him, and the first disciples knew enough to see that if they did not follow Christ they would miss the greatest opportunity of their lives.

As they followed, they saw more and more of His glory. He stilled the storm, healed the sick, cast out demons, fed five thousand people, and raised the dead. The strange thing was that other people saw Jesus do the same things, but they never saw His glory. All they saw was a remarkable man whose works could be included in a book about the unexplained.

When Christ was born, wise men and shepherds saw His glory, but the innkeeper, whose home was the venue of the greatest event in the history of the human race, only saw one more child born into an overcrowded world.

There was an occasion when Jesus invited a young man to follow Him (Matthew 19:16–22). He didn't do it. The immediate problem was that he had money and did not want to leave it behind, but the deeper problem was that he never saw the glory of Christ. He was given an opportunity to walk with the Son of God, something millions who have lived since would have given anything and everything to experience, but he did not see the glory of Jesus, and his life went on exactly as it had before.

The same thing happens in churches every Sunday. Crowds gather for worship, and some see His glory. Others hear the same music, read the same Scripture, and hear the same sermon but return home with nothing more than a religious duty fulfilled.

The Bible tells us the reason for this: "The god of this age [the devil] has blinded the minds of unbelievers, so that they cannot see the light of the gospel of the glory of Christ" (2 Corinthians 4:4). Satan keeps people from seeing the glory of Jesus. He must have his work cut out to obscure such a radiant light, but this is what he is up to.

To use our analogy from the office, he will be quite happy if the staff on the second floor believe that there is a CEO, just so long as they never meet him or follow him.

More than a Million Dollars

From time to time I have the opportunity of talking with people who tell me that they feel frustrated with their spiritual life. The conversation often goes something like this:

"So tell me: What's the problem?"

"Well, my spiritual life feels dead and dry; it doesn't seem to be going anywhere. Other people seem to be getting something out of it, but that doesn't seem to be happening for me."

"Talk to me a little about Christ."

"What do you mean?"

"Tell me what He means to you. Tell me what He has done for you."

"Well, I know all that stuff about He died on the cross . . ."

"Hold on a minute. You just rushed over the most amazing thing in the world like it was as common as tea! Suppose that you had a grandfather who died and left you a million dollars. If I asked you to tell me about him, you would sit forward in your seat and say, 'Oh, he was a great man!' You would tell me about what he did, and how he made his fortune, and then you would say with a smile, 'And of course when he died, he left me a million dollars. What he did has changed my life—his gift paid off the mortgage, enabled me to start my own business, and secured my retirement. Everything that I am enjoying today flows from what he did for me.'"

Keep this in mind: A million dollars is nothing compared with what Jesus Christ has done for you. He has paid your debt, given you a new purpose, and secured your future for eternity!

Jesus died not just for sin in general but for your sin in particular.

He took the guilt of your sin. He dealt with the charges against your name. Picture your sins as being written on pieces of paper and stuffed into a file that is marked with your name. God has taken all the charges against you and refiled them under "Christ." On the cross, Jesus died not just for sin in general but for your sin in particular. There was a long list of offenses against us, and He "took it away, nailing it to the cross" (Colossians 2:14).

When I came to Christ, God emptied all the damning records in my file into the file marked with the name of Christ. On the last day, when God opens the file of my offenses, it will be empty, not because there have been no offenses, but because the records have been removed.

The God who gave the Law on Mount Sinai took human flesh and was born under the Law. The One who said that it would take a sacrifice of blood for there to be peace with God took flesh and shed His own blood. Then on the third day He rose again and ascended into heaven. Now He invites you to follow Him. When you do, He will pour out the Holy Spirit into your soul so that the life of God will be within you, giving new life, direction, and power in your inner being.

Do you see the glory of this?

"Show Me Your Glory"

One day, Jesus asked His disciples, "Who do you say I am?" Peter answered, "You are the Christ, the Son of the living God." Then Jesus said something very significant: "Blessed are you, Simon son of Jonah, for this was not revealed to you by man, but by my Father in heaven" (Matthew 16:15–17).

This was not something that Peter had worked out for himself. Of course he had thought about the claims of Jesus and the miracles he had seen, but Jesus made it clear that there was something beyond the process of reason and deduction going on. God had opened Peter's eyes. The Father had given him the ability to see Jesus' glory.

Spiritual sight is the gift of God. If you don't have it, ask Him for it. Many people have never seen His glory, including some who attend church. For them, learning the Bible is like learning the history of the French Revolution at school. (I didn't enjoy that!) Prayer seems like leaving voice mail on a disconnected line. (I'm not sure that is possible, but you know what I mean.) The result is that obedience seems like a joyless chore to be postponed if at all possible.

If that's where you are, tell Him that you don't see and ask Him to open your eyes. Pray that you will see the glory of Jesus. That's what Moses did at a crisis point in his life. He knew that he could not go on without knowing the presence of God with him, and he prayed, "Show me your glory" (Exodus 33:18). Moses felt, "I can't move forward unless You do that." And God did.

Don't rest until God opens the eyes of your heart, and gives you some glimpse of the glory of His Son. When you see His glory, you will want to follow Him.

How to Make Disciples

"Go and make disciples of all nations." (*Matthew 28:19*)

I have read many books on discipleship and discovered many valuable things. Books on discipleship often emphasize the importance of small groups, spiritual disciplines, and accountability. I have no doubt that all these things are important. But behind and above them all is this whole matter of seeing the glory of Christ. You can be in a small group, practice spiritual disciplines, and be held accountable and still never see His glory.

If the church is *to make disciples, our first priority must be to declare the glory of Jesus.* It is not enough for us to promote a general faith in God or to announce a biblical set of moral values. The specific task of the church is to proclaim the Lord Jesus Christ in such a way that by the power of the Spirit there will be a community of people who are captivated by Him. That's where discipleship begins.

OUR MODEL OF MINISTRY

When Jesus called the first disciples, He said, "I will make you fishers of men" (Matthew 4:19). He was saying, "Place your life in My hands, and I will make something of it—something of eternal value." I'm glad it's in that order. Some people have the idea that they have to make something of their lives before they offer themselves to Jesus, but Christ accepts us as we are and promises to make something of us.

Disciples are active participants in the ministry of Jesus. We are "God's fellow workers" (2 Corinthians 6:1). I love the way Christ uses an analogy from their world of fishing and gives it a whole new dimension; they will be "fishers of men." He will take what you can do and use it in a whole new way in His kingdom.

Jesus trained the first disciples in ministry rather like a kindergarten teacher might show a young child how to write. The teacher draws beautiful vowels that sit like plump fruit on the line. The child watches the way in which these letters are formed and then copies them on the lines below.

That's exactly what you find Jesus did with the disciples. He showed compassion to people who were lost like sheep without a shepherd; He calls each of us to follow His example. As His Spirit flows into you, you will begin to feel compassion for a lost world. You will break free from the insularity of the world around you and begin to feel the heart of God for lost people.

Men and women who have followed Christ have changed the world.

When Jesus met a woman many people were ready to condemn, He reached out to her in love and showed her a whole new way of life. He calls us to follow Him, and when His Spirit flows into us, we will learn to show the same kind of grace.

On the other hand, when Jesus spoke with a young man who wanted to add eternal security to his self-centered lifestyle, Christ refused to compromise the challenge of the message. And when His Spirit is in us, we will find the courage to follow Him. We will not shape the message to suit the felt needs of the individual.

Men and women who have followed Christ have changed the world. Some disciples of Jesus have noted that He healed the sick. They have heard Him say, "Follow Me," and they have established hospitals in His name.

Others have noticed that He fed the hungry. They have heard Him say, "Follow Me," and they have established famine relief programs and launched agriculture projects in His name. Still others have noticed that children came to Him and He did not turn them away. They have heard Him say, "Follow Me," and they have established orphanages and schools in His name.

We are to show Christ to the world. Many will see nothing beyond the ministry that is offered, but some eyes will be opened to see the glory of Jesus.

The Cost of Discipleship

Following Jesus will be costly. There is no escaping this theme in the Bible. Jesus announced that He was going to Jerusalem to suffer, and then He called His disciples to follow Him. When the disciples heard this, they were extremely reluctant. Peter tried to persuade Jesus to pursue a less costly plan, but Jesus told him the problem. "You do not have in mind the things of God, but the things of men" (Matthew 16:23).

Jesus refused to hide the cost of following in the small print of His invitation. "If anyone would come after me," He said, "he must deny himself and take up his cross and follow me" (v. 24). He told His disciples plainly that He was sending them out like sheep among wolves (Matthew 10:16). "If the world hates you," He said, "keep in mind that it hated me first" (John 15:18).

The world will never tolerate the exclusive claims of Jesus Christ. It has a definite opinion about Him, and it is not favorable.

> Our culture would crucify Him again today . . . on talk shows.

Christ claimed that we cannot know God without Him (Matthew 11:27), and that insults our pride. He claimed that we are incapable of coming to God unless He brings us (John 14:6), and that emasculates our strength. He claimed the right to tell us what is right and what is wrong (John 5:27), and that restricts our freedom.

That's why they crucified Him. And our culture would crucify Him again today. Of course we would not do it with wood and nails; we would crucify Him on talk shows. Can you imagine what any of our talk show hosts would make of Jesus saying, "I am the way, the truth, and the life"? Can you imagine the lampooning? The world hates Christ. It has no room for His exclusive claims, and it will not look kindly on His disciples either.

If you follow Christ, you will have to take up a cross. He is on a collision course with the world, the flesh, and the devil, and if you follow Him, you will find yourself in conflict with all three. If you follow Christ, you will find yourself out of step with the thinking of our culture. Only those who have seen His glory will be ready to pay this price.

In the West, we have benefited from a culture that has been gentle toward the Christian faith for a long time. But that gentleness is fast eroding. So we must count the cost of following Christ, because increasingly our choice will be to abandon His distinctive claims or be regarded as bigots.

If we would settle for general statements about God, the world would have no problem with us. But that is one thing we cannot do, because He said, "Follow Me." We are followers of the Crucified One. The incredible thing is that even as He was crucified, some saw His glory.

Following All the Way

The cross was not the final destination for Jesus; if it was, the call to follow Him would be impossible. The way Jesus found strength to face the cross was to look beyond it. He endured the cross "for the joy set before him" (Hebrews 12:2). He did not look at the cross; He looked through it.

Remember that the word *disciple* literally means to go somewhere with someone, and Christ tells us where He is going. After His death and resurrection, He ascended to take His place at the right hand of the Father. And He says to His disciples, "Whoever serves me must follow me; and where I am, my servant also will be" (John 12:26).

At the end of the Bible, John was given a vision of the day when that promise will be fulfilled. Those who have followed Christ will be gathered with Him, and John says, "They follow the Lamb wherever he goes" (Revelation 14:4). On the last day, when you see Jesus, you will be so glad that you followed Him, whatever the cost.

UNLOCKED

There is only one motivation that will ultimately be strong enough to sustain a man or woman in following Jesus, and that is that they see His glory.

The challenge of following Christ is great, and the price can be high. If we are to make disciples, we must make much of Jesus. It was this compelling vision of His greatness and glory that led the first disciples to forsake everything and follow Him. The power of that vision is no less compelling today.

PAUSE FOR PRAYER

Gracious Lord,

Thank You for calling me to follow You and for Your promise to make something of my life that will be for Your eternal value. Show me Your glory so that I may be faithful in following You however difficult and whatever the cost.

Thank You that the path on which You lead me ends in Your presence. Give me grace to follow all the days of my life so that Your life may be seen in me and Your work may be done through me. In Jesus' name I pray. Amen.

Note

1. Colin Brown, gen. ed., *The New International Dictionary of New Testament Theology*, vol. 1 (Grand Rapids: Zondervan, 1975), s.v. "disciple."

5

Lord

MARK 4–5

Can I accept Jesus as Savior without owning Him as Lord?

5 Lord

MARK 4–5

DISCOVER

why the lordship of Jesus is central to the gospel.

LEARN

why Christ is waiting as well as reigning.

WORSHIP

because all of Christ's enemies will be placed under His feet.

HAVE you ever thought about the difference between a grocery store and marriage?

A grocery store is set out for choice. You make your selection as you go around with your cart, choosing what you want and leaving what you don't. You are under no obligation.

A marriage is different. Imagine a young couple at a premarital counseling session. He says that he likes her eyes but not her hair. He appreciates her interest in her sport but not her interest in music. He would like to spend time with her on Tuesdays and Thursdays but not on Mondays and Fridays. There is a serious problem! Marriage is all about taking a person as he or she is, for better, for worse; for richer, for poorer; in sickness and in health. It is a commitment to love whatever happens.

Some people think of the Christian life like a visit to the grocery store. They open the Bible and they go through the "aisles" to view what is most appealing. They find some things they would like: Forgiveness! Peace! Joy! Heaven!

Other "aisles" don't seem so attractive. One has a large sign saying, "Forgive others even as God in Christ forgave you"; another says, "Be holy because God is holy." The religious shopper does not feel a need for these things and so passes by.

The Bible never describes the Christian life as a visit to the grocery store, but it does describe the Christian life as a "marriage" in which two parties commit to each other just as they are.

Christ will receive you as you are, and you must receive Him as He is. Jesus Christ is Savior and Lord, and that is how you must receive Him. You cannot divide Him in two.

I have often heard people say that they have "received Christ as Savior, but never made Him Lord." The assumption is that we can somehow separate the Savior from the Lord; that we can have faith without repentance, blessings without commands, or forgiveness of sin without the pursuit of holiness.

That is a fundamental misunderstanding of the gospel. We cannot receive what He offers and at the same time resist what He commands. All through the Scriptures, Christ is presented to us as Lord and Savior. We can never separate the one from the other. Indeed, as we will discover, it is the fact that Jesus is Lord that makes it possible for Him to be Savior.

Junkyard Wars

When I was around five years old, my father took me on a number of occasions to a junkyard outside Edinburgh. The place was filled with scrap cars and trucks, and it was a marvelous place for a child with a vivid imagination to play.

Dad used to go there to get spare parts that he needed for our car. The system was simple: You could strip pieces that you needed off the cars, and then pay for them at the gate as you left. The problem was that some people were in the habit of throwing parts over the perimeter fence, walking past the gate without paying, and then picking up the stuff in the wasteland outside.

So the owners cleared a "no go" area around the inside of the fence and ran a rail about three feet off the ground around the perimeter. They brought in Alsatian guard dogs, which were leashed to the railing, so that they could patrol around the entire perimeter. As long as you did not go within a few feet of the fence, you were perfectly safe.

I enjoyed going to the junkyard with my father. One day he was taking a speedometer from a wrecked car, and while he was working, I found a truck and climbed up into the cab. I was lost in an imaginary world of truck driving, when suddenly one of the Alsatian dogs broke free from its chain and came bounding toward me.

I don't think that I have ever been more terrified in my life. I was quite convinced that I would be completely savaged by this aggressive and overwhelmingly powerful animal. I screamed as any small child would, and I remember seeing my father rushing over from where he had been working. He grabbed a stick, and after a struggle, he subdued the dog.

He saved *me* by subduing the dog. The fact that he was able to exercise authority over the dog was the reason he was able to deliver me from its power.

Christ is able to save us from our enemies precisely because He is able to exercise authority over them and subdue them. It is the fact that He is Lord that qualifies Him to act as Savior. That is why Scripture says, "Everyone who calls on the name of the Lord will be saved" (Romans 10:13).

Jesus could not be Savior if He were not Lord. So let's take a look at what He is Lord over, and what He is therefore able to save us from. We'll come to the Scriptures in a moment, but let's start with the newspaper.

THE DOGS OF HUMAN DARKNESS

Over time, your newspaper becomes a catalog of what we sometimes call "natural disasters." In one recent year alone, newspapers recorded a massive earthquake in India, a mud slide in Honduras, a volcanic eruption in Congo, and massive flooding in Mozambique. This is the world in which we live. No wonder the Bible says that the whole earth is groaning as if it were in a kind of labor pain (Romans 8:21–22).

The catalog of human evils is also painful to recount. I think of school shootings, gangland murders, crazed killers, and the men of violence whose distorted minds care nothing for their own lives or the lives of other people. Every time it happens, we ask, "How could we have stopped it, and how can we make sure it never happens again?"

The catalog of illnesses is no less alarming. For all the wonders of medical science, for which we are profoundly grateful, we live with the incurable injury, the irreversible condition, and the terminal disease. Billions of research dollars still find us with no cures for dozens of cancers, heart diseases, AIDS, and much more. Our hospitals are never short of business, and for many people, the ten most dreaded words of all time are "I'm sorry, there's nothing more I can do for you."

Which brings us to the last and the most obvious of the dogs of human darkness, death itself. The Bible talks about death as the last enemy, and anyone who has been near it with a loved one knows what a terrible enemy it is.

Watch any international news bulletin this week and you will find that it is dominated by these four dimensions of human darkness: disasters, the violent atrocities committed by deranged people, the effects of sickness and disease, and death.

These are the dogs of human darkness. They snarl at us, and when they come near, they bring terror to our lives. They have stalked every generation and every culture. They do not pay respect to boundaries of race, religion, gender, or wealth.

For all the joys of this life, we find ourselves asking, "Who shall deliver us?" "Who has the authority to subdue the destructive powers that bring such darkness?"

The answer to each dimension of darkness is the same: Jesus Christ. *He* is Lord.

Lord over Natural Disasters

Early in his gospel, Mark records four stories that illustrate the authority of Jesus over the dogs of human darkness. Mark shows us that Jesus is Lord, and this is why we can trust Him as Savior. The disciples learned this in stages. Every time they discovered a new dimension of His authority, they discovered a new sphere of His salvation.

It all began one evening, when Jesus told the disciples to row over to the other side of the lake. They did what He asked, and halfway across the lake they found themselves caught in a sudden storm.

Storms of this sort were not unusual in the area, and the disciples had made their living on the lake, so they would have seen a few in their time. They knew how to handle a boat, but on this occasion they were absolutely terrified. "Teacher, don't you care if we drown?" (Mark 4:38). They were picturing their obituaries in the following day's newspaper.

If the boat had gone down, the *Galilee Gazette* (or its first-century equivalent) would have had a familiar ring about it.

FREAK STORM CLAIMS 13 LIVES

Thirteen people died last night when a freak storm hit Lake Galilee. Meteorologists had failed to predict the weather system. Those who died included several local fishermen along with a former tax consultant, a religious teacher, and other unidentified friends. Eyewitnesses said the weather changed without warning. Rescue crafts were launched but were unable to identify any survivors.

We have all read similar reports many times.

The disciples were facing a life threatening natural disaster, and they must have been astonished at what happened next.

> *He [Jesus] got up, rebuked the wind and said to the waves, "Quiet! Be still!" Then the wind died down and it was completely calm. He said to his disciples, "Why are you so afraid? Do you still have no faith?" They were terrified and asked each other, "Who is this? Even the wind and the waves obey him!"* (vv. 39–41)

Think of the possibilities! If He can subdue a storm, what about a volcano, a mudslide, a tornado, or a hurricane? If He is Lord over nature, then He can save us from its destructive power.

LORD OVER THE DEMONS

> *When Jesus got out of the boat, a man with an evil spirit came from the tombs to meet him.* (5:2)

When they got to the other side of the lake, they were immediately confronted by a man who was out of his mind. He lived among the tombs, and night after night he would cry out and cut himself with stones (v. 5).

This man was clearly public enemy number one. People in the area would lock their doors at night because of him. You wouldn't want to leave your children playing alone in a park in case he came around. This man cared little for his own life and nothing for the lives of others. He was extremely dangerous.

The local authorities had tried all that they could to contain the problem. "He had often been chained hand and foot." But when they threw him in jail, he "tore the chains apart and broke the irons on his feet. No one was strong enough to subdue him" (v. 4). So the whole community lived in the shadow of violence, and nobody knew what to do about it.

The community had tried everything, and nothing had worked.

Every time there was another outbreak of violence, people would come up with their suggested solutions. "They need stronger chains at the jailhouse," or in our case today, "We need tighter gun laws or longer prison sentences." But the community had tried everything, and nothing had worked. The threat remained. Every night the locals would hear this man crying out on the hills. It couldn't have been easy to sleep.

This man had a family (v. 19). His wife and children must have gone through a thousand agonies as his self-destructive outbursts became worse. Eventually, when it got to the point where it was no longer safe to have him in the home, their hearts must have reached a point of despair.

The Bible is very clear that there were evil spirits (or demons) behind these great outbreaks of violence. This is not the case with every violent or self-destructive person, but it was the case with this man. Jesus described the devil as a thief who comes "to steal and kill and destroy" (John 10:10), and where stealing, killing, and destroying are most rampant, there his activity is most directly to be discerned.

Jesus came to this community where people lived under the shadow of this darkness. He commanded the evil spirits to leave the man and enter a herd of pigs. As soon as the people in the town heard, they came out to see what had happened, and they found the man who had been possessed by the demons "sitting there, dressed and in his right mind" (Mark 5:15).

Think of the possibilities! If Christ can pacify the man who was a terror to this community, what about the deranged gunman or the suicide bomber? Imagine how it would be if each of them were restored to a right mind. If He is Lord over the demons, He can deliver us from their destructive power.

LORD OVER DISEASE

> *A large crowd followed and pressed around him. And a woman was there who had been subject to bleeding for twelve years.* (vv. 24–25)

When Jesus returned across the lake, a large crowd was waiting. In the crowd was a woman who had suffered from a chronic and disabling illness for twelve years. She had spent all that she had in consulting various doctors, but in spite of their efforts, her condition was no better. In fact, it was worse. Her condition was beyond the frontiers of medical science in her time. She was suffering from an incurable disease.

She had heard about Jesus and joined the crowd that was following Him. In her condition, she would not have been able to move quickly, but crowds move slowly, and so she managed to push her way forward until she was just behind Jesus. She felt that if she could just reach Him, she would be healed. Finally she managed to touch Him, and immediately she was aware of a physiological change in her body. Mark reports, "Her bleeding stopped and she felt in her body that she was freed from her suffering" (v. 29).

Think of the possibilities! If He can cure diseases that are beyond the frontiers of medical science, what about cancer or AIDS? If He is Lord over disease, He can deliver us from its destructive power.

LORD OVER DEATH

> *While Jesus was still speaking, some men came from the house of Jairus, the synagogue ruler. "Your daughter is dead," they said. "Why bother the teacher any more?" Ignoring what they said, Jesus told the synagogue ruler, "Don't be afraid; just believe."* (vv. 35–36)

Jairus's daughter was just twelve years old. Her father had sent for Jesus, but the large crowd around Him and the time He spent with healing the woman had delayed His arrival, so that by the time Jesus came to the house, the wake had begun.

Jesus sent the mourners out of the house. Only the girl's father and mother, along with Peter, James, and John, remained with Jesus and the dead girl in the home. Jesus took the girl's hands. He said, "'*Talitha koum!*' (which means, 'Little girl, I say to you, get up!'). Immediately the girl stood up and walked around" (vv. 41–42).

Her parents stood watching in absolute amazement, and in a delightful touch, Jesus said to them, "Give her something to eat."

WHY DOESN'T HE DO IT?

Jesus is Lord over all the dimensions of human darkness. He is able to subdue the dogs of disaster, the demonic, disease, and even death. He is Lord over these enemies of the human race, and that is why He is able to save us from their destructive power. After thousands of years of human history marred by these enemies, here at last is someone who can deliver us.

So why doesn't He do it?

If Christ has the power to deliver us from these deadly enemies, why does He not exercise that authority? Many Christians can point to wonderful stories of healing, or deliverance from danger, or exorcism of demons, but anyone with a newspaper knows that the world still suffers from disasters, disease, death, and the madness of violent men.

Why?

Mark gives us the answer in the story of the demon-possessed man.

> *Those who had seen it told the people what had happened to the demon-possessed man—and told about the pigs as well. Then the people began to plead with Jesus to leave their region.* (vv. 16–17)

You would think that when Christ had delivered the town from public enemy number one, they would say, "Please stay." Imagine what Christ might have done about other problems in the area. But they asked Him to go.

It is important to grasp this. They were pleading with Jesus to leave. Pleading! "Please leave this area. We have seen what You did, but we don't want You here. This is not where You should be. Please go."

His name is not welcome in public.

Jesus gave the explanation on another occasion. "This is the verdict: Light has come into the world, but men loved darkness instead of light because their deeds were evil" (John 3:19).

Things haven't changed. Our culture has increasingly taken the position that we don't want Jesus around here either. Of course, many people have no problem with religious people exercising their freedom to worship as they choose, but as far as the country at large is concerned, the prevailing consensus is that we do not want Jesus here.

His name is not welcome in public unless it is placed alongside a list of alternatives. The suggestion that He is Lord is unacceptable because that would imply that He had authority over everyone, and we couldn't possibly have that—not here!

So Jesus left the area of the Gerasenes. What else would you expect? He does not force Himself on a community that does not want Him. But what will happen to the boy if the one who is able to subdue the dog leaves the junkyard?

There is only one way to make sense of your newspaper, and that is to read it alongside these words: "He came to that which was his own, but his own did not receive him" (John 1:11).

THE DAY THE DOGS BROKE LOOSE

Follow the gospel story, and you will find the same pattern of Jesus showing His power and then being rejected until eventually it leads to a cross, which was the ultimate expression of a community saying, "Go away."

When Christ was crucified, all the dogs of human darkness broke loose. Nature convulsed: "The earth shook and the rocks split." The demonic powers of hell were loosened as never before: Jesus described it as "[the] hour—when darkness reigns" Matthew 27:51; Luke 22:53). The suffering He endured in His body was beyond description, but it was foretold in part by the prophets. "I am poured out like water, and all my bones are out of joint. . . . My tongue sticks to the roof of my mouth. . . . Dogs have surrounded me; a band of evil men has encircled me, they have pierced my hands and my feet" (Psalm 22:14–16).

Then He entered death itself.

REIGNING AND WAITING

But this is not the end of the Bible story. On the third day, He rose from the dead and ascended into heaven. The Father said to Him, "Sit at my right hand until I make your enemies a footstool for your feet" (Hebrews 1:13).

Right now, He is reigning. He is on the throne with all power and authority given to Him. But He is also waiting until the Father God places all His enemies under His feet. That time has not yet come. The reigning and waiting are not in conflict. "He must reign until he has put all his enemies under his feet. The last enemy to be destroyed is death" (1 Corinthians 15:25–26).

We are living in the middle of this period. Jesus Christ is Lord. All power and authority are given to Him. But while He has power over all His enemies, He has not yet used that power to put all His enemies under His feet.

So we continue to live in a dangerous world that suffers under the curse of disasters, demons, disease, and death. But we do belong to the kingdom of Jesus Christ, who is Lord over these enemies, and we wait with Him for the day when He puts all these enemies under His feet.

God gave the apostle John a glimpse of that day in a vision recorded for us in the book of Revelation. John saw that the sea was like glass (see Revelation 4:6). There's no doubt in my mind that he would immediately have recalled the storm on the lake. God was showing him that the ravages of nature would be subdued.

Then John saw the devil and his angels cast into the lake of fire. God was showing him that all demonic activity will cease. John saw the dead raised to life. They were filled with inexpressible joy as they entered God's city, and John heard a voice saying, "There will be no more death or mourning or crying or pain, for the old order of things has passed away" (Revelation 21:4).

The message to John and to us could not be clearer. "You will face many storms throughout your life in this world," John was saying. "You will see the enemy at work, and you will shed many tears over disease and death. But Jesus is Lord over all these dogs of human darkness, and He will subdue them. The day is coming when they will be no more."

Until that day, Jesus has work for us to do. When He left the area of the Gerasenes, the man who had been delivered from the power of evil spirits wanted to get in the boat and go with Him. But Jesus refused. He said, "Go home to your family and tell them how much the Lord has done for you" (Mark 5:19).

Christ sent him back to be light in a culture that didn't want Jesus. The man returned to his family, and he was able to share the story of what Jesus had done for him in the ten cities on that side of the lake.

That's our calling. Christ will not force Himself upon our culture, but He sends us back as light in a dark place. As long as we are on earth, we will share in the sorrow that comes from the continuing activity of the great enemies of the human race. But we belong to a King who will subdue these enemies, and we wait with Jesus for the day when He will take His power and reign. Then the dogs of human darkness will be subdued forever. Lord Jesus, come quickly!

UNLOCKED

The good news is not just that Jesus is Savior; it is also that Jesus is Lord. In fact, it is precisely because He is Lord over the great enemies of the human race that He is able to save us from them.

The great invitation of the gospel is to give up our resistance to the lordship of Christ and receive His salvation. "Everyone who calls on the name of the Lord will be saved" (Romans 10:13). The Lord who is our Savior invites us to come to Him.

PAUSE FOR PRAYER

Gracious Father,

I confess that often I have claimed Your promises while resisting Your commands. Forgive my arrogance, and help me to place the whole of my life under Your sovereign rule.

Help me to share what Christ has done for me so that others may crown Him as their Lord and enter into His salvation. I look for the day when He will place all His enemies under His feet. Thank You that I will be among His people on that day through the powerful work of my Deliverer, the Lord Jesus Christ. Amen.

6

Hell

MARK 9

What is hell

and how can

I avoid it?

6 Hell

MARK 9

DISCOVER

Jesus' teaching about hell.

LEARN

the meaning of the worm and the fire.

WORSHIP

because Christ experienced hell so that you should never know what it is like.

SOMETHING remarkable happened at school when I was fourteen years old. I had been speaking to a friend about Christ and invited him to a rally where he heard the gospel. At the end of the meeting, he made a commitment to Christ.

This caused some interest in our class, and over the next few months, two other members of the class also professed faith. We used to wear red stickers with Christian slogans (it seemed cool at the time), and as the red stickers multiplied, the gospel became a topic of discussion. Those were exciting days.

One conversation stands out in my memory. I had been talking about the gospel with a lad in our school class and had emphasized the promise of eternal life in heaven. "I'm not interested in being with the holy crowd in heaven," he said. "I'd rather enjoy the party in hell." I have heard that response several times since, and it has caused me to think more deeply about the Bible's teaching on the subject of hell.

I do not find it easy to speak or write about hell. A large part of me would rather avoid the subject altogether, but we are committed to unlocking the Bible, and the Bible makes it clear that every person who has ever lived will one day see Jesus Christ and personally experience either heaven or hell.

Cartoonists and Brimstone Preachers

Heaven and hell are beyond our comprehension in this life. The danger is therefore that we either trivialize them by descending into fanciful speculations or ignore these awesome realities altogether.

Cartoonists have done a great deal to trivialize hell. Colorful imaginations have depicted devils in red tights, stoking fires with pitchforks. Some serious Christian art has gone in the same direction, and some preachers have fallen into the trap of preaching in a way that has amounted to a kind of psychological terrorism.

Many people have reacted to this speculation, and the result is that today the subject of hell is often completely ignored. This is a great mistake. God has revealed all that we need to know in His Word. There are promises to believe and warnings to heed. We need both.

God's salvation is about . . . where you will spend eternity.

Many people miss the power of God's warning not by denying what God says about hell but simply by ignoring it. If a church does not speak honestly and openly about the eternal destiny of human beings, the focus of its message will soon undergo a subtle change. The emphasis will be on coming to Christ to find a more fulfilling or satisfying life.

But this is not the heart of the gospel. Jesus Christ came into the world to bring us from death to life. He died to deliver us from hell, and to bring us into everlasting life in His presence. God's salvation is about more than your experience of life; it is about where you will spend eternity.

I believe in hell primarily because it was taught clearly by Jesus Christ. I do not believe that Jesus was a manipulator of people's minds and emotions. I do not believe for a moment that Jesus embellished the joys of heaven, or that He exaggerated the pains of hell. I believe that Jesus is the Son of God, and therefore I have to take every word that He spoke with equal seriousness. If you want to be a Christian, so do you; it's part of following Him.

Under a Storm Cloud

Nobody ever spoke more clearly or powerfully about the love of God than Jesus. But Jesus also spoke in the clearest terms about God's implacable hostility toward evil. "Whoever rejects the Son will not see life," He said. "God's wrath remains on him" (John 3:36).

Notice Jesus didn't say that on the last day God's wrath would suddenly come, but rather that it would "remain." The wrath of God toward sin is like a great storm cloud that hangs over us. It stays there unless and until it is taken away.

Jesus came into the world to take this judgment from us. He will do this for all who will come to Him in faith. But where He is rejected, the storm cloud of God's wrath remains.

The rest of the Bible story bears witness to God's relentless hostility toward all evil. God determined to destroy evil, and on the day Adam sinned in the garden, God pronounced a curse on the serpent. The evil he had introduced into the human race would not stand.

Throughout the Bible story, we have seen sin growing and God cutting it back. At the end of the story, God will destroy it altogether. When John was given a glimpse of this future judgment of God, he saw that the enemies of God would "drink of the wine of God's fury, which has been poured full strength into the cup of his wrath" (Revelation 14:10).

The Place of Punishment

Jesus spoke about hell as a place of punishment. He described a man who went to hell and said that "he was in torment" (Luke 16:23). The book of Revelation uses the same word and speaks about God's enemies being "tormented with burning sulfur in the presence of the holy angels and of the Lamb" (Revelation 14:10). John adds that "the smoke of their torment rises for ever and ever. There is no rest day or night" (v. 11). These are frightening words, but they are God's words, and so we must take them seriously, and consider what they mean.

Hell is a place of punishment, where God's justice is fully known. This world is riddled with injustice at every level. People who have been responsible for unspeakable evils have never been brought to face the evil for which they are responsible. Adolf Hitler would be one example, but there are many others who have slipped, by death, beyond the reach of justice in this world. And even with those who are living, the international community continues to struggle over how to bring justice to war criminals who have committed unspeakable atrocities.

But God has set a day of judgment from which nobody can escape. All secrets will be revealed, and there will be no evasions. The dead will be raised, and the wicked will be brought to face their own sins, as they stand before the judgment of God.

As awful as this is, it is something for which we should be thankful. It is for this reason that God urges us to leave vengeance in His hands. He will settle every score. "Do not take revenge, my friends, but leave room for God's wrath, for it is written: 'It is mine to avenge; I will repay,' says the Lord" (Romans 12:19). God will execute perfect justice with total knowledge. All evil will be brought to light by God.

Degrees of Punishment

God's justice is perfect, and that means that nobody will be punished for a sin he or she did not commit. The punishment experienced in hell by a person who rejects the Son of God will be a direct reflection of the particular sins committed by that individual.

Just as there are degrees of reward in heaven, so there will be degrees of punishment in hell. Jesus referred to this on at least three occasions. He spoke about a city that would not receive the good news, and He said, "It will be more bearable for Sodom and Gomorrah on the day of judgment than for that town" (Matthew 10:15). Receiving the good news brought a new level of responsibility and accountability.

In the same way, Jesus spoke about the people of Bethsaida, Korazin, and Capernaum (Matthew 11:20–24). Most of His miracles had been performed there, and yet these towns rejected Him. Jesus spoke of the responsibility these people had in the light of what they had seen. Again, He said, "It will be more bearable for Sodom on the day of judgment than for you" (v. 24).

On another occasion, Jesus distinguished between a servant who knew what his master wanted him to do and a servant who did not have that knowledge. Jesus said, "That servant who knows his master's will and does not get ready or does not do what his master wants will be beaten with many blows. But the one who does not know and does things deserving punishment will be beaten with few blows" (Luke 12:47–48). Jesus was making it clear that the greater the light we have received from God, the greater our responsibility to respond in obedience.

Other passages in the Bible also point in the direction of degrees of punishment in hell. The letter to the Hebrews speaks of the severe punishment of those who knowingly trample the Son of God under foot (Hebrews 10:29), and Paul says, "You are storing up wrath against yourself" (Romans 2:5).

This is an important truth, because there are some who imagine that having chosen the wrong path, they might as well take their chances, cut loose, and live wildly. Their logic is that if they are already headed toward hell, they might as well indulge the pleasures of sin to the maximum extent.

That is a desperate mistake. God will punish sins in hell with perfect justice. A person in hell would give anything to have committed even one less sin.

THE PUNISHMENT FITS THE CRIME

Some readers may be asking, Are any sins so serious as to deserve the punishment of hell? This is an important question, because it goes to the heart of the justice of God.

When we are considering what an appropriate punishment for sin would be, we have to consider not only the nature of the sin but also the person against whom it has been committed. The greater the person who is sinned against, the more severe the penalty for the offense will be.

My colleague Dave Gruthusen uses a helpful analogy to explain this truth to students in their early teens.[1] Suppose that a middle-school student punches someone else in his class on the nose. The matter is reported to his teacher, and he is given a detention. But suppose that during the detention he punches the teacher on the nose. The consequences are greater; he will be suspended from the school.

Now suppose that on the way home, the boy's father is stopped by a policeman who issues a ticket for speeding. The boy becomes angry with the policeman and punches him on the nose. Now he finds himself in jail. Some years later, he joins a crowd to see the president of the United States of America. As the president passes, the boy lunges forward attempting to punch the president on the nose. He is shot dead by the Secret Service.

In each case, the offense is the same, but the penalty is different. The greater the person against whom the offense is committed, the more severe the penalty for the offense.

It is a serious thing to offend against our neighbors, or against the laws of the land, but it is a much more serious matter to offend against God. Our sins are offenses against almighty God. That is why they are serious and bring such desperate consequences.

Jesus gave us two descriptions of what these consequences will be like when He spoke about a "worm" and a "fire."

THE WORM

> *"It is better for you to enter the kingdom of God with one eye than to have two eyes and be thrown into hell, where 'their worm does not die, and the fire is not quenched.'"* (MARK 9:47–48)

Some years ago, a severe storm destroyed three beautiful trees in our yard. One of them had become diseased, and when it fell, the extent of the damage was revealed. Worms had eaten away a large part of the inside of the trunk. Once the tree fell, the worms were exposed. We had never known that they were there.

Worms eat away on the inside. That's true of the woodworm, the tapeworm, or any other kind of worm.

Jesus spoke about a worm that never dies in hell. Notice that this worm belongs to the person in hell. Jesus uses a personal pronoun. It's not "the worm"; it's "their worm." Jesus is speaking of something personal and internal to every person in hell.

Given that worms eat away on the inside, it seems clear that Jesus was talking about something that eats away the inside of an individual in hell. He is talking about the conscience. There is nothing more crippling than a bad conscience that nags away and never rests. Jesus said that in hell, the sinner's "worm" will never die.

Consciences will be fully activated in hell.

This is important because many people go through this life with a minimal experience of conscience. My father was in the police force for thirty years. What surprised him most was that often people who had committed dreadful acts seemed to have a minimal understanding of what they had done, even after long periods in prison.

The conscience can be seared or stifled, and those who do the greatest evil are sometimes the least sensitive to wrong they have done. I have often spoken to people who have chosen an obviously sinful path but told me that since they made their choice, they felt at peace.

It will not always be so. Consciences will be fully activated in hell. Every sinner in hell will see his own life for what it is. Denial will be futile. Sinners will be unable to block out the knowledge of their own sins and their own responsibility. They will have twenty-twenty vision. We will see things as they are both in heaven and in hell. This is part of the justice of God.

In Psalm 51, David wrote, "I know my transgressions, and my sin is always before me" (v. 3). He had lived in denial about his sin for some time, but God brought him to the point of facing what he had done. God will bring every person who has ever lived to that point. He will do this either by bringing us to repentance in this life, or by showing the full horror of sin in hell itself.

In hell, the unbeliever's sin will always be before him. He will be in hell, but hell will also be in him. Those who loved sin will see it for what it is, and share God's abhorrence of it. This will be part of God's ultimate triumph and vindication.

THE FIRE

"The fire is not quenched." (v. 48)

There has been a great deal of discussion about the meaning of this fire that is not quenched. Often things that are unclear in one part of the Bible are illuminated by another part of the Scriptures. In the book of Revelation, John was told that the wicked would be punished "in the presence of the holy angels and of the Lamb" (14:10). The Son of God is present when the wicked are punished.

When Jesus spoke about the fire that is not quenched, He was speaking about the presence of God. Hell is sometimes described by Christian preachers as eternal separation from God, but it may be more biblical to warn of the danger of the eternal presence of God. Nobody can escape the God of the Bible.

The psalmist faced the awesome truth of God's inescapable presence when he said, "Where can I go from your Spirit? Where can I flee from your presence? If I go up to the heavens, you are there; if I make my bed in the depths, you are there" (Psalm 139:7–8).

Nobody can ultimately escape from God.

Many people spend their whole lives resisting the claims of God and seeking to put as much distance as they can between themselves and the Lord, and it is of very little value to tell such individuals that they will spend eternity outside the presence of God. That has been their choice in life and it would be their choice for eternity. They are like my high-school friend who thought that the company of the wicked in hell would be much more attractive than eternity in the presence of God.

But nobody can ultimately escape from God. When Paul wrote that the wicked will be "shut out from the presence of the Lord" (2 Thessalonians 1:9), he meant that they will be excluded from *enjoying* God's presence in the New Jerusalem.

Every eye will see Him. The righteous will see God in His beauty. The wicked will see God in His fury. Jonathan Edwards, perhaps the most famous American preacher on this serious subject, said that God will be the hell of one and the heaven of the other.

When Jesus spoke about the fire that is not quenched, He was referring to God's presence. God revealed His presence to Moses and Elijah through fire. Malachi spoke of God as being like a refiner's fire, and the writer of Hebrews described God as a consuming fire. That is why it is a fearful thing to fall into His hands.

In hell, sinners will have a full knowledge of themselves and a full knowledge of God. They will see their sins clearly, and they will know God clearly too. Perhaps the greatest pain of hell will be to know that there is a God of love, and yet to know that the opportunity of enjoying Him is past and gone forever.

Sin will be seen for the folly that it is. God will be known in the beauty of His holiness. Nobody will deny God's existence in hell. Nobody will promote sin, or commend ungodliness. In this sense, even God's enemies will bow before Him.

Hell on the Cross

The Bible's teaching on hell takes us to the very heart of the Bible's message. Jesus Christ came into the world so that you should never know what hell is like. He opened the way of escape for us by entering hell Himself on the cross.

Jesus was crucified at the third hour of the day (Mark 15:25), and for three hours, He suffered the mockery of men who despised Him. Then something wholly unexpected happened. "At the sixth hour darkness came over the whole land until the ninth hour" (Mark 15:33).

In these hours of darkness, Christ became our sin bearer. God "laid on him the iniquity of us all" (Isaiah 53:6). Martin Luther put it clearly when he said, "Our most merciful father, seeing us to be oppressed and overwhelmed with the curse of the law, and so to beholden under the same that we could never be delivered from it by our own power sent his only Son into the world and laid upon him all the sins of men saying: Be thou Peter that denier; Paul that persecutor, blasphemer and cruel oppressor; David that adulterer; . . . and briefly, be thou the person which hath committed the sins of all men; see therefore that thou pay and satisfy for them."[2]

Christ became the guilty one in the eyes of the Father. He committed no sin, but on the cross He bore the guilt of the sins of the world, and for this reason He began to experience the full force of the Father's judgment on sin poured out on Him. The storm cloud that loomed over us broke over Him.

In these hours of darkness, Christ entered the depths of His suffering. The comfort of the Father's love was taken from Him. He knew what it was to be shut out of the enjoyment of the relationship He had always known with His Father, and He cried out, "My God, My God, why have you forsaken me?" (Matthew 27:46). In Luther's words, God was forsaken by God.

In the darkness, Christ entered into all the dimensions of hell. Bearing our sins, He experienced the worm, and bearing God's judgment, He experienced the fire.

We may now know, we cannot tell what pains He had to bear;
But we believe it was for us He hung and suffered there.[3]

Jesus endured hell on the cross so that you should never know what it is like. God is just, and He will never punish the same sin twice. If Christ has taken your sin, then God will not, and even cannot, punish you for it. That is why there is no condemnation for those who are in Christ Jesus. The cloud of judgment that once hung over me has burst over Him. He entered hell in my place.

Christ has done this for you, and He invites your response. He calls you to turn to Him in faith and repentance, asking Him to be your Savior and beginning that pathway of following Him as your Lord.

UNLOCKED

The teaching of Jesus makes it clear that sinners in hell will know the full horror of their sin and live with that knowledge. They will also know God, but they will be excluded from enjoying His presence.

God has sent His Son into the world so that you should never know what hell is like. He experienced hell on the cross as He bore our sins and was cut off from the comfort of the Father's presence.

He invites us to come to Him, whatever our sins, and offers pardon, forgiveness, and release from condemnation. Turn to Him in faith and repentance.

PAUSE FOR PRAYER

If you have never taken that step of trusting Jesus Christ, use this prayer to come to Him now.

Lord Jesus, I believe that You died to take my sins and my punishment. I see that You did that to save me from hell, and I am truly grateful. I ask that Your death will cover my sins, and that You will deliver me from hell and bring me into everlasting life in heaven.

I trust You as my Savior and bow before You as my Lord. I ask for Your strength as I begin to follow You. Show me my sins and help me to turn from them and to live a new life for Your glory until I see You and enter the joy of Your presence. Through the name of the Lord Jesus, my Savior, I pray. Amen.

Notes

1. Dave is the middle-school pastor at Arlington Heights Evangelical Free Church. I am grateful for his insightful analogy and for his permission to use it.
2. Martin Luther, *Epistle to the Galatians*, 272; as cited in James Stott, *The Cross of Christ* (Leister, England: InterVarsity, 1986), 345.
3. Cecil Frances Alexander, "There is a Green Hill Far Away," verse 2.

7

Miracles

MARK 12

How can

I believe

in miracles?

7 Miracles

MARK 12

DISCOVER

how your worldview filters what you believe.

LEARN

Jesus' teaching about the resurrection.

WORSHIP

because the living God is at work in the world today.

WHEN I was young, I was quite convinced that Santa Claus came down the chimney on Christmas Eve. It wasn't difficult to find evidence for my belief. On Christmas Eve, we would hang our stockings and then leave out two plates, one with some cookies for Santa and the other with some peeled carrots for the reindeer. In the morning, the stockings were filled with presents, the carrots were gone, and only a few crumbs from the cookies remained on the plate, clear evidence that Santa had enjoyed our cookies before going on to visit the homes of other children.

Given my assumptions about Santa, the evidence all pointed one way. But eventually, I made some new discoveries, and from then on I had a different explanation for the filled stockings, vanishing carrots, and strategically placed cookie crumbs.

A worldview is a set of beliefs through which we filter information. It's like a software program running in the mind. Our worldview helps us to sort out what we receive as true and what we reject as false. And, of course, a worldview can be wrong, like my childish conviction regarding Santa Claus. A false worldview can blind your eyes to the truth.

It's not easy to change your worldview. Once we have grasped hold of a set of convictions, it is difficult for us to hear anything to the contrary. At one time, people believed that the earth is flat and that the sun moves around the earth. When someone discovered that the earth is round and rotates around the sun, it was very difficult for him to "unlearn" their old assumptions.

A SAD WORLDVIEW

The Sadducees held a worldview that made it very difficult for them to hear Jesus even when He spoke directly to them. There was one fundamental conviction buried deep in the mind of every Sadducee. As Mark reported,

> *The Sadducees . . . say there is no resurrection.* (12:18)

They didn't believe in any resurrection, and that is why they were sad (you see)!

This put them in dispute with the Pharisees, who did believe in a future resurrection. The Pharisees also believed in heaven and hell, but the Sadducees had a different brand of religion. As far as they were concerned, when you are dead, you are dead.[1] The book of Acts tells us that "the Sadducees say that there is no resurrection, and that there are neither angels nor spirits, but the Pharisees acknowledge them all" (Acts 23:8).

There's a pattern here. No resurrection, no angels, and no spirits. The Sadducees did not like anything that smacked of the supernatural. The Bible speaks of angels as ministering spirits (Hebrews 1:14). But the Sadducees did not buy any of that. As far as they were concerned, the only power available is the power inside you.

If you had asked a Sadducee for advice, he might have said, "Live for today. You only get one ride down the slide of life. If it doesn't happen for you here, it isn't going to happen anywhere else. And don't go looking to angels or spirits to help you. That's just an emotional crutch for weak people to lean on. Life is what you make it."

That was the Sadducees' worldview, and if you take off a Sadducee's robes and give him an Armani suit, take away his scrolls and give him a cell phone, and take him out of the temple and give him a job in the city, you have the picture of the twenty-first-century Sadducee.

His worldview is clear. "Don't look beyond the grave, because that cannot be known, and don't look to heaven for help, because it's all up to you."

Many of these modern Sadducees are to be found in church, just as their first-century counterparts were found in the temple. They are good, upright, and successful people, with sharp minds but blind eyes.

"BEAM ME UP, SCOTTY"

One day a group of the Sadducees came to Jesus with a question about the resurrection. They had debated this issue with the Pharisees many times and knew the questions that worked best in their argument, so they decided to try one of these out on Jesus.

They began by reminding Jesus about the Old Testament law of levirate marriage. This law said that if a man died without children, his brother must assume the care of the wife and raise children in his brother's name. The point of the law was, of course, to ensure the continuation of the line of Israel, which was central to the purpose of God.

The Sadducees then told a story about seven brothers. The first one died with no children, so the second brother took responsibility for the wife. Then the second brother died, and the third one stepped up to the plate, and so on. By the time it came to the seventh brother, he must have known that this woman was the kiss of death. Sure enough, he went the way of all the others, and last of all, this remarkable woman died.

Now the Sadducees come to their question.

> *"At the resurrection whose wife will she be?"* (MARK 12:23)

This is the Star Trek view of the resurrection. Captain Kirk says, "Beam me up, Scotty!" Kirk then disappears from view, only to rematerialize looking exactly the same but in a different place.

That's how the Sadducees thought about a future resurrection and, of course, that's why they rejected it. If the life of heaven were simply a continuation of this life as it is in another place, it would be horrendously complicated. Life creates so many anomalies that it would be impossible for it to continue in the same way after death.

Christ made this point clear when He said,

> *"When the dead rise, they will neither marry nor be given in marriage; they will be like the angels in heaven."* (V. 25)

In heaven, our relationships will no longer be exclusive. There will be no death, so there will be no need for procreation. Of course, for those who are happily married, this sounds like bad news because a happy marriage and the gift of children are among the greatest joys that God has given in this life, and so it is hard for us to imagine life without them.

But that is why God says that it has not entered into the mind of man "what God has prepared for those who love him" (1 Corinthians 2:9). Marriage and family are among God's greatest gifts in this fallen world. Wait till you see what God has prepared for the redeemed world. It is as if God would say to us, "You ain't seen nothing yet!"

When You Enter Heaven

When you enter heaven, you will know yourself to be there. Just as you are conscious of yourself being at a particular place on a given date as you read this book, so there will come a time when you are conscious of yourself being in the presence of God. You will be able to say to yourself, "I'm here."

You will also know God just as He knows you, and in the same way as you will know yourself to be there, you will know others who you love to be there also. But the life of heaven will not be a direct continuation of life as we know it here.

When you plant a bulb in the ground, what comes out of the ground is not a massive bulb, but a flower. When you enter into heaven, you will know yourself to be there, but you will not be the same. You shall be like Him, when you see Him as He is (see 1 John 3:2).

The Sadducees rejected the resurrection because they did not understand it. They created a caricature and then pronounced it ridiculous. Their first problem was that they did not know the Scriptures (Mark 12:24). But there was a second issue.

Don't Underestimate the Power of God

> *"Are you not in error because you do not know the Scriptures or the power of God?"* (v. 24)

Jesus' words to the Sadducees could hardly have been more direct. He said, in effect, "The fundamental assumption on which you are building your lives is wrong, and the reason for this is that you do not know the God of the Bible!"

Now the Sadducees believed in god. Jesus' point is that the god they believed in is not the God of the Bible, and that was why they had difficulty believing in resurrection. The god they believed in would not—and could not—do such a thing.

C. S. Lewis points out that this is precisely the problem for many people today.

> The sort of God conceived by the popular "religion" of our own times would almost certainly work no miracles. . . . Speak about beauty,

> truth and goodness, or about a God who is simply the indwelling principle of these three, speak about a great spiritual force pervading all these things, a common mind of which we are all parts, a pool of generalized spirituality to which we can all flow and you will command generalized interest.[2]

Do you recognize this kind of language in our daily TV talk shows? A generalized spirituality into which we can all tap is very popular.

> But the temperature drops as soon as you mention a God who has purposes and performs particular actions who does one thing and not another, a concrete, choosing, commanding, prohibiting God with a determinate character. People become embarrassed or angry. . . . The popular religion excludes miracles because it excludes the "living God" of Christianity and believes instead in a kind of god who obviously would not do miracles.[3]

That's precisely where thousands of people are today. They would say that they believe in god, but they would never expect the god they believe in to do anything in their lives. Praying to such a god would be like a child writing to Santa; it would merely be a way of expressing a wish. Nobody would expect anything to happen. Such a god is little more than a symbol of our aspirations. We might describe him as a gentle whisper, the ground of our being, or an inner voice, but this is not the God of the Bible.

Jesus had shown that the problem for these Sadducees lay in their worldview. The reason they did not believe in the resurrection was first, that they did not understand the teaching of the Bible, and second, that they did not know the God of the Bible.

THE GOD OF ABRAHAM, ISAAC, AND JACOB

So Jesus' first step in reaching out to them was to introduce them to the living God.

> *"Have you not read . . . how God said to [Moses], 'I am the God of Abraham, the God of Isaac, and the God of Jacob?'"* (v. 26)

If you want to know God, you need to know what He has revealed about Himself. This is why we are committed to learning the Bible story. God has made Himself known to particular individuals, and that revelation is recorded in Scripture. When God describes Himself as the God of Abraham, Isaac, and Jacob, He is saying to us,

"If you want to know what I am like, look at how I acted in the lives of these men. Look at what I did, and then you will know who I am."

Look at what God did in Abraham's life. Abraham was brought up worshiping idols, but God intervened to call him. God came down from heaven and made Himself visible to Abraham. He said, "Leave your country and your people . . . and go to the land I will show you" (Acts 7:3). So when God says, "I am the God of Abraham," He is telling us that He is the God who intervenes in human lives to call men and women to follow Him.

Look at what He did in Isaac's life. As a young man, Isaac watched as his father Abraham bound him to an altar on Mount Moriah. Can you imagine how Isaac must have felt? He was about to become a sacrifice when God spoke to Abraham in an audible voice. "Don't touch the boy!" God intervened to save Isaac by providing a substitute. Isaac was released, and an animal was bound to the altar in his place. The animal died, but Isaac's life was spared. So when God says, "I am the God of Isaac," He is telling us that He is the God who steps in to save His people.

He is the living God, . . . the God who calls and saves and fights.

God's dealings with Jacob show us that He never gives up on His people. Jacob lived a twisted life of lies and deceit and ran from both his family and God. One night, the angel of the Lord appeared to Jacob and wrestled with him. God had pursued Jacob through the troubled path of his life, and now God appeared and struggled with Him. That struggle changed Jacob. At the beginning, he was resisting God, but as the struggle continued, Jacob's hip was wrenched out of its socket. He could no longer stand up, and he found himself clinging to the Lord, desperate to know His name and to discover His blessing.

So when God says, "I am the God of Jacob," He is reminding us that He is a God who fights for His people. He is not a vague spirit standing aloof from the universe. A gentle breeze does not wrestle with a man and leave him with his hip dislocated from its socket! He is the living God, the God of Abraham, Isaac, and Jacob, the God who calls and saves and fights. He is the God who steps in to change things.

Once you know the God of the Bible, miracles don't seem so strange.

Twenty-first-Century Sadducees

There are thousands of people today who are just like the Sadducees. They are deeply religious. They say that they believe in God, but the god they believe in is a quiet breeze, a still small voice, a feeling best touched at weddings and funerals, a point of reference useful in inaugurations of presidents, a symbol worth mentioning on the back of a dollar bill.

The Sadducees then, and now, have their reasons for choosing this quiet god rather than the living God of the Bible. Sometimes we are not sure if we want the living God.

C. S. Lewis wrote:

> An impersonal God well and good. A subjective god of beauty, truth and goodness, inside our own heads still better. A formless life-force surging through us, a vast power which we can tap best of all. But God himself, alive, pulling at the other end of the cord, perhaps approaching at infinite speed, the hunter, king, husband—that is quite another matter.[4]

Imagine a group of children playing "burglars." In the middle of their game, they hear a sound and suddenly realize that a burglar is really there! We are happy to talk about our search for God, but as Lewis noted, "supposing we found him. Worse still, supposing he had found us!" With this God we have to be ready for anything. Certainly we should not be surprised if through the course of history He reveals Himself by breaking out of the normal routine in miracles.[5]

Once you know who the God of the Bible is, you have crossed a line in the sand. The God of Abraham, Isaac, and Jacob is free to do whatever He chooses. Christ came so that the Sadducees and their modern counterparts should have the opportunity of knowing the living God who calls, saves, fights, and raises the dead.

Take the Car, Not the Train

There is more than one way to commute into Chicago. You can drive the car, or you can take the train. Thousands of people travel by both means every day, and it's the same, boring routine. The train takes you down the line, stopping at all the same stations. You drive the car down the expressway, past all the same landmarks. The whole thing is entirely predictable.

That's how God has ordered the world. He holds the planets on regular courses, causes the sun to rise at predictable times, and makes things grow in consistent patterns. Science is able to observe these patterns. They are regular, just like the morning commute.

But there is one important difference between taking the train and driving the car. Suppose you are a passenger in the train and one morning you decide that you want to follow a different route. There is no way in the world you can do that, because you are only a passenger.

But if you are in the car, and you decide for some extraordinary reason that after twenty-five years of going down the same road, you are going to go by another route, you are at absolute liberty to do so, because you are the driver.

Here's the question. Is God like a passenger in the train, or is He like the driver of the car? Is God imprisoned in a closed system of the universe in which He has no alternative but to follow the tracks of natural law, or is God, despite the regularity of His actions, at liberty to do something completely different if He chooses?

The Sadducees said that God rides the train. Jesus said that God drives the car.

We can be thankful that God chooses to drive predictably. But if He should choose to do something completely different, He is at absolute liberty to do so.

Once we know the God of the Bible, miracles don't seem so strange.

God's Three Great Interventions

God does not shake miracles out evenly over human history. In the Bible story, miracles cluster around the key events in God's plan of salvation for the world. When human history is over and we look back on all that God has done, three great miracles will stand out from all the rest.

The first will be the great intervention in which the Son of God took human flesh and became a man. God normally gives life through the union of a man and a woman, but on this one occasion He stepped in and caused a virgin to conceive. The God of Abraham, Isaac, and Jacob can do that, and He did. The story of the Incarnation is a great mystery in itself, but it makes sense of everything else in the New Testament. Once we understand who Jesus is, His miracles will not surprise us.

If the Son of God has come into the world, is it really strange that He would display His glory in the most ordinary human situations by turning water into wine and feeding five thousand people?

Real Christianity is a resurrection.

And if the living God should take our flesh and then lay down His life, entering into death, would it be so strange that He should rise from the dead? A gentle breeze wouldn't do that, but when you know the God of the Bible, the Resurrection is really not so strange.

God's second great intervention is often called *conversion*. This is when God breaks into the life of an ordinary person bringing him or her to repentance and faith in Jesus Christ.

We are spiritually dead until God makes us alive in Jesus Christ. Real Christianity is not about turning over a new leaf or about realizing your potential. Real Christianity is a resurrection. It is about God pouring the life of His Spirit into your soul and making you alive with Christ. It is about God stepping in to make things different.

The Sadducees were convinced that there was no point in looking for help or power outside of yourself. But the God of the Bible tells us that the only way in which we can live a life that is pleasing to Him is by the power of His Spirit at work within us.

God's final great intervention will come when Jesus Christ returns in power and glory. The dead will be raised, wickedness will be judged, and God will create a new heaven and a new earth, the home of righteousness.

UNLOCKED

You need to know two things if you are to believe in miracles. The first is the Scripture and the second is the power of God. The God of the Bible takes the initiative and intervenes. He created the world, and He has come down to make Himself known. This living God is all powerful, and nothing is impossible for Him. When we know the God of the Bible, miracles will not seem strange.

As we come to know this God who makes Himself known to us in Scripture, we are faced with challenging questions. If it was the case that you are ultimately accountable to this God who calls and saves and fights and commands, how would you have to change? If it was the case that God is able to give life to your soul and speak strength into those who call upon Him, would you ask Him to do it?

PAUSE FOR PRAYER

Almighty Father,

I bow before You, the living God, in worship, adoration, and praise. You are the God of Abraham, Isaac, and Jacob, the God and Father of our Lord Jesus Christ.

Thank You that You have made Yourself known as my Creator and Savior through Jesus Christ. Thank You that You are able to breathe new life and strength into me, and to make me a new creation in Christ.

Open many eyes to see Your glory. Deliver many from the weak idols of our own creation who can do nothing.

Thank You that You have already set the day for Your ultimate intervention when Your Son, Jesus Christ, will return in glory. Thank You that by Your grace I may be among Your people on that day, through Jesus Christ my Lord. Amen.

Notes

1. The Jewish historian Josephus wrote, "While Pharisees believe that souls have an immortal vigor in them, the Sadducees take away the belief in the immortal soul, the Sadducees believed that when the body died, the soul dies as well. Cited in John Stott, *Christ the Controversialist* (Downers Grove,Ill.: Inter Varsity Press, 1974), 50.

2. C. S. Lewis, *Miracles* (Glasgow: Colins, 1947), 85.

3. Ibid.

4. Ibid., 98.

5. Ibid.

8

Born

LUKE 1

Why is Jesus different from any other person who has ever lived?

8 Born

LUKE 1

DISCOVER

God's incredible journey.

LEARN

why the birth of Jesus is different from other miraculous births in the Bible.

WORSHIP

because God has come to us in Jesus Christ.

IMAGINE that you are living on a large and beautiful island and that your home is located near a magnificent beach that stretches for miles.[1] Life is good on the island, and you are happy to be there.

From time to time, you have been able to explore the island, and you have been fascinated to find people with many different cultures. All the islanders are surrounded by the ocean, and over the years, they've held many discussions about what may lie beyond the horizon. But nobody has ever left the island, and so nobody knows. The discussions never really get anywhere, and since most people have full and busy lives, they aren't that interested.

The island is breathtakingly beautiful, and some islanders have spent many hours studying the wildlife, plants, weather systems, and rock formations. Islanders have also paid a great deal of attention to cultivating family life. Seminars have been held on how to have a healthy island marriage and how to bring up island kids. The land has all kinds of resources to help people develop in body, mind, and spirit.

You and the other islanders are all descended from castaways who were washed onto the island after a great disaster that happened many years ago—so long ago that many residents know little or nothing about it. In recent years, there has been a growing number of islanders who deny that there ever was a shipwreck. They dislike the idea of being descended from castaways and prefer to think of themselves as "natural islanders" who have always been there.

Besides, if the islanders were descended from castaways, it would mean that they were never intended to be on the island, but in some other place, and since there is no other place on the horizon, that seems rather self-defeating.

At the center of the island looms a high mountain with what looks like a crater at the top. One thing that has worried some people is the thought that it may be a volcano. At times the mountain seemed to throw up some ash, and there are stories of some people who got too close at the wrong time and were burned. But the horrendous scenarios of obliteration that have been predicted by some have never happened, and most people have come to the conclusion that they never will.

Message in a Bottle

Early one morning, as you are out strolling on the beach, you see a reflection in the sand. As you look more closely, you notice that a green bottle has been washed up on the shore, and inside there is a message: "Help is coming."

Strange. You have never seen anything like this before. *"Help"? What kind of help could possibly be needed on the island?* you wonder.

A few weeks later, you see another bottle, with another message: "Help will arrive soon!" *This is really strange*, you think. *Two bottles with the same message. Where could they have come from?*

Your curiosity is aroused, and so you begin to walk the beach regularly, looking for bottles. Sure enough, you find another, and then another, all with a similar message. "Help is coming." "Help will be with you soon." "I am sending help."

The discoveries are strangely unnerving. After all, you are living on an idyllic island and are enjoying a very full and satisfying life. But the notes in the bottles keep suggesting that there is some kind of problem. You don't know what the problem is, and you can't imagine what it could be.

You decide to tell your neighbor Bill about the bottles. After all, he also walks the beach; perhaps he has found some too.

"Bill, have you seen any bottles on the beach?"

"No. Why?"

"Well, a few weeks ago I found one, with a note inside. I didn't think much about it, but then I found others. The strange thing is that there seems to be one consistent message in all of them. I'm beginning to think someone is out there beyond the horizon, and they are trying to communicate with us. Whoever he, she, or it is, they are telling us that we are in some sort of danger here, and they obviously have a plan to do something about it."

"Oh, that sounds rather fanciful to me," says Bill. "It is much more likely that the messages were written by some kids further round on the island. If they threw the bottles out to sea, it's quite possible that the tide washed them back in. You don't want to worry about a few messages in a bottle!"

But somehow you can't get the bottles and their message out of your mind: "Help is coming."

The Islanders' Problem

The story of the islanders can help us grasp the big picture of the Bible story. Like an islander descended from castaways, you are not where you were meant to be. God created you to know Him, enjoy Him, and live in His presence. But there was a great disaster. Sin ruptured the relationship between man and God, and our first parents were driven out of Paradise. After they sinned, they found themselves in a fallen world which, for all its beauty, had a curse hanging over it.

But right from the beginning, God promised that help would come. Over hundreds of years God repeated that same message through the Old Testament prophets. "Don't despair; I am sending help. Someone will come to rescue you from the danger that you do not yet fully understand."

Our problem is not about finding fulfillment on the island; it is that the island will be destroyed. The island on which you were born is not where you ultimately belong, nor where you can remain forever. You were born for the mainland that you have never seen, but the only way you can get there is if someone comes from the mainland to rescue you.

That is why Jesus Christ came into the world. He has come from the mainland of heaven to the island of this world. He is the help that God promised at the beginning of the Bible story. He has come to save you from the destruction that will one day come on this world and bring you into an eternal life on the "mainland."

God Takes the Initiative

> *God sent the angel Gabriel to Nazareth, a town in Galilee, to a virgin pledged to be married to a man named Joseph, a descendant of David. The virgin's name was Mary.* (Luke 1:26–27)

The birth of Jesus was entirely at the initiative of God. Mary was a young woman, preparing for marriage to a man named Joseph. She was a virgin. God had chosen her as the one who would bring Jesus Christ into the world, and He sent the angel Gabriel to announce this to her. "The angel said to her, 'Do not be afraid, Mary, you have found favor with God. You will be with child and give birth to a son, and you are to give him the name Jesus'" (vv. 30–31).

Mary did not see how she could possibly have a child, given the fact that she was a virgin. The angel's answer takes us to the heart of the greatest and most wonderful mystery in the Bible.

> *"The Holy Spirit will come upon you, and the power of the Most High will overshadow you. So the holy one to be born will be called the Son of God."* (v. 35)

Mary's child would be born as the result of a direct initiative of God. Joseph had nothing to do with it. He was an outsider, a passive observer to the whole miraculous event. If God had not told him what was happening, he would not have had the faintest idea. God completely bypassed him; He made no contribution whatsoever.

The Bible contains other stories of miraculous births. Abraham and Sarah had longed for a child, and Isaac's birth was a miracle, because they were both well past the age of conceiving children. The same miracle of conception happened for Elkanah and Hannah (who was barren) when Samuel was born, and for Zechariah and Elizabeth (who was past childbearing years) in the birth of John the Baptist.

God acts. . . . God took the initiative.

Each of these children was born as a result of a special intervention of God. But in each case, God worked through the union of a father and a mother. But Mary was a virgin; Joseph had absolutely nothing to do with the child she bore. Not only did he have no union with her before the child was conceived, but Joseph had no union with her until the child was born (Matthew 1:25).

The life in Mary's womb came to be there through a creative miracle of God that is beautifully described in the angel's words to Mary: "The Holy Spirit will come upon you, and the power of the Most High will overshadow you."

It is significant that the angel did not tell Mary to do anything. All she was told was that *God* would do something. God acts; Mary is entirely passive. God took the initiative. Mary's privilege was that God's greatest miracle would take place in her body.

God takes the initiative throughout the Bible story. He does not wait for us to save ourselves. That would be like waiting for the islanders to mount their own rescue. Human history has thrown up many remarkable leaders. The Old Testament is full of them. But God did not wait for a deliverer to arise from the human race; He sent His Son to the human race. God the Son became a man, taking flesh from the Virgin Mary.

GOD'S INCREDIBLE JOURNEY

The New Testament teaches three foundational truths about the identity of Jesus: (1) He is God, (2) He is man, and (3) He is holy.

The angel announced to Mary that her child would be "the Son of the Most High" and "the Son of God" (vv. 32, 35). In Matthew's gospel, He is described as "God with us" (1:23). The apostle Paul explained that Christ was "in very nature God, [but He] did not consider equality with God something to be grasped." Instead He "made himself nothing, taking the very nature of a servant, being made in human likeness" (Philippians 2:6–7).

Speaking of Jesus' birth, Paul said, "He was rich, yet for your sakes he became poor" (2 Corinthians 8:9). Before He was born of the Virgin Mary, God the Son already enjoyed the most marvelous life. This is something that you could not say about any other person.

Before He was born in the stable, He shared the life of God.

Your life began when you were conceived in your mother's womb. Before that moment you did not exist. God used the union of your father and your mother to bring you into being. Before that, you were not, and without that, you would not have been.

But with Christ, it is different. His life did not begin in the Virgin's womb. Before He was born in the stable, He shared the life of God. He was there in the beginning. "In the beginning was the Word, and the Word was with God, and the Word was God" (John 1:1). This Word is the Son of God who took human flesh and was born of the Virgin Mary. The one who has always shared the glory of the Father came to us. He did not arise out of the human race by the union of a father and a mother, but He came as a gift to the human race.

This is of great importance, because only God can reconcile man to God. The Old Testament was full of prophets, priests, and kings, who were men and women just like us. They all belonged to the island. None of them had any means of reaching the mainland. The only way in which the islanders could be delivered was for someone to come from the mainland.

Think of an air-sea rescue. Suppose you are in a dinghy on the water, and you need to be rescued. There's a rope in the dinghy, but you cannot use it to climb up to the helicopter. Salvation has to be from the top down so someone who is secured at the top is lowered on the winch, and by embracing him you are lifted with him to the position from where he came. Salvation has to be from above. Only God can save. We cannot climb up, for the simple reason that we have nothing to climb on!

But Christ has come to us from the mainland. He came on an incredible journey from heaven to earth, and in Him, God is reaching out to every person on this planet.

The Mystery That Makes Sense of Everything Else

Once we have grasped that Jesus is God, it is every bit as important for us to grasp that He is a man. He took human flesh and was born as one of us, entering and sharing our life. He became an islander. This is the mystery that makes sense of everything else.

The fact that Jesus is a man is as important to our salvation as the fact that He is God. God the Son came from heaven because only God can reconcile man to God. But He became man, because only man can bear the punishment for man's sin.

Nothing like this had ever happened before or has happened since. In the Old Testament, there were many occasions when God appeared in a visible form. As we saw in the opening chapter of *Unlocking the Bible Story*, volume 1, these appearances are called theophanies. Right from the beginning of time, God was reaching out so that men and women could know Him. In the Garden of Eden, God took on a visible appearance and actually walked with Adam and Eve in the garden. Later, the Lord appeared to Abraham and ate a meal with him. But these appearances were only temporary.

> If God became man in Jesus, it all begins to fit.

The theophanies could be compared to an actor dressing up or putting on a disguise. When the show is over, the actor takes off his costume and leaves the theater. But the birth of Jesus is entirely different. Here, the Son of God took human flesh to Himself. He did not cease to be God, but He became a man.

Theologian James Packer expresses the wonder of this:

> The Word was made flesh. God became man. The Divine son became a Jew; the almighty appeared on earth as a helpless human baby, unable to do more than lie and stare and wriggle and make noises, needing to be fed and changed and taught to talk like any other child. And there was no illusion or deception in this; the babyhood of the Son of God was a reality. The more you think about it, the more staggering it gets. . . .
>
> The incarnation is in itself an unfathomable mystery, but it makes sense of everything else that the New Testament contains. [2]

In the words of C. S. Lewis, "We believe that the sun is in the sky at midday in summer, not because we can clearly see the sun (in fact we cannot) but because we can see everything else." [3]

You will never be able to fathom how God could become man, but when you believe that He did, you will not find it difficult to understand His claims, His miracles, or His resurrection. Everything else in the New Testament revolves around this one miracle. If God became man in Jesus, it all begins to fit.

If Jesus is "God with us," no one should be surprised that He claims to be the way to God or that He tells us there is no other way. If He has come from heaven, we may be astonished that He would allow His enemies to nail Him to a cross, but it will not surprise us that He should rise from the dead. Once you know who He is, what other outcome would you expect?

And if He is the help that God has promised since the beginning of time, you can be confident that He is able to do in your life what no other person and no other teaching could ever do.

THE HOLY ONE: A NEW KIND OF HUMANITY

"The Holy Spirit will come upon you, and the power of the Most High will overshadow you. So the holy one *to be born will be called the Son of God."* (V. 35, EMPHASIS ADDED)

Jesus Christ is like us in every respect except one. He is holy. This means that He did not at any time commit a single sin. But it means more than that. He was holy in His thoughts, in His intentions, and in His character. His nature was holy. He was not drawn to sin, and He had no inner propensity to sin. There has never been anybody else in human history about whom this could be said.

The apostle Paul was a good man who desperately wanted to live a holy life. He was born into a privileged family and educated in the finest schools. His parents gave him everything he could want, except for one thing. They could not give him holiness. He discovered from his inner struggles that the nature he inherited from his parents was far from holy.

When Paul tried to pursue a holy life, he found himself struggling upstream. There was a battle going on inside him, and for a long time, he did not know how to get deliverance from it.

We saw in volume 1 of *Unlocking the Bible Story* that sin is a power. When Adam sinned, it changed his nature. He became a different kind of man, and he passed that on to his children. Parents pass on many good things to their children, but holiness is not one of them. We do not have that in us.

> [Jesus'] holiness opens up a whole new world of hope for us.

What was born was not holy, and what was holy was not born until Jesus Christ came into the world. Christ broke the chain of the sinful nature, and when He was born there was, for the first time since Adam, a holy human being in the world.

We have become so used to fallen humanity that it is difficult for us to imagine a human being who is not subject to sin and death. "To err is human," we say, as if erring were inseparable from being human. When someone dies, we sometimes talk about them "going the way of all flesh," as if death and flesh were inseparable. Like the islanders who have never seen the mainland, we are so used to our condition that we find it almost impossible to imagine anything else.

But Jesus is the pioneer of a new kind of humanity. His holiness opens up a whole new world of hope for us. His purpose in coming into the world was to "[bring] many sons to glory" (Hebrews 2:10). We see that glory in Him. He was human and did not err. He committed no sin. When He entered death, it was only because He chose to, and it had no power over Him.

Jesus blazes the trail of a new humanity that will be holy, free from sin, and thus no longer subject to death. This has always been the purpose of God. Christ began where His people will end. He entered at birth what His people will enter at our death, and this is the life that He offers to you. When you see Him upon His return, you will be like Him, holy and rejoicing in God's presence as you enter all that God has prepared for His redeemed people.

When Paul confessed his struggles with his sinful nature, he asked the question, "Who will deliver me?" Thank God there is an answer to that question: Jesus Christ our Lord! (See Romans 7:24–25.) He will begin to deliver you when you come to Him. He will begin to make you holy by the power of His Spirit, and when you are in His presence, what He has begun will be complete.

Unlocked

Every child ever born has arisen from the human race by the union of a father and a mother, except for the Lord Jesus Christ. He is the gift of God the Father to the human race. He is God in the flesh, "God with us." He is the help promised by God since the beginning of time.

Stand back and see the magnificent sweep of God's saving work. God the Son came on an incredible journey. He took human flesh to Himself and was born of a virgin. He came down, lived among us, and went to the cross to bear our sin. As God, He was reconciling man to God. As man, He was bearing God's punishment for man. The Son of God became Son of man so that the sons and daughters of men might become the sons and daughters of God.

Pause for Prayer

Almighty Father,

As I consider this greatest miracle that Your Son should take flesh to become my Savior, I bow before You in worship and wonder. Thank You for sending Your Son on that incredible journey. Thank You that forgiveness and reconciliation and eternal life are all ours in Him. Thank You that having taken our flesh, He lives to be our Savior forever.

Help me to live for His glory, in Jesus' name. Amen.

Notes

1. Original idea adapted from a piece in Eugene Petersen, *Working the Angles* (Grand Rapids: Eerdmans, 1987), 139 ff. Petersen adapted it from an essay/parable by Walker Percy, *The Message in a Bottle* (New York: Farrar, Straus & Giroux, 1975).
2. J. I. Packer, *Knowing God* (London: Hodder and Stoughton, 1973), 53, 54.
3. C. S. Lewis, *Miracles* (Glasgow: Colins, 1947), 14.

9

Tempted

LUKE 4

Was Jesus

really tempted?

9 Tempted

LUKE 4

DISCOVER

why Jesus faced the power of temptation more than we ever will.

LEARN

how Adam's sin affects us, and why we should be grateful!

WORSHIP

because Christ has broken the power of the enemy.

THE major multinational companies that dot the downtowns of Seattle, Sioux Falls, San Antonio, and dozens of other metropolises across America typically can be spotted by their impressive skyscrapers, each containing a huge block of offices. Throughout each towering building, thousands of computers are linked together on a network.

Imagine that an enemy decided to sabotage the entire operations of one of these companies. What would he do? He could simply devise a deadly computer virus which, once loaded into the server, would transfer itself to every machine on the network. The virus would gradually corrupt the programs on each computer in such a way that, although some parts would work reasonably well, nothing would work as it used to.

Now suppose the computer geeks are called in, but nobody can find an antidote for the virus. Valuable work is lost, records are unavailable, and permanent loss looms ahead. Left unchecked, the whole system will be destroyed from within.

One virus can corrupt every terminal because all the machines are networked together. The enemy does not need to personally visit every terminal in the building because the network spreads the virus for him, and his objective is achieved.

But now suppose one computer is not linked to the network. While all the other machines in the office are corrupted, the one stand-alone machine remains free from the destructive power of the virus.

If the enemy wants to destroy this machine, he will have to come to the place where it is located and attack from the outside what he could not corrupt from the inside. Since he cannot access this computer via the network, he may resort to a more primitive method of destruction—like attacking it with a baseball bat.

No Virus Found

The computer that is not connected to the network can help us to understand how Jesus is fully human and yet free from the corrupting power of sin that affects every other member of the human race.

In the last chapter we saw that God the Son took human flesh and was born of the Virgin Mary. Jesus is God, He is man, and He is holy. He is like us in every respect except that He is without sin. *Sin had no connecting point to Him.* He had no propensity toward sin in His nature.

The Bible tells us that the human heart is desperately wicked (Jeremiah 17:9 KJV). But Christ's heart was different. There was nothing deceitful or wicked in Him. The Bible also tells us that when we are tempted, we are enticed by our own evil desire (James 1:14). But Christ did not have evil desires. He is the Holy One of God. It is important to understand this clearly, because if Christ were not holy, then He would not be God and He would not be in a position to offer His life as a sacrifice for sin.

Christ took human flesh and became a man, but He did not take *fallen* human flesh. The humanity He took was like the humanity with which Adam and Eve were originally created.

This raises the question of whether the temptations of Jesus were real. We struggle with sin in our nature, and if Christ did not have a sinful nature, how can He know our struggle?

The answer to that question is found at the beginning of the Bible story. When Adam and Eve were in the Garden of Eden, they walked with God and enjoyed His presence. They were holy, *and* they were tempted. In the garden, temptation did not come from within them but from outside them through a direct assault by the enemy. That is how it was in the temptations of Jesus.

It's rather like the difference between subverting a computer network through a virus that spreads to every terminal, and a direct attack on a machine that is not connected to the network and is not infected with the virus.

After the first couple fell into sin, our enemy the devil did not waste his energy in his attempts to destroy God's work. The "virus" of original sin is usually all that he needs to achieve his objectives.

Satan did not appear directly to Jacob, Moses, or David. He just relied on the network. The virus of sin was already in them. Jacob lied to fulfill his ambition. Moses lost his temper and murdered an Egyptian. David was captivated by another man's wife and committed adultery.

But where the tactics of sabotage fail, the Enemy has to use another approach. He has to come out into the open and marshal his forces for a direct assault.

Launching a Direct Assault

The Bible tells us about two occasions when he did this: with Adam and Eve in the Garden of Eden and with Christ in the wilderness. Let's look first at Satan's attack in the garden.

Satan had observed the creative genius of God in giving the man and woman the capacity to be holy and to love God freely. It was enough to make the Enemy sick. Ever since he had been driven out of heaven, he had been energized by his hatred of God and driven by a consuming desire to destroy the work of God. He hated the sight of God's glory, and now that glory was reflected in *people made in His image*. As if that was not enough, it was the purpose of God that they should have children. "Go forth and multiply," God had said. But if their children reflected the glory of God, it would not be long before the whole earth would be filled with His glory.

So Satan came into the garden to our first parents and launched a cunningly disguised assault on their holiness. As we saw in volume 1, he used three primary strategies.

First, the Enemy came to Eve with a question. "Did God really say, 'You must not eat from any tree in the garden'?" (Genesis 3:1). His aim was to introduce *confusion* in her mind about the Word of God.

Then the Enemy made a promise. "You will not surely die" (v. 4). Now he was trying to encourage *presumption* by assuring Eve that the judgment God had spoken about would not actually happen.

Finally, the Enemy appealed to Eve's *ambition*. "You will be like God," he said (v. 5). "Think what you can become," Satan was saying. "Life would be so much more interesting if you could decide what is good for yourself rather than depending on God. Wouldn't you like to be His equal?"

All these temptations came from outside. At that time, Adam and Eve were able to sin and able not to sin. They sinned. They disobeyed the single commandment of God and ceased to be holy.

THE SPREAD OF THE VIRUS

If this were just an ancient story, it wouldn't be worth our interest, but what happened in the garden has a direct consequence in your life and mine today. As the apostle Paul wrote,

> *Through the disobedience of the one man the many were made sinners. (ROMANS 5:19)*

Human beings are not like pebbles on a beach; we are like leaves on a tree. We are not disconnected units; we are one family, and we are descended from one stock.

If the root of the tree is diseased, then the disease will spread to every part of the tree. Adam's sin affected all who came from him. The disease flows from the root, and the blight of sin appears on every leaf of the human tree.

As I write, my home country of Great Britain is still recovering from a massive outbreak of foot-and-mouth disease. As soon as the disease is found in one member of a herd, the whole herd is destined for slaughter: From one infected cow, the whole herd can be lost.

That's why the apostle Paul wrote, "In Adam all die" (1 Corinthians 15:22). This is the tragedy of the human race. When Adam sinned, he sinned as the head of the human race, and his sin has brought death to the whole herd. To change the analogy, through his sin, a virus has entered into the human network, and communicated itself to every terminal that is added to the network through the generations. And there is no fire wall.

The virus in the network has changed everything. Adam and Eve were no longer holy. Their children never knew what it is to be holy. They discovered that sin was not an isolated event, but now had become an inner propensity—a desire that had taken root in their nature. As the years of history rolled forward, they saw what God meant when He said to Adam that sin leads to death.

When sin entered the world, God made two announcements to the Enemy. First, there would be a continuing battle. God said, "I will put enmity between you and the woman, between your offspring and hers" (Genesis 3:15). In every generation, men and women would try to rise above the power of evil. They would fight it, and have some victories, but they would never be wholly free from its power.

And so it was. That's why the sacrifices continued throughout the Old Testament. Year after year, the high priest came into the Most Holy Place knowing that he needed a sacrifice for his own sins and the sins of the people.

The tree was diseased. The herd was infected. The virus had corrupted every terminal. The race was under the condemnation of God. "In Adam all die."

But the ongoing conflict would not be the end of the story. God made a second announcement—a promise actually. A Deliverer would appear one day to crush the head of the enemy. Some day another man would triumph where Adam had failed.

Panic in the Operations Room

If the creation of Adam set alarm bells ringing in hell, what did the incarnation of our Lord Jesus Christ do? I love to think of the panic in hell when, after thousands of years of human history, what they could only have seen as God's "threat" was fulfilled.

Remember that the devil is not omniscient. He does not know all things. Imagine the panic in hell's operations room . . .

"Sir, reports are coming in of an as yet unidentified life that has been born into the world."

"What do we know about Him? Is He human?"

"Confirmed positive. He is definitely human."

"Well, then, let's use the usual channels at work in his nature."

"Confirmed negative! The usual channels are not at work in his nature. He is holy!"

"What? How come He has not inherited the nature that all the rest of them have?"

"He is born of a virgin. He is not part of the network. He is made like them in every respect, but does not appear to suffer from their disease."

"Call research—we need to know what's going on up there!"

A few minutes later the demon returns to relay the findings.

"Research reports that what's going on up there fits disturbingly well with what they call 'the enemy's book of threats.' This could be the initiative that we have feared, sir. What should we do?"

"Our best hope is to eliminate Him. Send someone to have a word with King Herod. If he fails, I will be forced to confront Him directly. We will employ the same strategies we used in the garden. They are well tested and extremely effective, and besides, they do not depend on the subject having a sinful nature. Maintain the operations room at the highest alert."

Herod proved ineffective, and so the enemy had no alternative but to resort to the strategy he had used in the garden: a direct personal attack. For the first time since the Garden of Eden, there was a confrontation between the Enemy and a Man with a sinless human nature.

STALKING THE ENEMY

> *Jesus, full of the Holy Spirit, returned from the Jordan and was led by the Spirit in the desert, where for forty days he was tempted by the devil. He ate nothing during those days, and at the end of them he was hungry.* (LUKE 4:1–2)

> Satan's strategies in the desert were the same . . . confusion, presumption, and ambition.

Notice how God always takes the initiative. The Spirit of God led Christ into the desert. Christ was stalking the Enemy. He came to confront Satan and to destroy his work. The first step in His public ministry would be to confront the Enemy and to triumph where Adam failed. So He went looking for him.

Despite the devil's direct approach on both the first man and the Son of Man, the circumstances in which Adam failed and those in which Christ triumphed contain marked contrasts. Adam and Eve were tempted in a garden; Christ was tempted in a desert. Adam and Eve's hungers were fully satisfied in the garden; Christ had been fasting for forty days, and His hunger was raging. Adam had the company of his wife Eve; Christ was completely alone.

Yet Satan's strategies in the desert were the same as those he had used in the garden: confusion, presumption, and ambition.

AN ATTEMPT AT CONFUSION

> *The devil said to him, "If you are the Son of God, tell this stone to become bread." Jesus answered, "It is written: 'Man does not live on bread alone.'"* (VV. 3–4)

Satan's first strategy was an attempt to create confusion in the mind of Jesus about His own identity. "*If* you are the Son of God," the tempter began.

"Are You really sure about that?" Satan was asking. "If God is Your Father, He doesn't seem to be taking very good care of You. Take matters into Your own hands—turn these stones into bread."

An Attempt at Presumption

The devil led him to Jerusalem and had him stand on the highest point of the temple. "If you are the Son of God . . . throw yourself down from here." (v. 9)

Now the Enemy switched tack and used an alternative argument. Consistency is not his strongest point. Instead of questioning Christ's identity, he now affirmed it and attempted to use Christ's security as the divine Son as the basis of a second temptation.

The devil's argument went like this: "Let's accept that You are the Son of God. Given, then, that God *is* Your Father, You can be absolutely confident that He will take care of You in every circumstance. So You can do anything You want. You could attempt things that other people wouldn't dream of. You could throw yourself off high buildings and God's angels would float You to the ground. So go ahead . . . Do it!"

An Attempt at Ambition

The devil led him up to a high place and showed him in an instant all the kingdoms of the world. And he said to him, "I will give you all their authority and splendor . . . if you worship me, it will all be yours." (vv. 5–7)

Obedience to the will of God would be incredibly costly for Jesus, and Satan used this in the third temptation. "Think of what obedience to the Father will cost You—the loss of Your own life! There must be an easier way."

Satan knew from God's words in the garden that Christ had come to crush his head, so Satan was doing what any general would do when faced with overwhelming opposition. He offered a truce. Satan was happy to offer his support to Christ in any project He chose except the full obedience to the Father.

Satan would have been happy for the Pharisees and Sadducees to give Jesus their full support. He would have done his part to deliver Judas as Jesus' greatest fan. He would have settled for a world filled with the teaching Jesus, just so long as Christ would not proceed with the Father's plan that would lead to a confrontation in which Satan would be crushed, and the people he had enslaved for so long would be set free by the ultimate sacrifice.

But Jesus was not negotiating. The strategy that worked so well in the garden failed completely in the desert. Where Adam collapsed in defeat, Christ rose in triumph. The battle lines were drawn.

FACING TEMPTATION'S FULL FORCE

When the devil had finished all this tempting, he left him until an opportune time. (v. 13)

The Enemy launched everything he had in his assault against our Lord Jesus Christ, but he could not break Him. After he had exhausted every strategy he knew, he was left with no alternative but retreat.

Christ faced the full power of temptation. Although He had a sinless nature, the temptation He faced was greater than we will ever know.

Imagine three airmen flying jets over enemy territory during a war. They are shot down, captured, and then taken by the enemy for interrogation. One by one they are brought into a darkened room.

The first airman gives his name, rank, and serial number. They ask him for the positions of his forces. He knows that he must not give this information, but he also knows that the enemy is cruel, and eventually they will break him. So why go through all that? He tells them what he knows.

The second airman is brought in. He also gives his name, rank, and serial number, and they begin to pump him for information. He is determined not to give in. So the cruelty begins. Eventually it overwhelms him. He breaks and tells them what he knows.

Then the third airman comes in and gives his name, rank, and serial number. "You will not break me," he says.

"Oh, yes we will. We have broken every man who has ever come into this room. It is only a matter of time; you'll see."

The cruelty begins, but he does not break. It is intensified, and still he does not break. So it is intensified again, until it becomes unbearable, but still he does not break.

Finally there comes a point where they have tried everything they know. "It's no use," they say. "He is not like any other person we've had in this room. We can't break him."

Which of the airmen faced the full force of the enemy?

The only one to know the full force of the enemy's assault is the one who did not break. So don't ever think that Christ's temptations were less than yours. Only Christ knows the full power of temptation, because only Christ has withstood the full force of the Enemy's assault.

Don't ever think that Christ's temptations were less than yours.

Adam capitulated early. Some of the heroes of the Old Testament put up a good fight, but at some point, all of them broke. When Christ faced the enemy, Satan threw everything he knew at the Savior. But at the end, Christ stood triumphant and the enemy had no alternative but to leave Him, hoping that in the future, there might be another more favorable opportunity.

Eventually the Enemy concluded, "We can't break Him; it looks like we will have to kill Him."

Plugging into the Network

We saw earlier that Adam's failure had consequences for every person who has ever lived. His sin became like a virus running through the human network. But the New Testament makes it clear that just as we are all descended from Adam, and in that way networked to him, so it is possible, by faith, for men and women to be "networked to Christ" or, as the Bible puts it, "united with Him."

Just as the consequences of Adam's failure in the face of temptation flow to us through our union with him, so the consequences of Christ's triumph over temptation will flow to us through our union with Him. Paul drew the parallel in Romans 5:19: "Just as through the disobedience of the one man the many were made sinners, so also through the obedience of the one man the many will be made righteous."

Paul called Christ "the second man" (1 Corinthians 15:47) and "the last Adam" (1 Corinthians 15:45). The first man sinned in the garden, and the result was the condemnation of the whole human race. Years of human history recorded in the Old Testament demonstrated conclusively that none of Adam's descendants was able to overcome the power of sin.

But God did not leave us there. The Son of God took our human flesh and became another Adam. This second man confronted our enemy, and just as the first Adam's failure spelled death for all his family, so the last Adam's triumph spells life for all his family.

THE POWER OF THE NETWORK PRINCIPLE

As in Adam all die, so in Christ all will be made alive.
(1 CORINTHIANS 15:22)

The whole of human history revolves around two men, Adam and Christ. The whole human race is networked to Adam, and so we all suffer from the disease called sin, which leads to death. If God had left us there, we would be without hope. In Adam all die.

But God decided to build another network—a network of those who are united with Jesus Christ. They are joined to Him not by physical birth, but by a new birth through the Holy Spirit.

Just as the consequences of Adam's sin run through his network, bringing corruption and death to all his descendants, the consequences of Jesus' righteousness run through His network, changing the eternal destiny of all who are joined to Him.

If you don't like computers, change the analogy. God has decided to plant another tree, and by faith you can be grafted onto it so that the life of Jesus will flow into you, as the life of a vine flows into its branches. Or recall the herd and its diseased cow: God has decided to gather another herd that will be free from the disease that condemned the herd descended from Adam.

God's "network principle" is terrible when we consider Adam's sin, but it is wonderful when we consider Jesus' righteousness. God's network principle means that one man's triumph can open the door of everlasting life for many, on the single condition that they are joined to Him.

You and I are both in Adam by nature. Are you "in Christ" by faith?

When we come to Jesus in repentance and faith, the Holy Spirit joins us to Him. Of course we are still in Adam—we have a sinful nature, we live in this fallen world, and one day we will die. But when you come to Jesus, the most important thing is that you are "in Christ," and that means that you will share in His triumph.

Of course, there is a great deal of repair work that needs to be done in us. But when you are in Christ, God begins His work of restoring you.

One day that work will be complete. Then all that was corrupted will fall away. Even your body will be transformed and equipped for everlasting life.

Don't go through life telling yourself what a miserable failure you are. If you are in Christ, hold your head high. You are a child of God, a member of His family. The

Holy Spirit is in you. His righteousness makes you righteous before God, and when you see Christ, you will be like Him.

Oh loving wisdom of our God when all was sin and shame

a second Adam to the fight and to the rescue came.

Oh wisest love that flesh and blood, which did in Adam fail,

should fight again against the foe, should fight and should prevail.

—JOHN HENRY NEWMAN
"PRAISE TO THE HOLIEST IN THE HEIGHT"

UNLOCKED

The Bible makes it clear that Christ was "tempted in every way, just as we are—yet was without sin" (Hebrews 4:15). The difference between the temptations Jesus faced and ours is that we are tempted by our own evil desire (James 1:14). Sin already resides within us. This was not true of Jesus. In His case, temptation came directly from the devil whom He confronted in the wilderness.

This does not mean that Christ's temptations were less than ours; in fact, they were greater. Christ stood against the full force of everything the enemy was able to throw at Him—and triumphed.

PAUSE FOR PRAYER

Almighty Father,

Thank You for the triumph of the Lord Jesus Christ over all the power of the enemy. Thank You that the reign of sin and death has been broken, and that all who belong to Christ are set free.

Help me to see where sin has gained a hold in my life and to gain victory over it by the power of the Holy Spirit. Thank You that one day I will be free not only from sin's guilt and power but even from its presence. Until then sustain me in the battle, for Christ's sake. Amen.

10

Transfigured

LUKE 9

How can I come to terms with the cost of the Christian life?

10 Transfigured

LUKE 9

DISCOVER

how Christ resolved a major disagreement with the disciples.

LEARN

about the magnificent future that lies ahead of every Christian believer.

WORSHIP

as you catch a glimpse of the glory of Jesus.

THE disciples had been with Jesus for nearly three years. They had seen His miracles, heard His teaching, and now Jesus discerned the moment had come to tell them what lay ahead.

He began by asking them a question about their culture. "Who do the crowds say I am?" (Luke 9:18). Jesus did not ask this because He needed the information. He was not doing market research on current opinion. The point of the question was to see if the disciples had understood their own culture.

They rose to the occasion and explained the three popular views about Jesus. "Some say John the Baptist; others say Elijah; and still others, that one of the prophets of long ago has come back to life" (v. 19). John the Baptist was a great moral teacher, Elijah was a worker of miracles, and the prophets stood in the presence of God to bring His Word to His people.

Many people in our culture today put Jesus in one of these three categories. The world's view of Jesus never changes, and disciples of Jesus today still confess their faith against the background of a culture that sees Jesus as a great moral teacher, a man endued with supernatural power, or a prophet through whom God speaks.

Then Jesus asked a second question: "Who do you say I am?" Having established the prevailing view of the culture, Jesus wanted to know if the disciples thought that He fitted into any of these three categories.

Peter stepped forward and said the one thing that his culture was not prepared to hear. "You are," he said, "the Christ of God" (v. 20). Peter was convinced that Jesus was the One the whole of the Old Testament had been pointing to. As he had watched Jesus and listened to Him, he had become persuaded that Jesus could not be slotted into the neat categories of a moral teacher, a wonder-worker, or a prophet. The prophets all pointed to someone who was to come. But Jesus did not point to anybody else. He was the One whom the prophets had been pointing to.

This was a great breakthrough in the disciple's understanding. Jesus said, "Blessed are you, Simon son of Jonah, for this was not revealed to you by man, but by my Father in heaven" (Matthew 16:17), and then He went on to tell them more of what lay ahead.

ARGUING WITH JESUS

"The Son of Man," He said, "must suffer many things and be rejected by the elders, chief priests and teachers of the law, and he must be killed and on the third day be raised to life" (Luke 9:22).

Peter was outraged at this suggestion. Having grasped who Jesus was, Peter found the idea of His suffering and dying to be unthinkable. He took Jesus aside and began to rebuke Him. "'Never, Lord!' he said. 'This shall never happen to you'!" (Matthew 16:22). This was a sharp exchange. The other disciples must have stood frozen to the spot wondering what would happen next.

"Jesus turned and said to Peter, 'Get behind me, Satan! You are a stumbling block to me; you do not have in mind the things of God, but the things of men'" (Matthew 16:23). There must have been a deathly silence.

Peter's great confession of faith was immediately followed by an argument in which Peter acted not as Jesus' disciple but as His adversary (that's the meaning of the name *Satan*). Peter became a stumbling block to Jesus, and Christ had to put that stumbling block behind Him.

There is no indication that this tense exchange was resolved. Jesus went on to tell the disciples plainly that if they were serious about following Him, they would also have their share of suffering. "If anyone would come after me, he must deny himself and take up his cross and follow me" (Matthew 16:24). But Peter remained utterly opposed to the idea of Jesus' suffering and dying.

EIGHT DAYS OF SILENCE

When a sharp disagreement is unresolved, a tension remains in the air, and it seems this is how it was between Jesus and the disciples for a whole week after Peter rebuked Jesus.

Luke skips over eight days in the life of Jesus and the other gospel writers do the same.[1] Matthew and Mark refer to six days. Luke is counting the first and the last days while the others only count the days in between. But the fact that three of the gospel writers record this period of silence indicates that it was significant.

Throughout these days, we may assume that there was a continuing distance between Jesus and the disciples. These were probably among the saddest days in the life of Jesus. There was silence for a whole week. Not one word is recorded. There was tension and estrangement as Jesus moved forward in a direction the disciples did not want to go. He was determined to go to the cross; they were equally determined that it should not be so.

Bible expositor G. Campbell Morgan wrote about the "desolate days in which He realized, and they proved, their present incapacity for fellowship with Him in suffering. He was moving in sublime loneliness to His Cross."[2]

During the week of silence, the disciples must have wondered what the future held. Like those disciples, we experience times in the Christian life where we follow Christ without a glad heart, because we don't like the direction He is taking us. So it is important for us to see how Jesus dealt with the problem.

A GLIMPSE OF THE FUTURE

After eight days, Jesus broke the silence. He took Peter, James, and John on a prayer retreat. They climbed a mountain together, and when they arrived at the top, Jesus gave these frightened and discouraged men a glimpse of the future.

> *As [Jesus] was praying, the appearance of his face changed, and his clothes became as bright as a flash of lightning.* (9:29)

As Jesus prayed, His appearance changed so that the disciples saw Him as He would appear in the future. His face shone, and His clothing dazzled (see Matthew 17:2; Mark 9:2). We call this event the Transfiguration. Jesus was showing His disciples the glory that He would enter after His death and resurrection.

An awesome brilliance radiated from Him, and it is clear that Peter, James, and John were at the limits of vocabulary to describe how He looked. Mark recorded

Peter's recollection, saying that Jesus' clothes appeared "whiter than anyone in the world could bleach them" (Mark 9:3).

The radiance and glory that the disciples saw when Jesus was transfigured is remarkably similar to the description John gave when He saw the glory of the risen Christ in a vision. He saw that Christ's face was like "the sun shining in all its brilliance" (Revelation 1:16). John saw the same glory that Jesus had revealed to him on the top of the mountain when He was transfigured.

The three disciples needed to see this. In the next few days, they would see the face of Jesus battered, bruised, scourged, and beaten. He would be so disfigured as to become unrecognizable. A crown of thorns would be forced onto His head, and after six hours hanging on a cross, the light in His face would go out, and His eyes would be darkened in death. The disciples needed to know that this would not be the end, so Jesus gave them a glimpse of the future.

Every person who has ever lived will see His glory.

The Transfiguration is full of significance. Peter understood what Jesus was saying about the cross (that is why he objected to it so violently), but he did not understand what Jesus said about the Resurrection. He thought that the death of Jesus would be a meaningless exercise in pointless suffering.

The Transfiguration revealed the glory that lay beyond the cross. There would be pain and suffering in Jerusalem, but Jesus wanted the disciples to see where the story would end. They would see Jesus rejected. He would die in ignominy. But that would not be the end of the story. They needed to see the glory that lay beyond the cross.

This glimpse of the future is of great importance when Christ leads us on a painful path. You need to know where the story will end. Christ's kingdom will not dwindle into failure. You are part of a kingdom that will never end. The path on which Christ leads you may be painful, but it does lead ultimately to glory.

We do not serve a weak or ailing Christ who is unable to stop the tide of secularism and pluralism in our world. We serve the risen Lord of Glory who sovereignly moves history forward toward its climax when His own glory will be revealed.

So when you see Jesus rejected, don't ever imagine that is the end. When you hear the world say, "We will not have this man to rule over us," don't ever imagine that you have heard the final word. When you find that His work seems to be set back and you don't understand it, remember the glory that lies beyond the cross.

History is moving toward the day when Jesus Christ will appear in glory. And through all the suffering and darkness of this world, God is moving toward the moment when His Son will be revealed and every person who has ever lived will see His glory.

You Can Be Transfigured Too!

Two men, Moses and Elijah, appeared in glorious splendor, talking with Jesus. (vv. 30–31)

Here is something really amazing. Two men appeared in glorious splendor, and they shared in the glory that was radiating from Jesus. This is full of wonderful significance for us. When Jesus gave the disciples a glimpse of the future, they saw that Jesus would be exalted in glory, and that other human beings would share in that glory as well!

This must have been absolutely staggering to the disciples. They had seen something of the glory of Jesus in the miracles, but who would have imagined that ordinary human beings could be transfigured into glory?

Moses and Elijah were both great men, but they both had their failures. Moses had a murder on his record and was unable to enter the Promised Land because of another failure at a later point in his life. Elijah had seen one of the greatest miracles in the Old Testament (calling down fire onto Mount Carmel), but at one point he regarded his ministry as a failure and lost faith in the ultimate victory of God.

Yet here were these two men, centuries after they had died, sharing in the glory of Jesus. This is telling us something important about our future.

Your Identity Will Not End at Death

God created you for eternity. You will never cease to exist and you will never become somebody else. The Bible emphasizes the continuity between this life and the next. Moses is still Moses, Elijah is still Elijah, and you will still be you.

The disciples immediately recognized Moses and Elijah. We are not told how they knew who these men were. They certainly hadn't seen photographs of them! But God caused them to know the identity of people from earlier centuries who they had never met.

Sometimes people ask if we will know one another in heaven. Of course! We will know others, because identity continues in heaven and because God's great purpose is to gather a great community of His people to share the joy of His presence. One of the greatest joys of heaven will be to see God's reflected glory in one another.

TALKING ABOUT THE CROSS

They spoke about his departure, which he was about to bring to fulfillment at Jerusalem. (v. 31)

It is fascinating that when Moses and Elijah talked with Jesus, the one subject of their conversation was His departure. They knew that it was through His suffering that they would be given a permanent share in the glory of Jesus. Indeed it is through His death and resurrection that all who believe are given the incredible privilege of sharing His glory.

Peter had no understanding of this. He had opposed Jesus' plan to go to Jerusalem and lay down His life, but Moses and Elijah understood that this was how God's promises would be fulfilled. They knew that their share in Christ's glory depended on His going to Jerusalem and giving His life on the cross. So they spoke with Jesus about it.

This conversation must have been a great comfort and encouragement to Jesus, especially after the eight days of strained silence in which the disciples had continued to resist Jesus' plan. Now Moses and Elijah ministered to Jesus as they affirmed what He was doing. When they spoke about His departure, they must have rejoiced with Him in the glory that lay beyond it and would come through it.

The Transfiguration gave the disciples a glimpse not only of the future for Jesus but also for them and for all His people. The disciples may have to take up their cross, but as followers of Jesus, they will also share in His glory.

This is the future for every Christian. Paul speaks about how God has called His people through the gospel so that they might "share in the glory of our Lord Jesus Christ" (2 Thessalonians 2:14). Perhaps John was thinking about how Moses and Elijah shared in the glory of Jesus when, years later, he wrote, "We know that when he appears, we shall be like him, for we shall see him as he is" (1 John 3:2).

THE OVERWHELMING CLOUD

While [Peter] was speaking, a cloud appeared and enveloped them, and they were afraid as they entered the cloud. (v. 34)

The cloud is very significant, because it represents the presence of almighty God. In the Old Testament, the pillar of cloud signified God's presence with His people.

The disciples would have been familiar with this. Now, at the climax of this story, God Himself enters on the scene.

Can you imagine being on the top of a mountain as this thunderous and terrifying cloud moves toward you, and then envelops you? It is hardly surprising that the disciples were terrified, as they "entered the cloud."

When God came down to meet with Moses at Mount Sinai, He spoke in an audible voice. Now the audible voice of God was heard again.

> *A voice came from the cloud, saying, "This is my Son, whom I have chosen; listen to him."* (v. 35)

The heart of the Bible story [is] the Father has made Himself known through the Son.

This invisible God whose presence was hidden in the cloud cannot be known directly. But He does want us to know Him, and He tells us that we may know Him by listening to His Son, whom He has chosen.

This takes us to the heart of the Bible story. The Father has made Himself known through the Son. "No one has ever seen God, but God the One and Only, who is at the Father's side, has made him known" (John 1:18).

If we try to understand God directly, He will always be mysterious to us. I have met people who say that they cannot understand God, and of course they are right! You can't understand God, but you can come to know Him if you will listen to what He says to you through His Son, Jesus Christ. This is how He makes Himself known.

That was precisely the problem for the disciples. They had heard the words of Jesus about the Cross and had refused to listen. Peter thought that he had a better handle on the ways of God, and during the eight days of silence he had resisted what God was showing him through the words of Jesus. Now he found himself enveloped in the cloud in the presence of the Almighty who said to him, "This is My Son; listen to Him."

Peter had resisted the word of Jesus about the Cross, and had tried to stand in His way. But now Peter's resistance was overwhelmed as first Moses and Elijah affirmed Jesus' plan to go to Jerusalem, and then God Himself spoke in an audible voice and told Peter to stop promoting his own ideas and start listening to what the Son of God was saying.

There may be times in your life when you find it very difficult to understand what God allows, and you find yourself resisting His purpose. In all your questions, doubts, and fears, God would point you to Jesus Christ and say, "*This is My Son; listen to him.*"

Cringing and Standing in the Presence of God

When the cloud rested on the mountain and enveloped the disciples, they reacted as any human beings would when confronted with the presence of God. They were terrified. Matthew reported that they could not even stand up; they fell with their faces to the ground, clinging to the grass in terror as the presence of God passed over them (Matthew 17:6).

I have heard people with grievances against God saying that they will have a few things to say to God when they see Him. It won't be like that. Peter fell facedown, and you would have done the same.

As the disciples lay terrified on the ground, something wonderful happened. "Jesus came and touched them. 'Get up,' he said, 'Don't be afraid' " (Matthew 17:7). This is very similar to the other occasion when John saw the glory of the risen Christ in heaven. He fell at the Lord's feet as if he were dead, and again, Christ placed His hand on him and said, "Do not be afraid" (Revelation 1:17).

The disciples must have been profoundly grateful that Jesus was with them when they entered the cloud of God's presence. One day, you will enter the presence of God. If Jesus is with you, you will be able to stand in the presence of God with nothing to fear.

This takes us to the heart of the message of the Bible. This awesome, hidden, and sometimes frightening God points you to His Son so that through Him you may be able to stand in God's presence.

The future is in the hands of God, and three things are absolutely certain: Christ will be glorified. He will share His glory with His people; and through Him, we can stand in the presence of God.

Coming down the Mountain

When the voice had spoken, they found that Jesus was alone. (v. 36)

Then the cloud vanished, Moses and Elijah disappeared from view, and they saw Jesus just as He had been before. Peter, James, and John had to return to the rest of the disciples and live by faith, not by sight.

As they went down the mountain, they must have had a different attitude toward the difficulties that lay ahead. To be a disciple of Jesus seemed the greatest privilege that anyone could know in life, whatever the cost. The way ahead may be hard, but they had seen a glimpse of the glory that lay beyond the Cross.

Unlocked

The Transfiguration reminds us of where the Bible story ends. It is a glimpse of the future. After His death, Jesus would be exalted in glory. Those who follow Him will share in that glory with Him. There is no greater encouragement when we feel the cost of following Christ than to look ahead, and see where this painful path will end.

The path of discipleship may be costly, but it does lead to glory.

Pause for Prayer

Heavenly Father,

Thank You for giving me a glimpse of the glory of Jesus, and for the knowledge that, in Your great mercy, I will one day share in it.

I do not find it easy to take up my cross and follow Your way. I confess that like Peter, I sometimes resist You when Your way seems to be costly. Help me to find strength and courage as I look to the glory that lies ahead. Help me to live in the light of that and find joy in following You whatever the cost.

Thank You for making it possible for me to stand in Your presence without fear and with great joy, through Jesus Christ. Amen.

Notes

1. See Luke 9:28; Matthew 17:1; Mark 9:2.
2. G. Campbell Morgan, *The Crises of the Christ* (Old Tappan, N.J.: Revell, 1936), 217.

11

Crucified

LUKE 23

What did the death of Jesus accomplish?

11 Crucified

LUKE 23

DISCOVER

how the death of Jesus is the centerpiece of the whole Bible story.

LEARN

the significance of Jesus' words from the cross.

WORSHIP

because in His death, Christ has splintered the gates of hell.

SOME years ago, I spent time with a missionary who was working among a primitive tribe in northern Thailand. He had gone there to teach the good news of Jesus Christ. Having gained acceptance, he built his own house in the tribal village and began to learn their language.

Try to picture yourself in his position. You are trying to communicate the gospel to people who worship the spirits of their ancestors. One night, you are sitting beside a campfire with the tribal chief, and he says to you, "Tell us, why have you come here?"

This is the opportunity you have been waiting for. You want to explain the message as clearly as possible, and so you take a deep breath and say, "Well, let me put it like this: 'God so loved the world that he gave his one and only Son, that whoever believes in him shall not perish but have eternal life.' "

You have quoted John 3:16, some of the greatest words ever written, and you have accurately stated the heart of the gospel. But there are some problems with your communication.

The tribal chief does not know who God is. He worships his ancestors. So when you say, "God," he thinks of his grandmother. She also loved the world; in fact the tribal chief cannot think of anybody who loved life more! And when you say, "God gave his Son," the tribal chief thinks about his grandmother having a son who was his father, and he understands that this is the way in which life has continued in the tribe for years; one generation gives birth to the next. And when you talk about "eternal life," the tribal chief is already quite sure that his grandmother is alive and well in the world of spirits, indeed that he offers her worship and hopes that she will afford him some protection.

So the tribal chief smiles and thanks you for coming. "But," he says, "we already know all this!"

I asked my missionary friend how he went about explaining the message of Christ in a way that these people would understand. "It's very simple," he said. "We tell them the Bible story."

He began by explaining who God is, how He made the world, and how He therefore owns the world and everything in it, including us. He explained how the first man and woman broke God's commandment, and as a result were driven from His presence. Then he took the villagers through the Old Testament story, explaining the life God calls us to lead, the sacrifices that were needed because we fail to keep His Law, and God's great promise to send help.

All of this built anticipation that when God finally did whatever He was going to do, it would involve the shedding of blood in a sacrificial death. From there, he told the story of how God Himself came into the world, taking our flesh and went to the cross to die for our sins.

"You have to explain the framework before they can understand the message," he said.

Postmodern America is very different from the jungles of Thailand, but we encounter some of the same problems in communicating the gospel. There was a time in this country when you could reasonably assume that an educated person would have a working knowledge of the main stories of the Bible. But that is no longer the case. The challenge of communicating the gospel has changed.

Spiritual Life in Two Generations

If we want unchurched people to understand the significance of the death of Jesus, we have to explain the Bible story. Let's take an example. Keith's parents brought him to Sunday school from his early childhood years. He discovered what happened in the Garden of Eden, learned about Moses, and especially liked the story of Elijah on top of Mount Carmel.

By the time he was eighteen, Keith knew about the God of the Bible; he also knew the Ten Commandments and the Sermon on the Mount. Of course, this did not make him a Christian. In fact, when he was eighteen, he left the church and told his parents that he no longer believed in God.

In his more honest private moments, Keith would admit to himself that the reasons for his unbelief were complex. He knew the laws of God, but he had chosen a different path, and he found that the best way of living with that tension was to sweep God away from the horizons of his life.

But Keith could not erase the knowledge of God from his mind. When he said that he did not believe in God, it was the God of the Bible that he did not believe in. Even his unbelief was defined by the knowledge of God that was imprinted in his mind.

Twenty-five years later, Keith formed a friendship with Dave, a Christian colleague at work. Dave invited him to a meeting where he heard the story of the Cross. The message of the love of Christ reaching out to those who despised Him awoke something inside Keith. Memories of God were rekindled, and he began to feel strangely drawn to return to the God he had known, but then denied.

Keith has a daughter, Lisa, who is at college. She has hardly been in church, except for a few family occasions when her grandparents were in town. Lisa hardly knows anything about the Bible, but she will tell you that spirituality is important to her. She is drawn to meditation, and says that it helps her get in touch with herself.

If you ask Lisa how she knows right from wrong, she will say that her conscience tells her. "If it feels wrong, you shouldn't do it," she says, "but if it feels right, then who's to tell you otherwise?"

With regard to the future, Lisa believes that we all go on forever, though nobody can know what this will be like. One day, Lisa is invited by a friend to a Christian meeting at her college campus. She hears the message of John 3:16, just as her father had: "For God so loved the world that he gave his one and only Son, that whoever believes in him shall not perish but have eternal life."

Where the Bible story is not known, the Cross will not be understood.

But she does not know who God is, and she cannot imagine why anybody should perish. So she finds it very difficult to make sense of the message. She assumes it is all a metaphor, a way of saying that God loves us all and wants us to have a wonderful life. She says that she really enjoyed the evening. She has heard the gospel, but like the tribal chief, she has not begun to understand it.

Where the Bible story is not known, the Cross will not be understood.

The Cross is God's answer to the problem presented in the Bible story, and if we have not seen the scale of the problem, we will not be able to grasp the magnificence of the solution. That is why it is so important to unlock the Bible story.

THE STORY OF THE CROSS

The Gospels record the story of the Cross with great restraint.

> *When they came to the place called the Skull, there they crucified him, along with the criminals—one on his right, the other on his left.* (LUKE 23:33)

Calvary is Eden in reverse. In the garden, God pronounced man guilty. At the Cross, man pronounced God guilty. In the garden, God pronounced the sentence of death on man. At the Cross, man pronounced the sentence of death on God. God had driven man out of His garden; now man would drive God out of His city.

The Cross reveals the full extent of human sin. Sin began in the garden but it did not end there. In our human nature, there is a deep resistance toward God. It is in our nature to hate Him. In the story of the Cross, this hatred reaches its full expression.

Jesus hung on the cross for around six hours. It was the third hour (9 A.M.) when they crucified Him (Mark 15:25), and darkness covered the land from the sixth hour to the ninth hour (Luke 23:44). These were six hours of unrelieved and excruciating suffering. All of the gospel writers focus our attention on what happened during those six hours. Luke records three events that take us to the heart of the story.

FORGIVENESS RELEASED

> *Jesus said, "Father, forgive them, for they do not know what they are doing."* (V. 34)

When God pronounced sentence on the first sin, Adam must have thought that the judgment of God was going to fall on him directly. But, as we saw in chapter 2 of the first volume of *Unlocking the Bible Story*, God diverted the curse onto the ground.

The principle is clear. Sin always leads to God's judgment. But in His great mercy, God allows the judgment to be diverted away from the sinner and to strike somewhere else so that room is created for reconciliation.

We saw the same principle in the story of Moses. When God was giving the Ten Commandments at the top of Mount Sinai, His people were busy breaking them around a golden calf on the plain below. The sin of the people caused God to remove His presence from them, so Moses went up the mountain to see what he could do about obtaining forgiveness.

He asked God if it would be possible for the consequences of their sin to fall on him. "Please forgive their sin—but if not, blot me out of the book you have written" (Exodus 32:32).

It was a remarkable offer, but not one that God could accept. Moses had his own sins, so he could not bear the sins of others. Instead, God allowed that a lamb could be sacrificed and, for the time being, His judgment would be restrained. The death sentence was diverted onto the animal, and in this way, God's mercy was extended to the people. Justice for the people's sin would be postponed for another day, and in the meantime, God's presence would return to them.

The same principle is seen in the story of Elijah. The priests of Baal had led many people away from obedience to God, and the time had come for God to reveal His awesome power. A large crowd was gathered around an altar at the top of Mount Carmel. Elijah prayed, and God's fire fell from heaven. When fire falls, people get burned, and if you had been in the crowd, you would have been quite certain that your final moment had come.

But God targeted His fire, and it struck the sacrifice on the altar. Not one of the people were burned, even though some were standing only a few feet away (see 1 Kings 18:20–39).

Man's sin reached its full horror and its most awful expression at Calvary.

God was teaching the principle that runs right through the Bible. Where there is sin, God's judgment must fall, but God is merciful and diverts His judgment to another place—the ground, the sacrifice, and the altar—so that those who would otherwise be consumed by it may be spared. God was building all this into the minds of His people so that we would be able to understand what was happening at the cross.

Man's sin reached its full horror and its most awful expression at Calvary. Not only had we disobeyed God's commandments and defied God's name, now we were crucifying God's Son.

If there was ever a moment in human history when God's judgment had to fall, this was it. But Jesus cried out, "Father, forgive them, for they do not know what they are doing."

Christ was isolating Himself under the judgment of God. He knew that judgment would come, but He cried out to the Father, "Don't let it fall on them. Let it fall on

Me, and on Me alone. Let Me be the lightning rod for Your judgment on their sin. Allow Me to be the sacrifice that is consumed, but don't let Your judgment fall on them."

I sometimes wonder what must have gone through the minds of angels as they watched what was happening on that cross. No doubt they gasped in wonder when they saw the Son of God take human flesh as He was born into the world.

> God's judgment for human sin is poured out on Jesus.

Now they saw that flesh torn by a whip. They saw thorns embedded in His brow, and nails piercing His hands and feet. Surely the eyes of angels must have been fixed on the throne of God, waiting for justice to be done. Now surely the judgment of God would be poured out on this human race. But then Jesus cried out, "Not on them, just on Me. Let Me be isolated under the judgment of God."

Just as God had spared Adam when the curse fell on the ground, and just as God spared the crowd on Mount Carmel when the fire struck the sacrifice, so God spared those who stood around the cross as His judgment for their sin fell on Jesus.

This is the heart of the gospel. Jesus stands under the judgment of God for sins that have been committed against Him. The victim asks that He may bear the sentence for the crime. Christ asks the Father to divert the punishment away from His enemies, and He absorbs it in Himself. That is how forgiveness is released.

God's judgment for human sin is poured out on Jesus. He bears it on the cross, while those who crucified the Son of God stand in the darkness unaffected by it.

When Christ prayed, "Father, forgive them," His prayer included the priests who condemned Him, the crowds who mocked Him, the soldiers who crucified Him, and the disciples who deserted Him. But it extended further. It included the Old Testament believers who had waited for Him and all those in every generation who would come to Him.

When Jesus isolated Himself under the judgment of God, His prayer was sufficient for every sin of every person who would come to Him. And if His prayer could cover the sins of those who nailed Him to the cross, then it will cover every sin you have committed or could commit. The Son of God took the punishment for your sins so that it would be diverted away from you and onto Him.

PARADISE OPENED

One of the criminals who hung there hurled insults at him: "Aren't you the Christ? Save yourself and us!"

But the other criminal rebuked him. "Don't you fear God," he said, "since you are under the same sentence? We are punished justly, for we are getting what our deeds deserve. But this man has done nothing wrong."

Then he said, "Jesus, remember me when you come into your kingdom."

Jesus answered him, "I tell you the truth, today you will be with me in paradise." (23:39–43)

Sin led to our first parents being driven out of Paradise. Adam and Eve had enjoyed a wonderful relationship together and with God. In the cool of the day, the Lord God walked with them in the Garden of Eden (Genesis 3:8). There was no suspicion, only trust; no fear, only love; no pain, only joy.

But when they chose the knowledge of evil, they could not stay in Paradise. They were driven out of the garden, and there was no way back. The entrance was guarded by cherubim and a flaming sword.

The Old Testament story emphasizes this exclusion. When the tabernacle and then the temple were set up with a holy place at the center, a heavy curtain was draped in front of the holy place. God said that He would appear in a cloud there, but ordinary people could never enter.

The Old Testament story raises one fundamental question: How can men and women get back into the Paradise that Adam lost?

The Old Testament contains no explicit answer to that question, only the promise that God would find a way to restore paradise. Men and women of faith believed that God would do something, but since they lived before He did it, all they could do was rest in His promise. They died in faith, waiting for God's promise to be fulfilled. As far as we can tell from the Old Testament, they went to a kind of waiting room, until Christ should come.

Then Jesus Christ came into the world with good news. "The kingdom of heaven is at hand," He said. "God is about to open access to His kingdom, and citizenship will shortly be made available to all who will come."

Now, three years later, He goes to the cross and finds Himself in the company of two men who had made a tragic waste of their lives. They had pursued lives of crime, and the long arm of the law has finally caught up with them. They are paying the price, and their sad lives are ebbing away.

This man . . . was about to enter the greatest joy a human being can ever know.

The criminals have no fear of God, and even in death, they join the crowd in heaping abuse on Jesus. But then something happens in the soul of one of them. He knows that death is drawing near, and it seems to dawn on him that in just a few moments, he may find himself in the presence of God.

"Don't you fear God?" he says to his friend. Then he turns to Christ and says, "Jesus, remember me when you come into your kingdom." Jesus turns painfully toward him and says, "I tell you the truth, today you will be with me in paradise" (vv. 40, 42–43).

This man's life had been a series of disastrous choices, but Jesus promises him an immediate translation, through death into a life of undiluted joy in the immediate presence of God.

The awful suffering that the thief was enduring would soon be past, and then he would enter eternity. But he would not face the condemnation of God, because Jesus was taking that for him. Before the day was over, Jesus would usher this man into the presence of God. Suddenly this man, for whom the world now held nothing, found that because of Jesus he was about to enter the greatest joy a human being can ever know.

When Jesus died, heaven was opened for all who would come.

When Jesus died, God gave one more sign that the way back into His presence and His blessing was now open. "The curtain of the temple was torn in two" (v. 45). Matthew adds that it was torn from top to bottom, almost as if God had reached down and personally torn it apart.

The curtain was, of course, the great symbol of exclusion from God's presence. Cherubim were embroidered into the curtain, as a reminder of the cherubim who blocked the way back into Paradise after Adam and Eve were driven out. Now it lay limp and torn on the floor. When Jesus died, heaven was opened for all who would come.

It was now about the sixth hour, and darkness came over the whole land until the ninth hour. (v. 44)

Jesus had suffered the judgment of men. Now He would endure the judgment of God. As Jesus entered into the heart of His sufferings, God kept the sun from shining.

Christ entered all the dimensions of hell while He was on the cross. In the hours of darkness, He bore our guilt, endured God's wrath, and suffered the taunting of evil. He endured all this alone, without the comfort of His Father's presence. That is why He finally cried out, "My God, my God, why have you forsaken me?" (Matthew 27:46).

But then, the darkness passed. The storm was over. The judgment poured out on Christ was exhausted, fully spent. And at the end of the three hours of darkness, Jesus cried out, "It is finished."

Death Subdued

Jesus called out with a loud voice, "Father, into your hands I commit my spirit." (23:46)

After three hours, the darkness cleared. The Son was no longer forsaken by the Father. He no longer bore the guilt of our sins. Sin had been dealt with. Justice had been satisfied, and Christ had bound the enemies in the valley of death for all His people.

Now all that remained was for Him to lay down His life. It was not a torturous process of wrenching the soul from His body. He placed His Spirit in the Father's hands.

Finally, the battle is over. The victory is won.

The last words of Jesus were not uttered with an exhausted sigh but "with a loud voice." There is a note of triumph here. He has released forgiveness to all who will receive, opened paradise for all who will come, drawn the sting of death, and bound the enemies who lurk in the valley. He has completed everything that the Father has given Him to do. It is finished.

On the third day, He rises from the dead. A few weeks later, on the Day of Pentecost, Peter begins to preach the Christian message: "God has made this Jesus, whom you crucified, both Lord and Christ" (Acts 2:36).

He is the one who brings God's salvation to you. He has cleared the enemies from the valley of death. He has opened paradise. He has borne the sentence of death for our sins and offers forgiveness to all who will come to Him in repentance and faith.

Don't push Him away. Come to Him and receive what He has purchased for you. Receive the gift of God by faith and make it your own. Understand the power and the promise of these words:

> *"For God so loved the world that he gave his one and only Son, that whoever believes in him shall not perish but have eternal life."* (JOHN 3:16)

UNLOCKED

Everything that God had promised to do since the beginning of time was accomplished through the sacrificial death of the Lord Jesus Christ on the cross. The whole of the Bible story has been preparing us to understand the meaning and significance of His death.

When Jesus died on the cross, He offered Himself as the sacrifice for our sins. Our sentence was passed onto Him. He bore our judgment in our place. In this way He opened the way back into paradise. Bearing our sin, He has opened the way for us to be righteous before God. Having been forsaken by the Father, He has opened the way for us to be reconciled to God. Having entered our hell, He has opened the way into heaven for all who will come to Him.

PAUSE FOR PRAYER

Gracious Father,

Thank You that Jesus suffered and died on the cross for me. Thank You that He bore the sentence of death for my sins, and that through His death Your mercy reaches me. Thank You that He has opened paradise, so that through His death, I may enter everlasting life in Your presence. Thank You that He was alone in the darkness so that I should never face darkness alone.

I am the sinner for whom Jesus died. Gladly I trust Him as my Savior, and receive by faith the amazing gifts that He has purchased for me. Receive my worship in Jesus' name. Amen.

12

Risen

LUKE 24

What can the

resurrection

of Jesus mean

for me?

12 Risen

LUKE 24

DISCOVER

how the first visitors to the tomb knew that Jesus had risen.

LEARN

why the Christian message is not "Jesus is alive" but "Jesus is risen."

WORSHIP

because Jesus Christ is risen from the dead.

IT must have been that old Monday morning feeling, as the three women made their way to the tomb. Their holiday, of course, was Saturday, the Sabbath, and it had been a miserable one. Now they had to face the first day of the week. Back to the routine, back to grinding out a living. Even after the greatest tragedies, life has to go on.

They had started early because they wanted time to cherish the memory of Jesus, who had died two days earlier, before they moved on to other things. These women were part of a group who traveled with Jesus and the twelve disciples (see Luke 8:1). They were from rural Galilee in the north of Israel, and they clearly had a deep commitment to Christ.

There was "Mary (called Magdalene) from whom seven demons had come out" (Luke 8:2). She must have had a remarkable story. For years, her life had been controlled by demonic powers. If you had met her at that time, you would have seen a woman who was driven by compulsive patterns of behavior that were beyond her own control. But Christ had set her free. He took authority over the evil powers that were destroying her life, and from that time forward, she was a devoted follower of Jesus.

Then there was "Joanna the wife of Cuza, the manager of Herod's household" (v. 3). Interesting: the manager of the king's household held a high-level position. Cuza was at the center of life in the royal palace, and Joanna was at his side.

The Gospels give us an insight into what was going on in the palace. John the Baptist had the courage to tell Herod that his relationship with his brother's wife was wrong. Herod responded by putting John in prison, and eventually had him beheaded. All that had happened after a party at which a young girl danced for the king, and who do you think would organize a party for the king? The manager of Herod's household.

Pilate tried to avoid taking responsibility for Christ by sending Him to Herod's palace. Yet here we find Joanna, the wife of Herod's household manager, in the inner group of Jesus' followers. Evidently she had come to know Jesus in Galilee and she had joined the group and followed Him to Jerusalem.

It was these same women, Mary Magdalene and Joanna, who came to the tomb along with Mary the mother of James on the first day of the week (24:10).

Love Without Faith

> *"Remember how he told you, while he was still with you in Galilee: 'The Son of Man must be delivered into the hands of sinful men, be crucified and on the third day be raised again.'" Then they remembered his words.* (vv. 6–8)

The women had heard Christ speaking about what would happen on the third day. On at least three occasions, He had specifically told them that He would rise from the dead.

They had heard His words, but it is quite clear that on this first day of the week, they did not expect anything unusual to happen. Their journey to the tomb was motivated by love, but it was absolutely devoid of faith. Whatever faith they had in Christ before had been overwhelmed by the darkness of Calvary. Faith was extinguished, and all that was left was love. So they went to the tomb with spices to anoint His dead body.

It is possible to have great love for Christ and absolutely no faith. These women believed in Christ's cause. They gave their money to support it. They had a deep love for Christ. But they were traumatized by the horrible reality of His excruciating death that they witnessed just two days before, and now they felt that death was stronger than His promise. Faith was gone; all that was left was love.

Today, many people have a deep affection for Christ but find it hard to believe. Having learned about the Christian faith, they were drawn to Christ and began to follow Him. But then they experienced great darkness in a personal tragedy, or in some great evil that was done, and somewhere in the darkness they stopped believing.

This has been a struggle for many who have served their country on the field of battle. The trauma of seeing the unspeakable cruelty and suffering of war has led some to say with sadness that they can no longer believe. The pain seems to extinguish the possibility of faith.

That was the position of these women on the first Easter morning, and it is the position of many today. Perhaps, like these women, you have seen unspeakable cruelty and suffering, and you simply cannot come to terms with it. In the darkness, faith has been extinguished and all that is left is love. You still attend church because there is affection for Jesus in your soul. You wish that it all might have been true, but the wish is filled with sadness and doubt.

Lost for an Explanation

> *They found the stone rolled away from the tomb, but when they entered, they did not find the body of the Lord Jesus. . . . They were wondering about this.* (vv. 2–4)

When the women arrived, they found that the rock in front of the tomb had been moved. When they went into the tomb, they found that it was empty. The women had absolutely no idea what to make of this. They were confronted with evidence, but they were lost for an explanation. The empty tomb left them "wondering."

It is important to notice that they did not immediately jump to the conclusion that Jesus had risen from the dead. When we have discussions about "what we should make of the empty tomb," we should remember that the first visitors had no idea how to answer that question.

When they found the body was missing, Mary did not say, "I have this feeling that He must have risen from the dead," and Joanna did not reply, "You know, I have that feeling too. I think you must be right." The thought did not even occur to them.

So how did they know what happened?

God told them.

GOD GIVES THE EXPLANATION

While they were wondering about this, suddenly two men in clothes that gleamed like lightning stood beside them. In their fright the women bowed down with their faces to the ground, but the men said to them, "Why do you look for the living among the dead? He is not here; he has risen!" (vv. 4–6)

God called two angels and said, "Go and tell them what I have done. These women love My Son, but there is no way in the world that they are ever going to work out what happened. Go tell them."

Suddenly the women became aware of "two men in clothes that gleamed like lightning" standing beside them. The other gospel writers identify them specifically as angels. Luke gives us a description. They looked like men and yet they were clearly not men because of the radiance of their appearance. They were given the privilege of announcing the greatest news the world has ever heard: "He has risen!"

A Christian is a person who has come to believe God's explanation of His own action. Christian faith rests entirely on grasping and believing what God tells us He has done. We have seen this pattern throughout the Bible story.

When Adam breathed his first breath and became aware of himself as a living being, he had no means of knowing who he was until God told him. God explained what had happened. Adam was made in God's image and for His glory.

When the Virgin Mary conceived a child, there was no way that she could have known what was happening to her. So God sent the angel to explain what was about to happen. It was the same with the shepherds and the wise men. How could they possibly have known that the child in a manger was God in human flesh? Without God's explanation through the angels and the star, they would never have known what was happening.

It was the same with the death of Jesus. Many people saw Him die, but few understood the significance of the Cross. But God tells us that on the cross, Christ bore our sin and endured our punishment, laying His life down as a sacrifice so that justice would be satisfied and we may receive mercy.

It was the same for the women at the tomb on the first day of the week. They would never have worked out what had happened for themselves. God told them. Christian faith does not rest on feelings, impulses, or personal insights. It is believing God's explanation of events, given to us in the Scripture: "He has risen!"

"RISEN" MEANS THAT DEATH IS DEFEATED

The word "risen" is full of significance, telling us first that death is defeated.

From the first sin in the Garden of Eden, death has been relentless. The apostle Paul wrote that "death reign[s]" (Romans 5:14, 17). It is like a tyrant exercising a reign of terror over the human race. Nobody can escape it. Everybody is subject to its awful cruelty.

In the Old Testament story, there were many great men of faith. Abraham, Isaac, Jacob, Moses, and David all believed God's promise, but death got every one of them.

What happened when they died?

We can be quite certain that they did not enter condemnation or judgment. They had trusted the Savior who was to come and looked for the sacrifice that would be made. They died before He came, and so we should think of them as waiting. They continued in a shadowy existence, separated from this life but unable to move forward into the presence of God. Death brought them to a place where there was a way in but no way out. They were stranded in a kind of "no man's land" with nothing to do but wait.

When I was around kindergarten age, my class at school had a pet mouse. On the weekends each of us had the opportunity to take the mouse home. Eventually my turn came, and one bright Saturday afternoon I brought the mouse outside into the sunshine.

I decided to bring several of my toys outside to make things more interesting for the mouse. One of them was a bright red double-decker London bus, about one foot long by six inches high.

The mouse found the red bus fascinating and before I knew it had climbed inside, run up the stairs, and was working its way along the top deck, clambering over the little plastic seats, and poking its nose out of the spaces for the windows.

This was tremendous entertainment, until it reached the front of the bus. Then we had a problem. The mouse couldn't move forward, and it couldn't go back. It was completely stuck.

Of course, I tried everything, including cheese at the back of the bus, but the poor animal had no room to turn. There was no way out.

I can still remember the sense of panic. What could I tell the rest of the class on Monday morning? "Sorry, the mouse is imprisoned in a London bus, but we can still feed it through the window!"

I remember my father saying, "There's only one thing to do, son. We'll have to destroy the bus!" And sure enough, he did. He took a knife and cut the roof open, and the mouse was free.

When Jesus died, He cut a hole in death itself.

I can't tell you what a relief that was. But my bus was never the same. It really was rather curious: a bright red London bus with half the roof missing. Of course, this made it even more interesting for the mouse. It could now go in the door, climb up the stairs, and come out through the roof.

Before, the bus had been like a dead end. There was a way in but no way out. Now, the mouse could go in knowing that there was also a way out. There is all the difference in the world.

From the time of Adam to the time of Christ, death had a way in but no way out. People went into death, but they could not emerge from it. But when Jesus died, He cut a hole in death itself. He changed its nature so that when I come to that moment of death, it will not be like entering a prison; it will be like going through a passage that leads right into the presence of God. There's all the difference in the world.

Before Christ, people went into death. But Christ went through death. Death could not keep its hold on Him. He is risen, and in His resurrection, He has destroyed the holding power of death. "Risen" means that death is defeated.

"Risen" Means the Whole Person Will Be Redeemed

The message of Easter is not that Jesus is alive. That is true, of course, but Easter tells us much more. The message of Easter is that Jesus has risen!

It is worth thinking about the difference. The Son of God was alive in heaven before He ever took human flesh. "In the beginning was the Word, and the Word was with God, and the Word was God" (John 1:1). He was not only alive but actively engaged in the work of the Godhead in creating and sustaining the world. The Son of God has life in Himself, and nobody can take it from Him. All this was true of Him *before* He took human flesh.

So why did He not simply leave the crucified body in the tomb and return to the Father? After all, it was only flesh and bone. Why did He bother with it?

The angels could still have appeared on Easter Sunday morning and said, "Now look, His body is here in the tomb, but you don't need to worry, because although you can see His body lying here, His Spirit is with the Father in heaven. He is alive, and He hears your prayers, and He is able to help you."

After all, when a Christian person dies, is this not precisely what we say at the funeral service? We bury the body. We know exactly where it is. We visit the graveside. But then we say, "Even though we know the body is here; nevertheless, the soul of the person is with the Father in heaven."

But the message of Easter is not that Jesus is alive in the presence of the Father. It is that Christ is risen! Do you see the difference? God has determined to redeem every part of you. Not just your soul, but your soul and body together.

[After] death . . . body and soul [will] be reunited in the power of a new life.

God has made human beings in a wonderful way. He created angels as souls without bodies. He created animals as bodies without souls. But He created men and women as a unique integration of body and soul together.

That is why death is such a terrible enemy to us; it is the separating of the soul and the body that God has joined together. It is the undoing of our very nature.

The survival of the soul without the body would mean only part of us being saved, and that would not be a victory over death. Since death is the separating of soul and body, the only way in which death can be defeated would be for body and soul to be reunited in the power of a new life.

> *While they were still talking about this, Jesus himself stood among them and said to them, "Peace be with you." They were startled and frightened, thinking they saw a ghost. He said to them, "Why are you troubled, and why do doubts rise in your minds? Look at my hands and my feet. It is I myself! Touch me and see; a ghost does not have flesh and bones, as you see I have."* (vv. 36–39)

The Bible places great emphasis on the physical nature of the Resurrection. When Christ appeared to the disciples, they thought that they were seeing a ghost, so

Jesus drew their attention to His hands and His feet and invited them to touch Him. "A ghost does not have flesh and bones, as you see I have," He said.

Jesus wanted them to know that what they were seeing was more than the spirit of Christ in a visible form. The flesh that lay in the tomb had been raised. When Jesus said, "It is I" (v. 39), He did not mean that a part of Him had survived death and lived on, but that the whole of Him had come through death and triumphed over it.

When Christ returns in glory and gathers all His people in His presence, every believer will be there, not only in mind but also in body. It is not just some spiritual capacity within you that will enter heaven. You will be there rejoicing in the presence of God. God has determined to redeem not just a part of you but the whole of you. And if we would believe more clearly in the resurrection of the body, we would have a much greater anticipation of the life in heaven.

Taking a Virtual Vacation

Suppose you have planned the vacation of a lifetime in Hawaii, but just before you are due to take the trip, you fall down the stairs and break just about every bone in your body. In good cartoon style, you wind up in the hospital, bandaged from head to toe, with a thermometer sticking out of your mouth.

There is absolutely no possibility of your going to Hawaii. Your body is simply not up to it. But you have a friend who is a wizard with computers, and he says, "Don't worry; I'm going to take you there anyway. You'll have the time of your life. I'll take you on a virtual tour of Hawaii on the Internet."

So he brings his laptop computer and sets it up on the bed in front of you. And sure enough, you can see Honolulu. You can view it from different angles. Then he gives you a pair of headphones and, sure enough, you can hear the sounds of the ocean. Then he produces his latest accessory—virtual smells. He places a little pad on your collar, and you can actually smell the flowers as you see them on the screen.

Your friend is excited about all this, and you are grateful that he has gone to all the effort. You thank him for his trouble.

"It's so beautiful," you say. "I just wish that I had been able to go."

"What do you mean?" he asks. "You have gone! You saw Hawaii, heard its sounds, and smelled its scents. What more could you want?"

Your friend is a computer geek, so you humor him and let him go. Whatever he says in his fancy world of computers, you know that you ain't been there! And the reason that you haven't been there is that your body is stuck there in the hospital. You may go there in your mind, or your imagination, or via the Internet, but if you do not go there in your body, you haven't really gone.

The Resurrection tells us that heaven is not some kind of spiritual experience; it is not a mind game, like a virtual tour. It is not that some spiritual capacity within you survives death to continue in an existence that is a shadow of the life you knew before. That's what the Old Testament believers had while they were waiting for the coming of Jesus.

It was not a part of Christ that ascended to the Father. It was the whole of Christ that ascended to the Father: mind, soul, spirit, and body. "It is I," He said to the disciples, "not a part of Me, but the whole of Me."

He is risen! "Risen" means that death is defeated. "Risen" means the whole person will be redeemed.

"Risen" Means We Will All Be Changed

When the body of Jesus was raised, it was also changed. Christ's flesh was raised, but it was also adapted to be appropriate for everlasting life. This was something that had never happened before.

There had been other examples of life returning to a dead person. Jairus's daughter, the son of the widow at Nain, and Lazarus had all been brought back to life by the power of Jesus.

These were wonderful miracles. But Lazarus came out of the tomb exactly as he had gone into it. I guess he might have been a few pounds lighter, but he was essentially the same! He carried on the process of aging at the point where he had left off, and then at some point, the poor fellow had to go through the whole miserable business of dying all over again. Jairus's daughter and the widow's son also would age and eventually die. Death was delayed but not defeated.

But when Christ was raised, His body was no longer subject to aging, sickness, or death. The resurrection body is not subject to pain or disability. It was His flesh, but it was transformed and adapted for eternity.

This is the glorious future that awaits every Christian believer. God has not prepared some kind of compensation package like a reduced pension plan for those who are unable to continue life on earth. He has sent Jesus Christ to redeem the whole of you, body and soul, and in the resurrection He will adapt your body even as He is preparing your soul for eternal life in His presence.

Wait till Everybody's Ready

The gift of the resurrection body is so wonderful that God holds it in reserve until the day when He will gather all His children together.

That's what it was like on Christmas morning when I was a child. We always had presents when we woke up early on Christmas morning. Stockings were hung beside the fire, and in the morning we were all eager to go into the living room and open the gifts. But we weren't allowed to go into the room until everybody was standing together at the door. Then, when everybody was ready, we all went in.

I think of Christian loved ones who have died. They are in the presence of Jesus, consciously enjoying the glory of His presence. That is far better than anything they could know here. But God has another gift for them and for us that He is keeping for the day when Jesus Christ returns to gather His whole family together.

When Christ comes, our Christian loved ones who are already in His presence will come with Him (see 1 Thessalonians 4:14). Then "the dead in Christ will rise" (1 Thessalonians 4:16). In other words, the souls of those who are with Jesus will be reunited with risen bodies adapted for everlasting life.

At the same time, believers who are still alive will be "caught up together with them in the clouds to meet the Lord in the air. And so we will be with the Lord forever" (v. 17). We will experience the same transformation in which our bodies are adapted for everlasting life. The gift will be given to the whole family together. Then all the faces of God's children will light up as together we enter all that He has prepared for us.

UNLOCKED

The resurrection of Jesus changes the face of death for all His people. Death is no longer a prison, but a passage into the immediate presence of God. Jesus said, "I am the resurrection and the life. He who believes in me will live, even though he dies" (John 11:25). The life that Jesus was talking about is more than a spiritual experience. God will redeem every part of you, including your body.

When Christ returns, all of His people will have new bodies, like the resurrection body of Jesus.

PAUSE FOR PRAYER

Almighty Father,

Thank You that when Jesus died, He changed the nature of death for all His people. Thank You that He is risen and that, by faith in Him, I will also rise. Thank You that when Your people die, what lies ahead is far greater than what lies behind.

Help me to live in the joyful anticipation of all that is to come. Through Jesus Christ my Lord I pray. Amen.

13

Ascended

LUKE 24, ACTS 1

Why were the disciples filled with joy when Jesus left them?

13 Ascended

LUKE 24, ACTS 1

DISCOVER

the significance of the resurrection appearances.

LEARN

how Jesus defends you against accusations in heaven.

WORSHIP

because Christ's people always live under His blessing.

AS everybody who has ever said a long-term good-bye knows, however well you are prepared, it's never easy when you actually come to the moment. I went through that experience repeatedly in 1995 before our move from Great Britain to the United States. We knew that we would keep in touch with friends, but it would not be the same as being physically present.

People have different ways of saying good-bye. I particularly remember the last time I was with one of my good friends. We had spent the day teaching a course together as we often did, and afterward we talked and reminisced about many things that we had shared over a period of about ten years.

Then it was time to go. He took what seemed like a deep breath, stretched out his hand, and said, "Well, Colin, good-bye." Then he turned on his heels in military style, got into his car, and roared off down the street. That's how the English do it!

It was somewhat more moist with the family as we gathered at Glasgow International Airport. We were well prepared, and everyone was agreed that the move was the right thing. But we were emigrating, so we would no longer be physically present, and however well you are prepared to say good-bye, when the moment comes it is never easy.

That's why I found the description of Jesus' ascension to contain some of the most surprising words in the whole Bible.

THE JOY OF PARTING

When he [Jesus] had led them out to the vicinity of Bethany, he lifted up his hands and blessed them. While he was blessing them, he left them and was taken up into heaven. Then they worshiped him and returned to Jerusalem with great joy. *(LUKE 24:50–52, EMPHASIS ADDED)*

I found those final words surprising. In fact, this has to be one of the most unexpected phrases in the Bible. If we had heard that family and friends had thrown a party as soon as our plane had taken off, we would have found that rather strange. So what are we to make of the disciples' joy when Jesus left them?

The disciples' joy is all the more strange when we remember that Jesus had spoken to them about His leaving during the Last Supper. At that time, they were horrified by the idea. But now, when it happens, we find them filled with joy!

Something must have happened so that what they once dreaded now became a reason to celebrate. Our aim in this chapter is to discover what that was.

BEYOND REASONABLE DOUBT

After his suffering, he showed himself to these men and gave many convincing proofs that he was alive. He appeared to them over a period of forty days. (ACTS 1:3)

Although the gospel of John comes between them, Luke and Acts are two volumes of one book, so there is a natural link between the end of Luke's gospel and the beginning of the Acts of the Apostles. Acts begins where Luke ends—with the ascension of Jesus. By putting the two accounts together, we get a fuller picture of what was happening.

The physician Luke, who wrote both books, tells us that after the Resurrection Jesus appeared to the disciples during a forty-day period. The first reason for these appearances was to give "many convincing proofs that he [Jesus] was alive." It was important that the resurrection of Jesus should be established beyond reasonable doubt. So Christ appeared to them not once or twice, but repeatedly.

Putting the accounts in the Gospels and 1 Corinthians together, Christ appeared to the disciples (either as a group or to one or two of them) on at least nine different occasions. Once Christ appeared to a group of more than five hundred people, most of whom were still living at the time Paul wrote about it and were able to bear witness to the truth of his account (1 Corinthians 15:6).

After the Ascension, however, the appearances stopped. Their sudden ending is one of the clear evidences that they were actual events in which Christ appeared. They were not a projection in the mind of the disciples. Hallucinations fade gradually; they don't stop suddenly. These appearances were not wish fulfillment for those who believed. Jesus had risen, and He wanted His people to know that He is alive.

Kingdom Business

> *He appeared to them over a period of forty days* and spoke about the kingdom of God. *(v. 3, emphasis added)*

The resurrection appearances were not only to give convincing proof that Jesus was alive, but also to prepare the disciples for the kingdom work that lay ahead.

Over a period of forty days, Jesus taught the disciples and brought them to a new level of understanding. Previously, they had thought of the Cross as an unmitigated disaster. Now, they saw that everything had happened exactly as God had planned it.

Christ was not with them constantly throughout those forty days. He appeared to them, taught them, and then He disappeared. In this way, Christ began to wean them away from dependence on His physical presence. For three years they had been used to talking with Jesus directly, face to face. They had witnessed His miracles, heard Him speak, and asked Him their questions.

Their faith was built on sight. But now things would be different. They would have to learn to walk by faith without sight (2 Corinthians 5:7). So over a forty-day period, Jesus introduced them to this, and gradually they became used to trusting Him without seeing Him. From this time on, that would be how kingdom business would be done.

The End of the Appearances

After the forty days, Jesus led the disciples out of Jerusalem and up the Mount of Olives that overlooked the city. They were retracing the route they had taken some weeks earlier when Christ had entered Jerusalem to the acclaim of crowds on Palm Sunday. Jesus had come into the city to face the horrors of His crucifixion, but now all that was behind Him. He walked away from Jerusalem knowing that He had accomplished everything He came there to do.

Then He ascended into heaven and they saw Him go (Acts 1:9). On other occasions when Christ had appeared, He had simply vanished. But on this occasion they saw

Him go. This was the end of the resurrection appearances to the disciples. The evidence had been given, the training was complete, and now Jesus was returning to the Father.

The Rapture of Jesus

> *He was taken up before their very eyes, and* a cloud *hid him from their sight*. (v. 9, emphasis added)

You can be certain that when Luke tells us about a cloud, he is not giving a report on the weather conditions in Jerusalem forty days after Easter! The Bible is one story and God has tied His story together in a wonderful way.

Though God is invisible (nobody has ever seen God), He wants to make Himself known to His people. So throughout the Old Testament God gave certain visible signs of His presence. When God's people were in the desert, the visible signs that He gave them were a pillar of fire and a pillar of cloud. When the people saw the cloud, they knew God was with them. Similarly, when Solomon built the temple, God gave His people a visible sign of His presence—the cloud again filled the temple. Solomon explained the meaning of this to the people. God had come down among them; He was present in the cloud (see Leviticus 16:2; 1 Kings 8:10–13).

Significantly, when Christ was transfigured and the disciples saw His glory, the cloud came down on the mountain. The disciples fell on their faces, because they knew that they were in the immediate presence of almighty God.

Now Jesus is taken up, and as the disciples look up, what do they see? The cloud! Literally translated, Acts 1:9 reads, "He was taken up . . . and a cloud hid him from their sight."

God reached down and snatched Him up.

Christ was received into the cloud. Could anything be clearer than this? The same Christ who had come from the Father was now returning to the Father, and having finished His work, He is received by the Father, represented in the cloud. This was what filled the disciples with joy. Jesus had not simply disappeared into the sky; He was taken up into the cloud.

The Bible is such a wonderful book. It is so profound that it exhausts the most brilliant mind, but it is so simple that a young child can understand. You could draw this in pictures. The cloud represents the presence of God. Where the cloud is, God is. When Jesus ascends, He is taken up into the cloud. He is received right into the presence of God.

Notice that Jesus was "taken" into the cloud. God reached down and snatched Him up. Just as the Father had raised Him from the dead, so now the Father received Him into His presence.

A Man in Heaven

Think about the significance of Jesus entering heaven. For the first time since Adam was expelled from the garden, there was now *a Man* in the presence of God. The Lord Jesus Christ not only assumed our humanity on earth, He has also taken our humanity into heaven. No wonder the disciples were filled with joy!

Can you imagine the celebration of Christ's entrance into heaven? Angels had seen Adam driven out from the presence of God. Now heaven erupts as, for the first time, a Man walks right into the presence of God!

Adam was expelled from God's presence, and as a result, all his children were alienated from God. Christ is welcomed into the Father's presence, and as a result, all His children will be welcomed by the Father. The first Adam led us all out. The last Adam leads us all in. No wonder the disciples went back to Jerusalem with joy.

Get a Good Attorney

When Christ ascended into heaven, the disciples knew that He was exactly where they needed Him to be. It is far more important that Christ should represent us in heaven than that He should be physically present with us on earth.

Suppose that you are in prison on a charge that carries the death penalty if convicted. You need a good attorney, the very best you can get.

As you get to know your attorney, you find that he is not only a skilled lawyer, but he is also a man of great compassion. When he visits your cell, you find his presence comforting. You build a relationship, and you find that you can talk to him about how difficult life is on the inside.

All that is of great value. But of course, what you need from your attorney most is not comfort in the cell but an effective performance in the court. My greatest need, as a sinner, is not comfort on earth but defense in heaven. I need a representative who will speak to the Father on my behalf, an advocate who will plead my case in heaven. So when Christ ascended into heaven, He went to the place where I most need Him to be. John explained, "We have one who speaks to the Father in our defense—Jesus Christ, the Righteous One" (1 John 2:1).

There are many ways of getting through this life with success and happiness, but what use will that be if on the last day you find that almighty God has a case against you and you have no effective defense?

The apostles were filled with joy because they understood that, having entered heaven, the ascended Christ was able to speak to the Father on their behalf.

The apostle Paul speaks about this in Romans 8:34. "Who is he that condemns? Christ Jesus, who died—more than that, who was raised to life—is at the right hand of God and is also interceding for us."

IN THE COURTROOM

Imagine yourself standing in the dock in the courtroom of heaven: Satan, your accuser, has a case to present against you. Let's face it, someone wanting to accuse you or me of not shaping up to the Law of God wouldn't find it hard to make a case against us.

The courtroom is filled with angels, who rise as God the Father takes His place as the Judge. Then the diabolical prosecutor takes his papers and begins to stride around the court as he presents his case against you. The sum of it is that you are guilty of sin and that you should be condemned.

He begins by stating that you were born in sin and that your nature is corrupt. Then he proceeds with allegations about particular sins committed when you were young. He follows your life story, identifying moments of weakness, cowardice, complacency, pride, pettiness, and greed. You cringe as you listen and find yourself thinking of other things that he may use in his case against you and fearing what may happen if he brings them to light.

"I have here a full pardon. . . . It was purchased by My own blood."

Finally, he clinches his argument by appealing to the weakness of your faith. He points out that even though you may have professed to be a believer in Christ, your faith was often weak, and you had many doubts. His case is so compelling that you find yourself shaking and wondering how there could be any hope.

Then Jesus steps forward. He takes His brief in hand and begins to argue in your defense. "My client admits that every word spoken by the prosecution is true. We do not contest any of the charges, nor do we claim any mitigating circumstances. My client is guilty as charged."

"But," He continues, "I have here a full pardon that is signed by God's own hand. It was purchased by My own blood." Then stripping off His robes, He shows His hands and His side.

The accuser has no answer to that. His whole case against the believer crumbles and will be thrown out of court. Our defense is not that we are without sin but that Christ has died for our sins. Our sins have already been judged at the Cross, and once a charge has been dealt with, it cannot be brought again.

Aren't you glad that when we fail, we are no longer faced with the daily question of what we have to do to get right with God, what sacrifice to make, what offering to bring?

The hymn writer C. L. Bancroft pictures it well:

Before the throne of God above I have a strong and perfect plea,
A great high priest whose name is Love, who always lives to plead for me.
My name is printed on His hand, my name is written on His heart;
I know that while in heaven He stands, no one can tell me to depart.
When Satan tempts me to despair, and tells me of my guilt within,
Upward I look and see Him there who made an end of all my sin.
Because the sinless Savior died, my guilty soul is counted free;
For God, the just, is satisfied to look on Him and pardon me![1]

The disciples rejoiced because they knew that Christ was right where they most needed Him to be.

THE BLESSING THAT NEVER ENDS

When he had led them out to the vicinity of Bethany, he lifted up his hands and blessed them. While he was blessing them, he left them and was taken up into heaven. (LUKE 24:50–51)

As anybody who has lost a loved one knows, last impressions usually make a powerful impact on the mind. The last impression the disciples had of Jesus was full of significance.

Luke tells us that Jesus lifted up His hands and blessed the disciples. Can you imagine what this must have been like? Try to imagine yourself kneeling down, as Christ lifts His hands and begins speaking the blessing of God into your life.

In the Old Testament story, the blessing was of great importance. It was much more than kind words expressing best wishes for the future. Jacob was prepared to deceive his father to get his blessing, because the blessing was a prophetic statement of what God would do through a person's life. When Isaac's blessing was given to Jacob, it was irreversible. God's hand would be on Jacob and his children, and this man would be used to fulfill the purposes of God. That's what Jacob had wanted.

But now we come to something far greater. Christ raises His hands over the disciples and imparts His blessing to them. God's anointing would be on them, and they would be used to fulfill the purposes of God.

Luke tells us that "while he was blessing them, he left them and was taken up into heaven" (v. 51). The last glimpse the disciples had of Jesus was with His hand raised blessing them. He hadn't finished! This blessing is His unfinished work. He is still doing it. If we ask what Jesus is doing for His people now, the answer is that He is continuing the work He was doing when He left them; He is still blessing His people.

"He sat down at the right hand of the Majesty in heaven."

The ascension speaks to us both of the *completed work* and the *continuing work* of Christ. His completed work is the work of offering a sacrifice for sin. He cried out from the cross, "It is finished." Then He ascended to the Father, and the Bible says that "after he had provided purification for sins, he sat down at the right hand of the Majesty in heaven" (Hebrews 1:3).

The priests in the Old Testament never sat down. There was a table and a lamp in the tabernacle, but there was no chair. The absence of a chair was full of significance. It was a visual reminder that the priest's work never ended. There was always another sacrifice to be made for another sin. They literally never sat down. Their work must have been exhausting.

But Christ's work is finished. There is no more sacrifice to be offered, no more atonement to be made, nothing more that needs to be done to placate the wrath of God and release forgiveness to His people. That work is complete, and that is why Christ sat down.

But there is also a work that continues. The unfinished work of Christ is to bless His people, and it will go on until He returns. "He always lives to intercede" for us (Hebrews 7:25). As He sits at the right hand of the Father, He continues what He was doing when the Father took Him up into the cloud. He pours out His blessing into the lives of His people. No wonder the disciples went back to Jerusalem with joy.

The Promise of His Presence

> *"Do not leave Jerusalem, but wait for the gift my Father promised, which you have heard me speak about. For John baptized with water, but in a few days you will be baptized with the Holy Spirit."* (Acts 1:4–5)

After Christ ascended into heaven, His presence was with His disciples by the Holy Spirit. Jesus would no longer be visible to them, but His presence would be just as real as when they could see Him. This new situation offered one wonderful advantage: The presence of Jesus would now be with all of them, in every place at the same time.

Of course, this was not possible while Christ was on earth. He took our flesh, and human flesh can only be in one place at any given time. Even after the Resurrection when Christ was able to appear and disappear, there is no indication that He was in more than one place at one time.

Over the previous three years, there were times when Christ was away from even His closest disciples. On one occasion, they faced a storm on the lake and Christ was with them, but there was another occasion when they faced a storm on the lake and Christ was not with them; He was back on the shore (Matthew 8:23–27; 14:22–33).

When Jesus took Peter, James, and John up the mountain and they saw the Transfiguration, the other nine disciples were at the bottom of the mountain, trying to help a boy who was possessed by demons. Christ was not with them, and they found themselves in all kinds of trouble!

Now Jesus tells the disciples that they are to be His "witnesses in Jerusalem, and in all Judea and Samaria, and to the ends of the earth" (Acts 1:8). As they are sent out into ministry, they will be scattered across the face of the earth, but Christ will be with each of them in every place (Matthew 28:19–20).

This is what Christ was referring to when He said, "It is for your good that I am going away. Unless I go away, the Counselor will not come to you; but if I go, I will send him to you" (John 16:7). After the Ascension, they did not have the visible presence of Jesus with them, but they had the Spirit of Jesus in them.

So the presence of Christ is with us in the cell as well as in the courtroom. Our advocate operates in two places at the same time. The Lord Jesus Christ is at the right hand of the Father, and at the same time the Spirit of Jesus is present in the heart of the believer. The Son of God represents us to the Father, and the Spirit of God represents the Father and the Son to us.

This is Christ's promise to every one of His children. Jesus is with you by His Spirit, and He will never leave you nor forsake you. Are you beginning to see why the Ascension was such a cause for celebration?

THE PROMISE OF HIS RETURN

> *"Men of Galilee . . . why do you stand here looking into the sky? This same Jesus, who has been taken from you into heaven, will come back in the same way you have seen him go."* (ACTS 1:11)

God's promise is that just as Jesus was snatched up into the cloud, so when He returns, we will be caught up to meet Him in the air. The Ascension is the model for the rapture of the church. What happened to Jesus in His ascension will happen to us when He comes in glory.

No wonder Luke recorded that the disciples were filled with joy! What they had just seen happen to Jesus would one day happen to them. Of course, the disciples all died long ago, and Christians are still waiting for the great day when Christ will come again. But, as we saw in the last chapter, every Christian will be part of that day. Those who have already died will not miss out, but they will all be caught up to meet the Lord in the air.

So the disciples "went back to Jerusalem with joy." They were just a handful of people, and they faced a monumental task, but they knew that Christ was where they needed Him to be, at the right hand of the Father. Whatever they faced, they knew that they were living under the blessing of God and that they could count on the promise of His presence and His coming.

Unlocked

The disciples were filled with joy when Jesus left them, because they knew that He had returned to the Father. This meant that, for the first time in human history, there was a Man in heaven. The disciples knew that Jesus would represent them before the Father and act as their counselor or advocate there.

The last glimpse they had of Jesus was while He was still blessing them, and so they returned to Jerusalem knowing that, although they could no longer see Him, they would live under His continued blessing. They also understood that just as He had been taken up to heaven, the day would come when all His people would be caught up to meet Him in the air.

Pause for Prayer

Gracious Father,

Thank You that Your Son, the Lord Jesus Christ, is my Savior and that He sits at Your right hand. Thank You that He defends me from all accusations and that I live under His blessing. Thank You that He is coming again and that when He does I will ascend into Your presence as He snatches me up.

Help me to live in the light of that day with the confidence of one whose sins are forgiven, and whose destiny is secure. In Jesus' name I pray. Amen.

Note

1. C. L. Bancroft, "Before the Throne of God Above"; adapted.

14

Coming

JOHN 14

What is the

practical value

of the second

coming of Jesus

for my life today?

14 Coming

JOHN 14

DISCOVER

how Jesus helps us when we have to handle devastating news.

LEARN

about the home Christ has prepared for all His people.

WORSHIP

because you have a glorious future with Jesus Christ.

THE Bible story is like a necklace in which many pearls are joined together on a string. Just as a necklace falls and rises, the Bible story shows us the magnificent sweep of God's plan for history. The story begins at a high point in the Garden of Eden, where God made everything good. But there was a great disaster when sin entered the world, and we have followed the downward sweep of man's rebellion against God to its lowest point, when men nailed the Son of God to a cross.

God set His greatest pearl at this lowest point in history. In the darkness of Calvary, God did His greatest work. The Cross was not only the greatest expression of human sin; it was also the greatest outpouring of the love and grace of God.

But the necklace doesn't end at the lowest point. It not only falls; it also rises. Christ rose from the dead and ascended into heaven. He sends His Spirit and builds His church. He will come again, appearing in glory, and when He does, He will bring His people into their ultimate destiny in the new heaven and the new earth.

The great pearl of the Cross is not only tied back to the problem of our sin, it is also tied forward to our final destiny. If someone were to cut a necklace, the pearls would fall to the floor. You could pick up a few pearls and keep them, but that would not be the same as owning the necklace.

Many Christians have gathered a few disconnected pearls of God's truth, but they have not grasped the magnificent sweep of God's plan for history. They know about the Cross and may believe that this is how God deals with our sins, but they have not seen that through the death and resurrection of Jesus, God will bring all His people into His presence and glory.

God has been working to a definite plan throughout the entire history of the human race. The Cross is the center point, but it is not the end point of God's plan. The Bible story began when God walked onto the stage of human history, revealing Himself as the Creator of everything that exists. It will end when God reveals the glory of His Son, Jesus Christ, and ushers in a new creation that will be home for all His people.

THE DINNER WHERE EVERYTHING SEEMED TO GO WRONG

Jesus spoke about His second coming often, but never more clearly than on the night before He died. Significantly, Jesus spoke most directly about His return when the disciples were deeply shocked by a series of unthinkable events. As we follow the story of that evening, we will discover the importance of the second coming of Jesus in our struggle to live the Christian life today.

The Passover was the greatest celebration of the year, and Jesus had been looking forward to this last opportunity of time with His disciples before He went to the cross.

Early in the evening, Jesus shocked His friends by saying that someone at the table would betray Him. One after another they began to say, "Lord, is it me?"

Nobody said, "Lord, is it Judas?" It is quite clear that he was trusted and respected. Nobody imagined that he would do such a thing. After all, they had put Judas in charge of the money, and you don't give a man your money unless you trust him completely.

Eventually Peter prompted John, who was sitting next to Jesus as they reclined at the table, to ask Him whom He was speaking about. Jesus said, "It is the one to whom I will give this piece of bread" (John 13:26). Then He dipped a piece of bread in a dish and offered it to Judas. Can you imagine that moment? The whole group must have been looking at Judas. What would he do?

Judas had already planned to betray Jesus. He had taken the money offered by the chief priests for his help, but now the final decision was made in his mind. Judas reached out and took the bread. He made his choice.

John tells us that "as soon as Judas took the bread, Satan entered into him" (v. 27). Notice the order of events. Satan entered into a mind that had been fully opened to his activity. Then, Judas went out and John says, "It was night."

How do you carry on a dinner party after that?

There was more bad news to come. Jesus said, "My children, I will be with you only a little longer" (v. 33).

Can you picture the expressions on the faces around the table when Jesus said this? These men had left everything to follow Christ. They had staked everything on Christ and built their whole lives around Him. The last three years had been the best because of Him. And now, after just three years, He told them that He would be with them only a little longer.

To be told that the person who means most to you in the world will only be with you for a little while longer is one of the hardest experiences a human being can endure. This was what the disciples faced at the Last Supper. They must have wondered what kind of future they would have without Jesus with them.

Standing on the Brink of Failure

Peter could not bear to think of being separated from Christ. He reacted to Jesus' announcement of the unthinkable by announcing that he would lay down his life for Jesus. But Jesus answered, "Will you really lay down your life for me? I tell you the truth, before the rooster crows, you will disown me three times!" (v. 38).

There had never been a day when the disciples had to deal with news like this. In a matter of a few moments in one evening, they discovered that a trusted leader would betray the Savior, Jesus Himself would be taken from them, and His leading disciple would make a total denial of his faith before the night ended.

When You Hear Disastrous News

What Jesus said next must have seemed absolutely staggering.

> *"Do not let your hearts be troubled."* (John 14:1)

How could Jesus possibly say this in the light of all that had just happened? The disciples must have been staggered by His words. I can imagine several of them saying, "Jesus, You tell us that Judas is bailing out, that You are about to leave, and that Peter's testimony will collapse, and then You say that we are not to be troubled?"

Imagine a church meeting where the congregation gathers for a few items of business. The chairman opens the meeting in prayer, and then says that he has three important news items to share.

"First, I have to announce, with regret, that our senior pastor is leaving in a few days' time. Second, you should be aware that the church treasurer has resigned, and at this point we are not quite sure what he has done with the money. Third, our senior elder has denied the faith and no longer wishes his name to be associated with the church."

The congregation is reeling at this triple announcement of disastrous news, but the chairman continues with his announcement. "I know that some of you may have some questions," he says, "but the first thing I want to say is, 'Do not let your hearts be troubled!' "

There may be a time in your life when you face disastrous news. What do you do if there is a scandal in the church and someone betrays the trust you have placed in him or her as Judas did? What do you do when a leader whose example you have looked up to shows himself to have feet of clay like Peter? And how do you cope when the person around whom you have built your life is no longer with you?

TRUSTING IN THE DARKNESS

It was common in the time of Jesus for people to recline at a low table when they ate, but by this point in the evening, I cannot imagine that anyone was reclining. After all that had happened, everyone would be sitting bolt upright. Jesus looked around the room, His piercing eyes looking deep into the souls of every one of His eleven disciples. "Here's what I need you to do right now," He was saying. "Trust God! Trust in Me!"

Jesus was not asking them to take a blind leap of faith. They had seen His miracles, heard His words, confessed their faith, and walked with Him for three years. Now they had to lean into all that they knew of Jesus. It was time to draw deeply on what they had said they believed. In this moment of great darkness, Christ called them to trust what He had taught them in the light.

Then, having called them to exercise faith, Jesus began to speak to them about the future.

ONE HOUSE WITH MANY ROOMS

"In my Father's house are many rooms." (v. 2)

When Jesus spoke about His Father's house, the disciples must have wondered what that had to do with Judas's defection, Christ's departure, and Peter's denial; but Jesus had asked them to trust Him, and so they listened carefully.

Many older Christians remember this verse from the King James version of the Bible, which reads, "In my Father's house are many mansions," and there have been a number of hymns that take up the theme of having a mansion in the sky or over the hilltop. This has led many people to a picture of heaven as an upmarket housing estate with extremely large buildings on generous lots of gently rolling countryside. Others, who think they have lived less worthy lives, have the idea that they will find themselves in second- or third-class heavenly accommodation—a heavenly equivalent of a garden shed!

There really is no basis for this in the Bible. Jesus spoke about one house with many rooms. The picture He was using was of one great extended family being brought into the Father's home. It was not that everyone would be given a building plot, but that all of God's family would be together in the Father's house.

There was a special irony in Jesus speaking about the many rooms in His Father's house. When Jesus was born, there was no room for Him in Bethlehem. The innkeeper had a small house and every room was taken. I cannot help but think that there must have been a smile on the face of Jesus as He was telling His friends, in effect, "Now don't worry; when you come to My home, it won't be as it was when I came to your home! You won't find it overcrowded like Bethlehem when I came. In My Father's house are many rooms!"

God will move in with you until one day you move in with Him!

Jesus used the same word again later that evening, when He said, "If anyone loves me, he will obey my teaching. My Father will love him, and we will come to him and make our home with him" (v. 23). Literally Jesus said, "We will room with him."

Jesus was telling the disciples that God would "room" with them by the Holy Spirit until He came again, and then they would "room" with God. God will move in with you until one day you move in with Him!

Jesus emphasized the absolute certainty of the disciples' future in heaven. "In my Father's house are many rooms; if it were not so, I would have told you." This is the candor of Jesus. If the future of the disciples were in any doubt, He would have told them. But the fact is that they had a magnificent destiny ahead of them, and it is for this reason that they were not to be troubled, but were to put their trust in Christ even when the bottom seemed to be falling out of their world.

Having described the Father's house, Jesus went on to explain how they would get there.

The Way to the Father's House

"I go to prepare a place for you." (v. 2 KJV)

Jesus' promise to prepare a place for His followers does not mean that Christ was going to heaven to get the place organized for our arrival! If God can create the cosmos out of nothing, and hold the moon and stars on their courses, He can certainly get heaven organized for believers with a single command.

When Jesus said that He was going to prepare a place, He was telling the disciples that the place would be prepared by His going. Jesus was about to go to the cross. He was going to die, be buried, rise, and finally ascend to heaven.

It is through Christ's death, resurrection, and ascension into heaven that the place for all His followers is prepared. His death and resurrection have made the place ready and reserved a block booking for all who would believe.

That is why His disciples are not to be troubled by the fact that He is being taken from them. It is through His going to the cross that the way will be opened up for them to enter into the home that Christ has described.

"I Will Come Again"

"If I go and prepare a place for you, I will come back and take you to be with me that you also may be where I am." (v. 3)

Jesus was about to endure indescribable suffering on the cross, and it was in this way that reservations would be made in the Father's house for all His people. Since He would pay such a price for the reservations, the disciples could be absolutely certain that Jesus would bring them into the Father's home. The logic of Jesus' words is powerfully persuasive: "If I go . . . I will come back and take you to be with me."

Jesus was saying, "If I go through the agony of death and then rise on the third day and ascend into heaven, all for the single purpose of preparing a place for you, then is it conceivable that I would not bring you there?"

If I were to spend my life savings on a priceless ring, it is inconceivable that, having written out the check and made the purchase, I would then leave the ring on the counter. Having paid the price, the ring would become my treasured possession, and I would bring it home.

This is why Jesus told the disciples that they were not to be troubled but rather to trust in Him. They had seen Judas leave, they had heard that Peter would fail, and they had been told that Jesus would be taken from them. They felt that their world was falling apart, but it was not.

Jesus was going to prepare a place for them, and they could be absolutely confident that He would bring them home.

Two Ways of Going Home

There are two ways in which Christ's people may enter into the Father's house. One is to die before Christ comes; the other is to live until Christ comes. Christ will bring every believer into the presence of the Father either one way or the other.

It really doesn't matter which way it happens, because either way, it is Christ who is taking you. If you die, Christ will take you into His presence without the body. If you are alive when He comes, He will take you into His presence in the body. He could choose to take any one of us at any time, in either way. The important thing is that Christ will gather all His people together to share in His final victory.

When the Roman army came back from a military campaign, there was always a procession of triumph through the streets of the city. The Romans wanted to make it clear the victory of the army was also the victory of every citizen. So when the army returned, they would set up camp outside the city while the preparations were made for the great celebration. At that time anyone who was a Roman citizen could come out of the city and join the soldiers in the camp.

Then when the time for the procession came, the citizens would form a procession behind the army. They shared in the glory of the homecoming, because the triumph of the army was the triumph of every citizen.

You will reflect His glory for all eternity.

That is how it will be on the last day. The citizens of God's kingdom will be called out to join the King in preparation for His triumphal entry at the close of history. Then every eye will see Him. "Every knee [will] bow . . . and every tongue confess that Jesus Christ is Lord, to the glory of God the Father" (Philippians 2:10–11). His people will confess this to their everlasting joy. His enemies will confess this to their everlasting regret.

We tend to think of some people as very near to eternity. If someone is very old or sick, we may visit the person and then say quietly, "He doesn't have very long." But actually that is true for all of us. I do not know how long I have before Christ will come, or before He will call me home. This didn't scare the disciples; it brought them comfort. We are not to be troubled, because He is coming again.

One day you are going to look into the face of Jesus Christ and you will reflect His glory for all eternity. He died and rose and ascended into heaven to make that possible, and He will come again to bring you into all that He has prepared for you. That is His promise; it is absolutely certain.

AN UNFINISHED PROJECT

Over the last few weeks, I have been working on a home improvement project. We are remodeling a bathroom, and it isn't finished yet.

There are some bare studs, and a few pipes are exposed. Some areas have unfinished drywall, and there is a hole in the ceiling for a new light. Some areas are better than they were; others are still to be tackled. The place is functional, but nothing is as it finally will be.

When my wife comes into our bathroom and looks at the state of the place, I remind her that she is looking at an unfinished project, and that it will not always be like this. I say to her, "Do not let your heart be troubled. Trust me."

God's plan for redeeming the world is in process, but it is not yet complete, and there will be times when life looks like a jumbled mess. That is how it was for the disciples at the Last Supper, and it is often the same for us.

We find ourselves asking "Why?" and some answers are not given to us this side of heaven. But Jesus says, "Do not let your hearts be troubled." Remember that you are looking at an unfinished project. What you see now is not as it will be.

When I look in the mirror, I am looking at an unfinished project. God has given His Spirit to every believer. The new life has already begun in us. But we still battle with the pull of the flesh, and we are not yet what we shall be. Like Peter, we have our failures as well as our successes. But it will not always be like this. Christ is coming, and on the day He appears, you will be everything God has made you to be, so do not let your heart be troubled.

UNLOCKED

Jesus comes to us in the devastating crises of life and invites us to trust Him. He reminds us that we are not looking at the finished picture. Through His death and resurrection, He has prepared a place for us. Christ will come again, and when He does, we will be caught up to meet Him and then we will be forever with the Lord.

The second coming of Jesus is one of the most important and practical truths that we need to grasp for living the Christian life today. Christ could come at any time and may well come in our lifetime. But even if He does not, the truth of His second coming is still of vital importance.

There will be times when we are faced with devastating news. We may wonder what God is doing and what the future holds. But Jesus tells us that we are not to let our hearts be troubled. He invites us to trust Him and lean on what He has revealed about Himself. God's work in us and in the world is an unfinished project, but it will be brought to completion when Jesus Christ returns in glory.

PAUSE FOR PRAYER

Almighty Father,

Thank You for the glorious hope of the second coming of Jesus Christ in glory. Thank You that when He comes, all His people will be caught up to meet Him and in that moment made like Him. Help me to live in the anticipation of His coming.

Help me to trust You in the things that I cannot understand. And when life seems to be a mess, help me to remember that Your work is an unfinished project, and that You always complete what You have begun. Help me to live in confident hope, until my faith is turned to sight, in Jesus' name. Amen.

15

Father

JOHN 14

What does it

mean to know

God as Father?

15 Father

JOHN 14

DISCOVER

the mystery of the Trinity.

LEARN

why we can only come to the Father through Jesus.

WORSHIP

because through Jesus, we are adopted into the family of God.

THE old pastor's brow was furrowed as he peered over his half-moon spectacles at the scattered congregation and began the message he had been pondering all week. "First," he said slowly, "I am going to search the unsearchable. Then," he said with increasing confidence, "I am going to explain the unexplainable. And finally . . ." He paused as he searched for the words. "I'm going to unscrew the inscrutable!"

I'm not so ambitious, and it is with a sense of awe that I begin to write about the most distinctive but also the most difficult doctrine in the whole of the Christian faith: There is one God, and He is Father, Son, and Holy Spirit.

Nobody can understand the nature of God. This should not be surprising. I assume that fish have a very limited understanding of human nature, and in the same way, it is beyond the range of human ingenuity to figure out the mystery of the nature of God.

You can't run a high-tension voltage through a flashlight. It does not have the capacity to hold that kind of charge. In the same way, the human mind does not have the capacity to comprehend the nature of God.

But God has revealed Himself to us, and even though we cannot know Him fully, we can know Him truly. In the Old Testament, God reveals that He is one. In the New Testament, God reveals that He is Father, Son, and Holy Spirit.

GOD IN THREE PERSONS

The Old Testament raises some questions about the nature of God that are not resolved until God reveals Himself more fully in the New Testament. For example, at the Creation God says, "Let us make man in our image" (Genesis 1:26). One of the Hebrew words that is used for God is in the plural. Why would God use a name that has plurality built into its grammar when He tells us so clearly and distinctively that He is one?

The Bible tells us that God is love. But love needs an object. Who did God love before the Creation, when nothing existed except God Himself? God has always been love, and before anything else ever existed, that love was shared among the Father, the Son, and the Holy Spirit.

In the Old Testament, God said, "I am." In the New Testament, God was saying, "I am the Father, I am the Son, and I am the Holy Spirit." If we are going to know God, we must come to know Him as Father, Son, and Spirit. If we do not know Him in this way, we do not know Him as He is.

SATURATED IN THE LIFE OF GOD

This is not just a matter of knowledge but also a matter of experience. At the end of Matthew's gospel, Jesus tells His disciples that they are to "go and make disciples of all nations, baptizing them in the name of the Father and of the Son and of the Holy Spirit" (Matthew 28:19).

The word *baptize* literally means "to dip" or "to drench." In the early church, believers were baptized in rivers. They were either plunged under the water or water was poured over their heads. Either way, they emerged extremely wet! Jesus said that baptism was to be given "in the name of the Father and of the Son and of the Holy Spirit." The Christian life is all about being drenched in the Father, plunged into the Son, and soaked in the Spirit. That's what baptism symbolizes.

The Father, the Son, and the Holy Spirit permeate every part of a believer's life. You cannot separate one from the other. The Spirit draws you to the Son, the Son brings you to the Father, and the Son pours out the Spirit into your heart. You cannot know the Father apart from the Son or the Son apart from the Spirit.

So while we may not be able to understand the nature of God, we must grasp what is revealed about the Father, Son, and Holy Spirit if we are to know God as He is.

FIXING THE ANCHOR POINTS

We may summarize what God has revealed to us in three statements.

First, there is one God. This is clear in both the Old and New Testaments. God says, "Hear, O Israel: The LORD our God, the LORD is one" (Deuteronomy 6:4). There is "one Lord, one faith, one baptism; one God and Father of all" (Ephesians 4:5–6). Christians do not believe in three Gods. There is one God.

Second, God is three persons. It is important to say that the word *person* is not used in the Bible; neither is the word *trinity*. There is no place in the Bible where we read, "God is three persons." But within the limitations of human language, *person* is the best word that we can use to describe the identity of the Father, the Son, and the Spirit.

The distinct identities of the Father, Son, and Spirit are written all through the New Testament. The Father sends the Son (Galatians 4:4). The Son prays to the Father (John 17:1). The Spirit glorifies the Son (John 16:14), and the Son sends the Spirit (Acts 2:33).

The three persons of the Godhead are not to be confused. The Father did not die on the cross. The Son did not send Himself into the world. The Spirit did not rise from the dead. There is one God, and God is three persons.

Third, each person is fully God. The Father is God, the Son is God, and the Spirit is God. Christ said, "I and the Father are one" (John 10:30), and He talked about the glory He shared with the Father before the world began (John 17:5). And when Christ spoke about sending the Holy Spirit, He was not talking about an alternative to His own presence; He was promising that His presence would be with the disciples, even though He was returning to the Father (John 14:16–18). If the Spirit was with them, Christ was with them; and if Christ was with them, the Father was with them (John 14:23).

There is one eternal God who is Father, Son, and Holy Spirit.

The Father is God, the Son is God, the Spirit is God, but there are not three Gods. There is one eternal God who is Father, Son, and Holy Spirit.

The more you think about this, the more staggering it gets.

All praise and thanks to God the Father now be given,
The Son and Him who reigns with them in highest heaven,
The one eternal God, Whom earth and heaven adore;
For thus it was, is now, and shall be evermore.[1]

The Problem with Analogies

Through the centuries, people have used analogies to try and explain the nature of God. I have never found any of them very helpful. It seems to me that if there were an analogy in the natural world that would help us grasp the nature of God, then God would have put it in the Bible. The fact that He didn't is significant.

So beware of analogies of the Trinity. They usually help us to see one part of the truth, but at the same time they distort or obscure something else. Some people use the analogy of one person playing three different roles. For example, I am a husband and a father and a pastor. But the analogy falls short because there is only one person fulfilling these three roles. God exists in three persons; the Father is not the Son, and the Son is not the Spirit.

Others use the analogy of water existing as ice, water, and steam. The problem here is that the same water cannot be ice, water, and steam at the same time. But right now, the Son is seated at the right hand of the Father and the Spirit dwells in the hearts of believers. These things are true simultaneously.

Perhaps the best-known analogy was used by Saint Patrick in Ireland. He spoke about the three leaves on one shamrock. The problem here is that each leaf is only part of the shamrock, and not the whole of the shamrock. The persons of the Trinity are not "part of God." Each one is fully God. "In Christ all the fullness of the Deity lives in bodily form" (Colossians 2:9). Christ is not some kind of "cutting" as if part of God came to earth, while the remainder stayed on in heaven. Christ is God with us!

Beware of analogies of the Trinity. They appear to suggest a solution, but they always do so by obscuring part of the glory of what is revealed.

Mist on the Mountain

There is a mountain in Scotland I love to climb. We often take a trip there as a family when we are on vacation. I have climbed it in all kinds of weather conditions, including drifting snow, and it is absolutely magnificent. But there is one occasion I will never forget.

As we were climbing, a mist came down and surrounded us. We thought about turning back, assuming that there would be nothing to see from the top, but we decided to continue and eventually climbed out of the mist. The sky was clear, and the view was magnificent. When we got to the top, we looked down on the blanket of mist that had settled over the town in the valley below.

We couldn't see the town, but we could see everything above. We could see people walking on other hills and sheep on the high ground. We couldn't see into the mist, but we could see everything outside of the mist.

I have found that picture helpful when thinking about the mystery of the nature of God. There is a little town called Truth. It is shrouded in mist, and we cannot see into it. I cannot explain to you how one God can exist in three persons. I have to confess humbly that I am gazing into a mystery that is beyond my comprehension.

But at the same time, I can clearly identify what lies outside the town called Truth. For example, if someone says that Christ is less than God, or that there are many gods, I can immediately see from the Scriptures that this is outside the boundaries of truth. The mist covers the town itself, but that which is outside the town can be clearly seen.

I cannot describe the mystery of the truth, but I can clearly identify teaching that is outside of the truth, and that is something the church must always do.

How to Respond to a Mystery

The nature of God is a mystery, but it is not a contradiction. If Christians believed both that there is one God and there are three Gods, that would be a contradiction. Or if we believed that there are three persons and there is one person, that would be a contradiction. But to say that there is one God who exists in three persons is not a contradiction; it is a mystery.

There are a number of places in the Bible where we are presented with a mystery, and it is important to know how we should and shouldn't respond.

First, don't turn away from a mystery. Some people instinctively throw up their hands and turn away from anything they cannot understand, as if something that cannot be understood could not possibly be true. They miss the unfathomable splendor of the glory of God.

Second, don't try to explain a mystery. You can't put "understanding the nature of God" on your To Do list and expect that one day some publisher will bring out the book that will explain it all, so that you can cross it off your To Do list and say, "It all makes perfect sense to me now; I don't know why I didn't see it before." God will never let you get there, because if you did, you would cease to worship.

After twenty years of marriage, my wife often seems to know what I'm thinking and can anticipate what I'm going to say. It happened the other day, and she said, "I knew you would say that. I've been married to you over twenty years, and I've figured you out."

> Let [the mystery] lead you into worship.

That's an interesting and rather intimidating phrase. "I've figured you out." And she has; I can't deny it. After twenty years there isn't much mystery left! It's getting harder to spring a surprise. There isn't much she doesn't know about me and what there is isn't much worth knowing!

God has revealed Himself in such a way that we may truly know Him, but we will never come to the point where we have "figured Him out." Even in heaven, when you see God as He is, you will be lost in wonder and love and praise. You will look into the face of God, and you will find yourself filled with more wonder than ever before, and you will spend all eternity enthralled with the mystery of His glory.

The way to respond to a mystery is to let it lead you into worship. That should always be our response to the mystery of the nature of God.

Holy, Holy, Holy, Lord God Almighty!
All Thy works shall praise Thy name in earth and sky and sea;
Holy, Holy, Holy! Merciful and Mighty!
God in three Persons, blessed Trinity![2]

COMING TO GOD THE FATHER

Jesus answered, "I am the way and the truth and the life. No one comes to the Father except through me." (JOHN 14:6)

Suppose you want to visit the president of the United States. It would be difficult, because he is not easily accessible, but there are a number of possible approaches that you might try.

The reason that there are many ways to the president of the United States is that there are many people near to him. For example, if you knew his wife, she could bring you to him. If you knew his father or mother or brother, the person might arrange a meeting. Or if you knew the secretary of state, the press secretary, or the chief of staff, he might grant you access.

There are many ways to the president of the United States, because there are many people next to him. But who is next to God the Father?

Jesus makes it clear that nobody is next to the Father except the Son. The Son is the only one who has seen Him and who knows Him (Matthew 11:27; John 6:46). It follows that He is the only one by whom we can come to the Father. John wrote, "No one has ever seen God, but God the One and Only, who is at the Father's side, has made him known" (1:18). Only the one who is next to the Father can bring you to the Father.

JESUS' FATHER AND YOUR FATHER

"In my Father's house are many rooms." (JOHN 14:2)

"If you really knew me, you would know my Father as well." (V. 7)

"On that day you will realize that I am in my Father, and you are in me, and I am in you." (V. 20)

It is very significant that when Jesus spoke about the Father, He regularly spoke about "My Father."

Jesus distinguished clearly between His own relationship with the Father and that of the disciples. "I am returning to *my Father* and *your Father*" (John 20:17, emphasis added). Why did He not say, "Our Father"?

There is only one occasion when Christ used the phrase "Our Father" referring to God, and that was when He was teaching His disciples how *they* should pray. In the Lord's Prayer (Matthew 6:9–13), He told them that *they* should say, "Our Father." There was never an occasion when Christ referred to His relationship with the Father and that of the disciples in the same way. The distinction is always preserved.

This is the highest privilege . . . to know God as our Father.

The good news is not that God is everybody's Father. The good news is that Christ knows God as His Father, and for that reason, He is able to bring us to know God as our Father as well.

This is the highest privilege offered in the gospel—to know God as our Father. God offers more than forgiveness. That is our greatest need, but it is not our highest privilege. God acquits us in the court where He presides as Judge, but He also adopts us into the family where He is Father. "When the time had fully come,

God sent his Son . . . to redeem those under law, that we might receive the full rights of sons" (Galatians 4:4–5).

Christ is the one and only Son of God, but He took our flesh, making us His brothers. If we receive Him, God the Father will adopt us into His family so that we may become sons and daughters of God!

This is more than a name or status; it is a living experience. God sends His Spirit into our hearts so that we cry, "Abba, Father" (Romans 8:15). The Spirit confirms within our hearts that we are indeed God's children so that we can live in the enjoyment of it.

If we want to know what a relationship with God the Father looks like, we must begin by looking at what it means for Jesus to call God His Father. If we can grasp what it meant for Him to know God as His Father, then we will be able to grasp what it will mean for us to know God as our Father as well.

SUBJECT TO THE FATHER'S AUTHORITY

Christ invites us to a relationship in which we are subject to the Father's authority. You can't miss this in the life of Jesus. He placed Himself under the authority of the Father. He brought glory to the Father by completing the work that the Father gave Him to do (John 17:4). He said, "My food . . . is to do the will of him who sent me and to finish his work. . . . I have come down from heaven not to do my will but to do the will of him who sent me" (John 4:34; 6:38).

The whole of His life was aligned with the Father's purpose, and that was never seen more clearly than in the Garden of Gethsemane, where Christ said, "My Father, if it is possible, may this cup be taken from me. Yet not as I will, but as you will" (Matthew 26:39). If it were possible to fulfill the Father's purpose without the awful pain of the cross, that would have been Jesus' choice, but if the Father's purpose required Him to go through this agony, He was ready.

If we would come to the Father, the first question is whether we are ready to be subject to His authority. That was the big decision the prodigal son had to face (see Luke 15:11–24.) He had resisted his father's authority for a long time. Then there came a point where his father's house seemed very attractive. But before he could return, he had to decide if he was ready to be subject to his father's authority.

The reason some people know little of the Father's love is that they are continually resisting His authority, and nobody can enter the relationship Jesus offers like that.

When you say, "Our Father," it will not be long before you are saying, "Your will be done." Christ brought these two things together in the Garden of Gethsemane. He submitted Himself to the will of the Father even when that was indescribably painful. Are you ready for that?

It is very significant that the first time the most intimate word "Abba" is used in the New Testament is not from the lips of an ecstatic worshiper but from the agonized voice of Christ in the Garden of Gethsemane (Mark 14:36).

To know God as Father is to be subject to His authority. The Christian life does not begin with me deciding I would like to go to heaven, but when I come to the place of saying, "Not my will but Yours be done."

ENJOYING THE FATHER'S LOVE

Submitting to the Father's authority may sometimes be painful, but it is the gateway into experiencing the Father's love. The Father loves the Son, and Jesus offers to bring us into that love. "As the Father has loved me, so have I loved you," He said (John 15:9). Think of how the Father loves the Son. Jesus speaks of experiencing that love before the world began (John 17:24).

Jesus brings us into the Father's love, and it is the special work of the Holy Spirit to let us know that we are loved. The Spirit pours out the love of God into our hearts (Romans 5:5). Love is not something that we believe, but something that we experience. It is a wonderful gift to be enjoyed.

This is a sensitive issue for some people. I was privileged to be raised in a happy family and thank God for a loving father. The security and love I knew makes me sensitive to the pain of those who did not know that privilege.

Sometimes folks whose experience of family life has been painful suggest that talking of God as Father is unhelpful and misleading. If that's how you feel, I have a question for you. How do you know that your experience of your father was a bad one?

You know because God has placed within your heart a sense of what a father should be. The very fact that you can identify your disappointment is an indication that you have a sense of what "ought to be." God put that sense there.

Ask the Holy Spirit to pour out the Father's love in your heart.

Christ has come to bring you into a relationship in which you know the unfathomable love of God the Father to His children. Christ will bring you into the family of God as a wanted, loved, and welcomed child. The Holy Spirit will bond you to the Father so that you know you are secure in His love.

This kind of assurance does not always come immediately in the Christian life. Paul regularly prayed that Christians would experience more of God's love (Ephesians 3:18–19). Sometimes our pain numbs us to the warmth of God's love for a time. But this is what a relationship with God the Father looks like. Don't settle for anything less. Believe God's promises. Ask the Holy Spirit to pour out the Father's love in your heart. Go on asking. You will receive.

SHARING THE FATHER'S GLORY

Jesus said to the Father, "I have given them the glory that you gave me" (John 17:22). Before the Son of God came into the world, He shared the Father's glory (John 17:5), and when He came into the world, the glory of the Father was revealed (John 1:14). When Christ brings us into a relationship with the Father, He brings us into that glory.

This is the highest privilege of the Christian's relationship with God. Jesus brings us into a relationship with the Father in which we submit to His authority, enjoy His love, and share in His glory.

There are times when it may be costly to submit to the authority of the Father, but Paul reminds us that this is "not worth comparing with the glory that will be revealed in us" (Romans 8:18).

John revels in the privilege of this relationship. "How great is the love the Father has lavished on us," he declares, "that we should be called children of God!" And then he reminds us of what this means: "When he appears, we shall be like him" (1 John 3:1–2).

Christ is not ashamed to call us His brothers (Hebrews 2:11). He brings us under the Father's authority and into His love. Eventually, Christ will bring us into the Father's presence. He will stand before the Father with us and say, "Here am I and the children You have given me."

UNLOCKED

Knowing God as Father is not natural for us. As descendants of Adam and Eve, we are born in alienation from God and need to be brought into a relationship with Him. This is why Jesus Christ has come into the world. He has come from the Father's side to make Him known and to bring us to the Father.

For Jesus to know God as His Father meant submitting to His authority, enjoying His love, and sharing His glory. When Jesus invites us to come to the Father through Him, He is inviting us into the same kind of relationship.

PAUSE FOR PRAYER

Almighty Father,

I bow before You with awe and wonder as I contemplate Your greatness and Your glory.

Thank You for making Yourself known to me through Your Son Jesus Christ, and for making it possible for me to call You Father. Help me to live in a growing awareness of Your everlasting love for me. Create within my heart a deeper love for You. Help me to live in submissive and joyful obedience to Your will, and so to offer worship that is in Spirit and in truth, until the day when I see Your glory, through Jesus Christ my Lord. Amen.

Notes

1. Martin Rinkart, trans. Catherine Winkworth, "Now Thank We All Our God," verse 3.

2. Reginald Heber, "Holy, Holy, Holy," verse 4.

16

Son

JOHN 5

Why is it so

important that

Jesus is God?

16 Son

JOHN 5

DISCOVER
what it means for Jesus to be the Son of God.

LEARN
how you can be sure about your salvation.

WORSHIP
because God has made Himself known through His Son, Jesus Christ.

MY birth certificate announces that I am the son of George and Violet Smith, born on April 27, 1958, in a small hospital in Edinburgh, Scotland. The hospital has now been turned into an old people's home, and so there is a distinct possibility that I could end my days where I began!

I became a father in 1986, when my son Andrew was born. Before I had a son, I could not have been described as a father. It is the birth of a son or daughter that makes a man a father or a woman a mother.

When did God become Father? The answer is that He has always been Father. He is the everlasting Father, and His nature never changes.

When did Christ become the Son? The answer is that He has always been the Son. He is the eternal Son, and His nature never changes.

The Father was never without the Son, and the Son was never without the Father. God did not gain a Son when Jesus was born. God sent His Son, who was already at the Father's side, into the world to be born of the Virgin Mary. Christ did not begin to exist in the Virgin's womb. Before He took our flesh, God the Son shared the Father's glory, the Father's life, the Father's activity, and the Father's love.

The Son has always been with the Father, and the Son has always been equal with the Father. There is no ranking of Father, Son, and Spirit in order or priority or importance.

The Bible makes it clear that the Son is equal with the Father; He is "in very nature God." However, He did not count this "equality with God something to be grasped" (Philippians 2:6). He placed Himself at the disposal of the Father and took on the form of a servant. For the purpose of our salvation, the Son subordinated Himself to the Father and became obedient to Him, not because He was less than the Father but because the Father and Son chose that it should be so. Being equally God, the Father and the Son assumed different roles in accomplishing our salvation.

On one occasion, Jesus said to His disciples, "If you loved me, you would be glad that I am going to the Father, for the Father is greater than I" (John 14:28). This is like me saying, "The president of the United States is greater than I." When I say that, I don't mean that the president is more human than I. I mean that he has a far more exalted position or role.

Similarly, when Jesus said, "The Father is greater than I," He did not mean that the Father is more divine than the Son, but that the Father had a more exalted position, a fact that was very obvious since at that point Jesus was about to take the lowest position as He went to the cross.

So Christ was saying to His disciples, "If you loved Me, you would be glad that I am going to the Father, because that means that I am returning to share His exalted position."

LIKE FATHER, LIKE SON

When I use the word *son*, I am speaking about someone who was born when I was twenty-seven years old. I existed before my son Andrew, and could have continued to exist without him. But God the Father was never without God the Son, and God the Son was never without God the Father. The relationship of this Father and Son has no beginning and no end. So it is quite clear that when God speaks about His "Son" in the Bible, He is using the term in a quite different way.

The word *son* is used in two ways in the Bible. It can mean a dependent relative (Isaac was Abraham's son), but it can also mean a reflected nature.[1]

In the ancient world, life followed a very simple path: If you were a boy, you did what your father did, and if you were a girl, you followed in your mother's footsteps. Your father or mother would show you what you needed to know. As you watched them, you would learn how things were done, and then you would do them.

If it were like this today and your father was a plumber, you would be a plumber as well. Indeed, if your father was a good plumber, the chances are you would be a good plumber too. If your father was a bad plumber, the chances are your work would spring leaks all over the place. The character of the father's work is normally reflected in the work of the son. As the old saying goes, "Like father, like son."

Names That Tell a Story

In the ancient world, names described character. If a person was really wicked, someone might describe him as a "son of Belial." The name meant that the person showed such unusual wickedness that he reflected the character of the devil himself; it was as if the devil were his father.

In 1 Samuel 2:12 we are told that "the sons of Eli were sons of Belial" (KJV).[2] Notice that the word *son* is used in two completely different ways in the one verse. These men were Eli's dependent children, but the character they reflected was not Eli's, but the devil's. It is not a very complimentary description.

On a more positive note, God referred to Israel as His "son." He said to Pharaoh, "Let my son go, so he may worship me" (Exodus 4:23). The Hebrew people were descended from Abraham, but God called them to reflect His holiness and to express His character in the world, so God called them His son.

The same was true of the king. Psalm 2 was used at the coronation of a king in Israel. God said, "You are my Son; today I have become your father" (Psalm 2:7). This meant that from that day, God was calling the king to reflect His dignity and glory among the people. The kings of Israel and Judah were called to be "Godlike," sons of God. Most of them made a pretty poor job of it.

In the New Testament, we read about a man called Joseph, whom the apostles called Barnabas. The name Barnabas means "Son of Encouragement" (Acts 4:36). Barnabas was a nickname, and it's not difficult to imagine why the apostles gave it to him. They saw that Joseph was a great encourager, and so they called him "Son of Encouragement." He was encouragement personified, encouragement in human flesh.

Jesus used the word *son* in the same way in the Sermon on the Mount. "Blessed are the peacemakers," He said, "for they will be called sons of God" (Matthew 5:9). God is the great peacemaker, and people who make peace are reflecting His character and activity. They are doing what God does, and so they are called "sons of God."

So when the Bible describes Jesus as "the Son of God," the word *Son* does not mean that He is a "dependent relative" of the Father, but that He exactly reflects the nature of the Father. He is everything that God is, in the flesh.

The full glory of what it means for Jesus to be the Son of God is opened up for us in John chapter 5, where Jesus makes two remarkable statements.

DOING THE FATHER'S WORK

Jesus [said,] "I tell you the truth, the Son can do nothing by himself; he can do only what he sees his Father doing, because whatever the Father does the Son also does." (v. 19)

First, Jesus tells us that His activity is limited to what He sees the Father doing. "The Son can do nothing by himself; he can do only what he sees his Father doing" (v. 19). Christ is saying that He never does anything that is outside the range of what the Father would do.

I wish that I could say that everything I do is a reflection of the activity of God, but of course, I can't. If that were true, I would be perfect. Yet that is exactly what Jesus is saying. "You will not find a single thing in My life that is outside of the range of the activity of God."

Then Jesus makes a second statement that is even more astonishing. "The Son can do nothing by himself; he can do only what he sees his Father doing, because *whatever the Father does the Son also does*" (emphasis added).

Not only is all of Jesus' activity a reflection of the activity of God, but all of God's activity also finds its reflection in Jesus.

In other words, Jesus is saying, "Everything that I do reflects what the Father does, and everything the Father does is reflected in what I do."

We may do *some* things that reflect what God does. We may love or forgive or make peace, and in that limited sense, we may reflect the nature of the Father. But there are some things that God does that we can never do. When did you last make a universe?

Only God gives life. Only God raises the dead. Only God is in the position to pronounce final judgment. These are God's things, and Jesus tells us that He does them.

WOMB, TOMB, AND DOOM

"Just as the Father raises the dead and gives them life, even so the Son gives life to whom he is pleased to give it. Moreover, the Father judges no one, but has entrusted all judgment to the Son. . . . I tell you the truth, a time is coming and has now come when the dead will hear the voice of the Son of God and those who hear will live." (vv. 21–22, 25)

The church I serve recently completed a building extension. When the work was completed, keys were distributed. There was quite a bit of discussion about who should have which keys. Keys are interesting because they reflect authority. If you have the keys to a place, you have the right of access to it.

Only God gives life, . . . raises the dead, and . . . pronounces final judgment.

Some keys belong to God alone. They are the keys of womb, tomb, and doom. Only God gives life, only God raises the dead, and only God pronounces final judgment.

But Jesus says, "Whatever the Father does the Son also does. For the Father loves the Son and shows him all he does" (vv. 19–20). Jesus holds all of the Father's keys in His hand.

Jesus is speaking to people who were amazed at the miracle they had just seen as Jesus healed a man who had been paralyzed for thirty-eight years. But Jesus tells them that they should not be surprised. The Son is simply doing a few of the things that the Father does. And Jesus promises that they would see Him doing greater things than healing a crippled man.

Jesus does everything that God does, and that means that He will raise the dead and pronounce final judgment (vv. 21–22). These are God's things, and Christ says that they are His things. They belong as much to the Son as they do to the Father.

The Son Who Has Life in Himself

"As the Father has life in himself, so he has granted the Son to have life in himself." (v. 26)

God has given us the wonderful gift of life, but we do not have life "in ourselves." Our lives are the gift of God to us through our parents. Without them, we would not be.

Only God has "life in himself." He is the only being whose existence does not depend on anybody else.

Jesus' statement helps us to gaze with wonder into the mystery of the Trinity.

Notice that Jesus did not say, "The Father has life in himself and the Son has life in himself." That would mean that there are two gods, both with life in themselves. Nor did Jesus say, "The Father has life in himself and he has granted the Son to have life." That would mean that the Son was a created and dependent being just like you and me.

Jesus said, "The Father has life in himself, so he has granted the Son to have life in himself." The Father has always had life in Himself, and the Son has always had life in Himself, but there is one life. The Father and the Son share in the one eternal life of God.[3]

Put all this together and you will begin to see the glory of our Lord Jesus Christ. Everything about the Son reflects the Father, and everything about the Father is reflected in the Son. The Son holds all the Father's keys and does everything the Father does. The Son has life in Himself, and He is able to give life to all who come to Him. He will one day raise the dead and pronounce final judgment on all people.

The New Testament places great stress on this teaching about the identity of Jesus: He is God with us. As we will see, this truth is of central importance for three reasons: If the Son is not God, (1) we could not know the Father, (2) the Cross would be an act of cruelty, and (3) we could never be sure of our salvation.

Knowing God: A Guess or a Revelation?

On one occasion, Philip expressed his deep longing to know God. He said to Jesus, "Show us the Father and that will be enough for us." Jesus replied, "Don't you know me, Philip, even after I have been among you such a long time? Anyone who has seen me has seen the Father" (John 14:8–9).

I have a brother in England. He is like me in some ways but very different in others. There is no way I could say to you, "If you have seen me, you have seen my brother," because even though we come from the same parents, we are entirely different. To know me is not to know my brother.

If the Son was not God, then we would not know the Father. The best we could say would be that someone who was with the Father and in some ways is like the Father has come to tell us about Him.

If anyone ever tells you that the Son is not fully God, that person has removed the possibility of knowing God. How else could the invisible God be known?

If the Son is close to God but not God, then we are left guessing about what God is like. We can assume that Jesus is like the Father in some respects, but how could we know which ones? And if the Son is not God, then, by definition, He must in some ways be different from God. In what ways is He different? If the Son is not God, then we do not know the Father.

But the central claim of the gospel is that the Son is one with the Father. "No one has ever seen God, but God the One and Only, who is at the Father's side, has made him known" (John 1:18).

Jesus is not a companion of God who can tell us about Him. He is God with us. Whoever has seen Jesus has seen the Father. As the apostle Paul wrote, "God . . . [gave] us the light of the knowledge of the glory of God in the face of Christ" (2 Corinthians 4:6). How else could the invisible God be known?

The Cross: An Act of Cruelty or a Gift of Love?

If the Son is not God, the Cross would be an act of cruelty, not a gift of love.

The Bible tells us that the Father laid the guilt and the punishment for our sins on the Son. Think about that. If the Son is not God, then the Cross was an act of utter cruelty on the part of God.

If the Son is not God, it means that God picked on some person in His creation and poured out on Him what everyone else deserved. What kind of justice is that?

If the Son is not God, He was victimized by the Father—sentenced for crimes He did not commit. If the Son is not God, the Cross was the greatest miscarriage of justice in history, and not just by Pontius Pilate—it would be the ultimate miscarriage of justice by God Almighty. If the Son is not God, we would have to rewrite Romans 5:8: "God demonstrated his injustice in this: While we were still sinners, Christ died for us."

God's Eternal Purpose

God had always planned to redeem men and women from the clutches of sin. The Bible speaks about God's eternal purpose (Ephesians 3:11). Before God created the world, He knew the choice that Adam and Eve would make and the disaster that would follow. But God had planned to redeem men and women out of this fallen world so that they would share His eternal glory forever.

That plan involved a great cost. It would mean God giving Himself, and that self-giving would be the ultimate display of His own nature and His own glory.

God's self-giving would involve all the persons of the Trinity. One would be the giver, one would be the gift, and one would bring the gift to all who would receive.

> Here is the great mystery: . . . God was reconciling the world to Himself in Christ.

Before the world began, the Father said, "I will be the giver." The Son said, "I will be the gift," and the Spirit said, "I will bring the gift to all who will receive." The Father would send the Son; the Son would come and lay down His life. The Spirit would deliver this priceless gift and make it yours.

If you are trying to evaluate the difficulty of the role of the Father and the Son, think about Abraham and Isaac climbing Mount Moriah. Which of them had the easier part to play? The one who would give up his son, or the one who would lay down his life? The question is unanswerable. The Father and the Son were locked together in a mystery of self-giving and sacrifice at infinite cost.

Here is the great mystery: As the Father gave the Son and the Son laid down His life, God was reconciling the world to Himself in Christ. When the Father poured out the judgment for sin upon the Son, *God was bearing the wrath of God.*

That is why Romans 5:8 actually reads, "God demonstrates his own *love* for us in this: While we were still sinners, Christ died for us" (emphasis added). The Father demonstrates His love in giving the Son. The Son demonstrates His love by becoming the gift. The Spirit demonstrates His love by opening our hearts to receive this gift.

The Cross was not the act of a cruel and vindictive God. It was the outpouring of love by the God who chose to redeem His enemies at infinite personal cost. And the reason it is so is that the Son is God.

Salvation: Being Sure or Hoping for the Best?

If the Son was not God, you could never be sure of your salvation.

I phoned my credit card company recently because I wanted to change my card into a new one that had some extra benefits. "Can I do this over the phone?" I asked.

The assistant was very helpful and assured me that I could.

I spent about fifteen minutes on the phone answering every question imaginable and a few more, but at the end she assured me that I would have the new card within a few days.

A few days later I received a letter.

> Dear Colin Smith,
>
> Thank you for your recent inquiry regarding your credit card account. Unfortunately we are unable to change your account as you requested.
>
> If you would like to change your account, please contact our customer service at the telephone number listed above.
>
> If you have any questions or if we can help you in any other way, please call us. Serving you is very important to us, and we appreciate your business.

The letter came from the financial services adviser, though he didn't bother to sign it.

Now you know what has happened here. Some poor telephone operator has been overruled! From the information I gave her, she sincerely believed that my account could be changed over the phone, so she led me through the process and assured me that all was well.

But she was overruled by a higher authority who presumably told her that she had no right to make such rash promises to me, and that what she had told this "Smith fellow" in Arlington Heights was quite beyond her authority and that she should send the appropriate letter immediately and without fail!

Now, what if it was like that with Christ? If the Son is not God, there is always the possibility that however well intentioned, He may ultimately be overruled by a higher authority.

Christ presides over the supreme court of the universe. . . . There is no higher authority.

If the Son is not God, we have to face the distinct possibility that we might arrive at heaven's gate only to be issued an unsigned letter from a higher authority informing us that the heaven we hoped for is currently not available, and that we had better begin some entirely new application process for which we may or may not qualify.

If the Son is not God, then we have an attorney acting for us, but at the end of the day everything depends on whether he can persuade the judge.

But suppose that the Father entrusted all judgment to the Son (John 5:22). Suppose that the Son is in very nature God. Then, if the Son said, "You are forgiven," you would be forgiven!

Christ presides over the supreme court of the universe. If He settles your case, there is no other place of appeal. There is no higher authority. There are no other proceedings. There can be no overruling.

RESPONDING TO THE SON

When you have seen who the Son of God is, faith will be the most natural thing in the world. When Jesus revealed His true identity, He invited people to trust Him. His words in John 5 are emphatic:

> *"I tell you the truth, whoever hears my word and believes him who sent me has eternal life and will not be condemned; he has crossed over from death to life."* (v. 24)

You can put your trust in the Lord Jesus Christ. In His hand He holds the key to your destiny. He offers you eternal life. He promises that if you will believe His words and believe the Father who sent Him, you will not be condemned. That's His promise and He will never be overruled. Do you believe Him?

When you see who the Son of God is, your response will also be one of worship. Jesus said, "The Father . . . has entrusted all judgment to the Son, that all may honor the Son just as they honor the Father" (vv. 22–23). Those who honor Him begin a new life, "by faith in the Son of God, who loved [us] and gave himself for [us]" (Galatians 2:20).

UNLOCKED

Jesus Christ is the Son of God. He shares the Father's nature and glory; He is the image of the invisible God, "the exact representation of his being" (Hebrews 1:3). This teaching runs throughout the New Testament and is of foundational importance to the whole Christian faith.

Jesus is God with us, and for this reason we can truly know the Father in Him. His death on the cross is the ultimate demonstration of the love of God for us. On the cross, God was bearing the wrath of God. God was reconciling the world to Himself in Christ. The deity of the Lord Jesus Christ is also the basis of our assurance of salvation. The Father has trusted all judgment to the Son; there is no higher authority. His word is final.

PAUSE FOR PRAYER

You can use the following words to reflect on the glory of the Son of God, and express your worship to Him:

You are the everlasting Word, the Father's only Son;
God in the flesh now seen and heard, You're heaven's best loved one.
But the high mysteries of Your Name, not even angels know;
All that's in God is seen in You, living with us below.
In You we see the face of God, whose nature is concealed;
You know the Father; through You alone, the Father is revealed.
In all the joy of heaven's bliss, the center is God's Son,
Through time and through eternity, we'll sing of what You've done.
Worthy O Lamb of God art Thou
that every knee to You should bow.[4]

Notes

1. I gladly acknowledge my debt to Professor Don Carson for his work on the "Son language" of the New Testament. See especially D. A. Carson, *The Difficult Doctrine of the Love of God* (Wheaton, Ill.: Crossway, 2000), 31ff.
2. The New International Version translates the verse "Eli's sons were wicked men; they had no regard for the LORD."
3. I am again indebted to Don Carson for this point, particularly in *The Difficult Doctrine of the Love of God*, 37–39.
4. Adapted from the hymn "Thou Art the Everlasting Word," Josiah Condor (1789–1855).

17

Spirit

JOHN 16

Who is the Holy Spirit and what does He do?

17 Spirit

JOHN 16

DISCOVER

how the Holy Spirit delivers the gift that Christ has purchased for us.

LEARN

how to recognize the work of the Holy Spirit.

WORSHIP

because God is at work throughout the world by the Holy Spirit.

IMAGINE a man who is fabulously wealthy. His name is Stavros, he is a Greek shipping magnate, and over the years he has amassed billions of dollars.

One day Stavros dies, and his lawyer opens the will. It's a very lengthy document, running to hundreds of pages. The lawyer already knows the contents because he was there when the will was written. He knows that Stavros chose to distribute his wealth to many people.

The beneficiaries of Stavros's will are all over the world. Every one of them has to be found and told about the legacy, and, according to the terms of the will, every one of them has to be brought to Stavros's home in order to receive what has been promised to them. The lawyer has his work cut out for years to come.

The Bible tells us that through His death, Christ has purchased a marvelous inheritance for us. Through His death and resurrection, He has opened the way for sinful men and women to be reconciled to God and to enter everlasting life. The will of God has been signed by the Father and sealed by the blood of Christ. But what has been signed and sealed still needs to be delivered.

It is one thing for a gift to be offered; it is another thing for that gift to be received. And all that Jesus Christ has done will be useless and of no value to us until we receive what He offers.

> Without the Spirit of God, salvation would [be only] a theoretical possibility.

So how can the will of God, signed by the Father, and sealed in the blood of Christ be delivered to us? The answer is, "By the Holy Spirit."

The Holy Spirit brings what Jesus has accomplished on the cross and applies it personally to us. He takes what Christ has made possible for all people and applies it to your particular case.

If the Son of God had not come, you *could not* be saved. If the Spirit of God had not come, you *would not* be saved. Without the Spirit of God, salvation would remain a theoretical possibility, but it would never become a reality for any of us. If there were no Holy Spirit, nobody would arrive in heaven. Without the Spirit, all that Jesus has done would be like a will that was never read, a gift that was never received, an inheritance that was never made known.

So when we talk about the work of the Holy Spirit, we are right to the center of the Christian faith. It is the Spirit who brings us to Christ, and it is the Spirit who keeps us in Christ.

Jesus highlighted three distinctive activities of the Spirit: disturbing, illuminating, and indwelling.

God's Disturber of the Peace

> *"When [the Holy Spirit] comes, he will convict the world of guilt in regard to sin and righteousness and judgment."*
> *(John 16:8)*

People in the world of business know that you can't sell what people don't want to buy. That's a fundamental rule of the marketplace. You may have the most marvelous widget, but if people can't see a need for your widget, then you don't have much hope of success.

Christ offers us forgiveness of sin, righteousness from above, and deliverance from the judgment to come. The problem is that most people do not feel that they need what Christ offers.

This is nothing new. The Gospels tell us about an occasion when Jesus was approached by a successful businessman who wanted to know what he had to do to have eternal life. When Jesus spoke to him about the Ten Commandments, he said that he had kept them all since his youth.

He was absolutely sincere. "You don't understand," the businessman was saying. "You're not talking to a lowlifer who has trashed his life. You're talking to a highly successful, upwardly mobile achiever, and I've kept all of these commandments since my youth."

He wasn't suggesting that he was perfect. No sane person thinks that. But he was not aware of any obvious sin in his life, and he felt that he was making a commendable effort to walk the right path. As he looked at his own life, his honest opinion was that overall he measured up to the Law of God rather well. He expected to have eternal life; he just wanted to be sure.

It is very interesting that the first thing Christ did with this man was to expose his need. He said, "Go, sell everything you have and give to the poor, and you will have treasure in heaven. Then come, follow me" (Mark 10:21).

In a moment, the man saw himself for the self-centered person he was. His whole view of himself as someone who measures up to what God requires was completely blown apart, and he saw for the first time that he knew nothing about the love of God.

Jesus had to illuminate this man's need because the man would never progress until he discovered his need of Christ.

Think about opening a can of paint. You would probably use a screwdriver or some other kind of lever to pry the lid open. Round the edge of the can there is a rim that functions as a pivot for the lever. If there were no rim, you would not be able to pry the lid open. There would be nothing for the lever to pull on. A lever has to pull on a pivot.

The gospel is like a lever, and it depends on a sense of sin as its pivot. If a person has no sense of sin, the gospel will have no "pull" in that person's life. The gospel is addressed to the sense of sin, and where that does not exist, it is like a lever without a pivot.

[The Spirit's] first work is to disturb by convincing us of sin, righteousness, and judgment.

The gospel will only have its effect in our lives if the Holy Spirit creates a sense of sin within us, and that is why His first work is to disturb by convincing us of sin, righteousness, and judgment.

If it were not for the Holy Spirit, we would never see our need for Jesus. Indeed, it is frightening to observe that as a man's deeds grow more evil, his capacity for denial often seems to increase. The more a person engages in sin, the easier it gets to live with it, and those who continue longest in patterns of sin are least sensitive to the sinfulness of their behavior.

FALSE GUILT . . . AND TRUE GUILT

I recently watched a film about the Nuremberg trials. After the Second World War, the Allies set up a legal process for trying war criminals of some of the most horrendous crimes, and the hearings were held in the town of Nuremberg, Germany. The highest-ranking defendant was Hermann Göring.

What was truly staggering, as the story unfolded, was that when survivors of the most appalling violence were brought forward and film of the concentration camps in all of their horrors was shown, Göring could still not see that the cause that he had supported had been wrong. He felt that there was good justification for what he had done and that there was no good reason for judgment to be passed upon him.

We hear a great deal today about false guilt. False guilt is an inappropriate feeling of guilt over something that we did not do and for which we were not responsible. There is nothing useful about false guilt. It is a snare of the enemy, and we need to expose it so that we can be free from it.

But there is such a thing as true guilt, and true guilt needs to be embraced. True guilt relates to sins we have committed, righteousness we have not fulfilled, and judgment that is due on account of these things. True guilt is about facing reality and taking responsibility. A person who never discovers his or her true guilt will continue down the path of sin and never find reconciliation to God.

There is a huge gulf between what we are and what God calls us to be. When the Holy Spirit enables us to see ourselves clearly, we will quickly realize that righteousness is far beyond our reach and that without Jesus Christ we would be liable to the judgment and the condemnation of God.

The first work of the Holy Spirit is to show us what's wrong, so that we will see our need and be ready to listen to the gospel. This is never comfortable. Nobody likes to be wakened when they are sleeping, but if there is a fire in your house, you will be deeply thankful to the person who wakens you. You may be angry at first, but as soon as you realize the danger you are in, you will be grateful.

GOD'S THREE ALARM CLOCKS

Karen and I have three alarm clocks in our bedroom. The first one to go off wakens us gently with music. The second is set for a few minutes later and is more disturbing. We have it set in case we sleep through the first one. The third is set later still and is a last resort if all else fails. It makes a horrendous sound, and the day begins much better if we are up before it sounds its deafening blast.

God has three ways to intercept sin in a person's life. You could think of them as three alarm clocks. As you consider them, think about which you would most like God to use in your case.

The first is the quiet and gentle work of God's Spirit opening up the conscience and revealing what's wrong to your mind so that you can change it.

If you sleep through that, the Holy Spirit may speak more loudly and directly. That's what God did with David. The king wasn't listening to the Holy Spirit's prompting in his conscience, so God revealed David's secret sin of adultery to the prophet Nathan and sent him to speak to David. David's sin was exposed. It became public knowledge, and at that point, David turned to God in repentance. If that's what it takes, that is what God will do.

If a person ignores God's second alarm, his or her situation becomes perilous. That is what happened with Pharaoh. God sent Moses to him, but Pharaoh refused to listen to God's command, even when he was confronted with it directly. He continued to harden his heart, and eventually God took direct action. Pharaoh came under the judgment of God.

Consider these three alarms: the quiet work of God's Spirit in opening the conscience, confrontation by another person, and the direct judgment of God Almighty. Which of these three ways would you like God to use to stop you sinning? I have no doubt about the way that I want God to work in my life.

We should be deeply thankful to God for the disturbing work of the Holy Spirit, and determine to be sensitive to His voice. Those who refuse to face their sins eventually find that God has other ways of speaking.

Nothing could be more foolish than to resist the Holy Spirit when He speaks to you about your sin. God is reaching out to you in the gentlest of ways. It's always disturbing, but this work of the Holy Spirit is a wonderful expression of God's grace.

TURNING ON THE FLOODLIGHT

"When the Counselor comes, . . . the Spirit of truth who goes out from the Father, he will testify about me." (JOHN 15:26)

"He [the Holy Spirit] will bring glory to me [Jesus] by taking from what is mine and making it known to you." (JOHN 16:14)

I love to drive past our church at night when it is floodlit. The building looks magnificent, but if it were not for the floodlights, its beauty would be hidden in the darkness. I have often driven friends past the floodlit building, but I have never yet heard anybody comment on the floodlights. People always talk about the building.[1]

The second distinctive work of the Holy Spirit is to floodlight Jesus Christ. He illuminates the truth that once was obscure to us; He opens our understanding so that we see the glory of Jesus. Like the floodlight, the Holy Spirit does not draw attention to Himself; He directs our focus to Jesus Christ.

The Holy Spirit is heaven's matchmaker. He brings us to Christ.

The Father, the Son, and the Holy Spirit are equally God. There is no order or rank or precedence. But for the purposes of our salvation, the Father, the Son, and the Spirit have different roles. The Father chose to be the giver, the Son chose to be the gift, and the Spirit chose to bring the gift. The Son placed Himself in the service of the Father, and the Spirit placed Himself in the service of the Son.

The Holy Spirit has a beautiful ministry. He shows me my need of a Savior, and at the same time, He shows me that Christ is the Savior I need. Then He brings the two together.

The Holy Spirit is heaven's matchmaker. He brings us to Christ and joins us to Christ so that everything Jesus accomplished on the cross becomes mine. He delivers the gift, signed by the Father and sealed by the death of Christ.

THE HOLY SPIRIT IS A PERSON

"And I will ask the Father, and he will give you another Counselor to be with you forever." (JOHN 14:16)

Donald Grey Barnhouse pointed out that our English word *another* is ambiguous because it can mean "different" or "the same." If I go into a shop and buy a pen, and when I get home I find that it's a roller ball when I thought it was a fountain pen, I might take it back and ask for "another" one, by which I mean one that is different. But if I like the pen and then lose it, I might go back to the shop and ask for "another" one, by which I mean one exactly the same.[2]

Thankfully, the Greek language in which the New Testament was written distinguishes these two uses of "another," and the word Jesus uses here to describe the Spirit as "another Counselor" is the word that means "exactly the same."

"Over the last three years," Jesus was saying, "I have been your counselor. But when the Holy Spirit comes, He will be everything to you that I have been."

This tells us two very important things about the Holy Spirit. If the Holy Spirit is to be everything to us that Christ was to the disciples, it follows that the Holy Spirit is a person and that the Holy Spirit is God.

Jesus never referred to the Holy Spirit as "it," and neither should we. Jesus always spoke about "He" or "Him." When speaking about the Spirit, Jesus said, "The world cannot accept *him*, because it neither sees *him* nor knows *him*. But you know *him*, for *he* lives with you and will be in you" (v. 17, emphasis added).

The Holy Spirit is as much a person as the Father and the Son. So we should not think of the Spirit simply as a power or force. The Bible speaks about lying to the Holy Spirit and grieving the Spirit (Acts 5:3; Ephesians 4:30). You cannot lie to a force, and you cannot grieve a power. A burst of energy could never be to the disciples everything that Jesus was.

The Holy Spirit is a person. He speaks to us and works with us. The Holy Spirit is as much God with you as Jesus was God with the disciples.

The Holy Spirit Is God

The Holy Spirit has been at work from the beginning. At the creation, the Spirit of God hovered over the waters (Genesis 1:2). He was at work throughout the Old Testament, especially through prophets, priests, and kings. David asked where he should run from the Spirit or go from His presence (Psalm 139:7–10).

The Father is the fullness of God invisible. The Son is the fullness of God made flesh. The Spirit is the fullness of God with us and in us. Once again we stand in awe of the mystery of the Trinity: one God in three persons.

Notice how Jesus spoke about the unity between the Father, the Son, and the Spirit. He called the Spirit "another Counselor" (John 14:16). So the Spirit is not to be confused with the Son. They have a distinct identity. But then Jesus added, "I will not leave you as orphans; I will come to you" (v. 18). In other words, where the Spirit is, Christ is.

Then Jesus said something even more astonishing. "If anyone loves me, he will obey my teaching. My Father will love him, and we will come to him and make our home with him" (v. 23). So now, we learn that where the Spirit is, both the Father and the Son will make Their home.

One thing that is absolutely clear is that you cannot know one person of the Trinity without the others. There is no such thing as knowing the Father apart from the Son. It is through the Son that the Father has made Himself known. And nobody knows the Son apart from the Spirit. It is the Holy Spirit who opens our eyes to know who Jesus is, and it is the Holy Spirit who brings us to repentance and faith in Him.

"IN" AND "WITH"

> *"You know him [the Holy Spirit], for he lives* with *you and will be* in *you."* (JOHN 14:17, EMPHASIS ADDED)

Notice the two distinctive words Jesus used to describe our relationship with the Holy Spirit. The Holy Spirit is "with" me. That reminds me that there is the "Holy Spirit" and there is "me," and I must never get the two confused!

Have you ever met someone who did confuse the two? You know them by their assumption that everything they say is something that God is saying. They cannot distinguish between themselves and the Spirit. It is almost impossible to reason with such a person. This error is at the root of a great deal of fanaticism, and has led to many disasters that have tarnished the church.

We must never confuse what we think and say with the mind of the Spirit. If we are wise, we will humbly allow others to test what we say. The Spirit is with me, and I often need Him to correct me.

> He is able to touch all the deep places of your soul.

The Holy Spirit is not a spiritual capacity within us. If that were the case, we would be alone and would have no help outside of ourselves. When Jesus says that the Spirit is "with" His disciples, He is reminding us that God Himself comes to us. He is our help and our shield. God is with you in the hardest situations of your life.

But Jesus also said that the Spirit would be "in" His disciples. The third distinctive work of the Holy Spirit is to indwell believers. The Holy Spirit is more than a mentor who shows us what to do. We need more than advice; we need the power to change. The ministry of the Holy Spirit goes beyond the work of a counselor, pastor, or friend who may be able to shed light on problems and suggest possible ways forward. The Spirit works *in* us.

He is able to touch all the deep places of your soul, renewing your mind, redirecting affections of the heart, molding and reshaping the will, cleansing the imagination, and healing the memory. He can create new desires within you so that you follow Christ not out of a sense of duty but from a heart that hungers and thirsts for righteousness. He can give you the power to live a new life for the glory of God.

If you have come to faith in Jesus Christ, God's Spirit is with you and in you (see 1 Corinthians 6:19; 12:13). There is one God and He is Father, Son, and Holy Spirit. You can come to the Father only through the Son, and those who come through the Son have the Spirit. Indeed, it is the Spirit who draws us to the Son and shows us our need in the first place.

So don't ever say that you can't change. Don't allow your enemy to talk defeat. The fullness of God is with you, in Christ, and by the Spirit. Think about the Spirit who dwells in you! The blessed third person of the Trinity is at work in you and is with you in everything you face from here to eternity.

UNLOCKED

God the Holy Spirit is the third person of the Trinity, and His ministry is central to our salvation. We could not be saved without the work of God the Son on the Cross, and we would not be saved without the work of God the Holy Spirit in our hearts. The promises that are signed by God the Father and sealed by the death and resurrection of God the Son are delivered and made effective in our lives by God the Holy Spirit.

The Holy Spirit disturbs us so that we see our sin and grasp our need of the Savior. As He disturbs, He also illuminates, so that we can see that Jesus is precisely the Savior we need.

Then as heaven's matchmaker, the Holy Spirit forms the bond between the believer and Christ as faith and repentance are formed in our hearts. The Holy Spirit is both with and in every Christian believer, giving us the knowledge of God's presence and the gift of His power.

PAUSE FOR PRAYER

Almighty Father,

Thank You for sending Your Holy Spirit into my heart, so that I may know You and Your Son Jesus Christ.

Show me the secret sins that lurk in the dark places of my soul so that I may be able to see myself and grow in repentance. Give me a fresh and clear understanding of the love of the Lord Jesus Christ so that I may trust Him more fully and worship Him from a full and thankful heart.

Thank You that Your Spirit is with me in every situation I face. Give me a deeper appreciation of His power that is at work in me, and help me to know that I can do everything You call me to do by the power of Your Holy Spirit. In Jesus' name. Amen.

Notes

1. I owe the illustration of the floodlight to Dr. J. I. Packer. See Packer, *Keep in Step with the Spirit* (Old Tappan, N. J.: Revell, 1984), 65 ff.

2. The illustration of the pen is from Donald Grey Barnhouse, *Illustrating the Gospel of John* (Grand Rapids: Baker, 1973), 189–190.

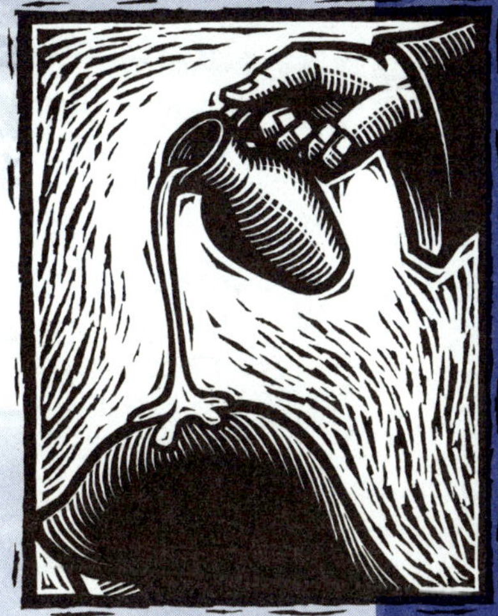

18

Christ

JOHN 20

What does

the name

Christ mean?

18 Christ

JOHN 20

DISCOVER

the evidence for believing that Jesus is the Christ.

LEARN

why salvation does not rest on you but on Jesus.

WORSHIP

because those who trust in Jesus Christ will never be put to shame.

SUPPOSE you are in a large city and that you don't know how to find your way to a particular destination. There are two ways in which you might proceed.

You could ask for directions. Someone might tell you that you need to catch the number 29 bus, get off at the second stop past the old cement works, take the third street on the left, go over the bridge, across the field, through the underpass, and then take the fourth block on your right.

A second approach would be to take a taxi. You would ask the taxi driver if he knows how to get to your destination, and assuming that he did, you would get in.

Now suppose, in the first case, that just after you get on the number 29 bus, the man who gave you the instructions has a heart attack and dies. This unfortunate event will make no difference to your journey because you have the instructions. All that matters, as far as your journey is concerned, is that he gave you the information before he died.

But suppose you are in the taxi, and just as you are going past the old cement works, the taxi driver has a heart attack and dies. Then you are completely stuck. You do not know the way to your destination, and the one in whom you put your trust is unable to take you there.

The heart of Christianity lies not in a set of instructions but in the ability of Jesus to take us to heaven. It is not the teaching of the New Testament that will save you; it is Jesus Christ Himself who will save you, and that is why Christianity stands or falls with Jesus' ability to do what He promised. Everything depends on whether He is able to take us to the promised destination.

Are we ready to stake our destiny on Him?

That is why the New Testament insists that if Christ is not risen, our faith is futile (1 Corinthians 15:17). We would be the most miserable people in the world, because we chose to trust our journey to one who was unable to deliver us to our destination. Everything stands or falls with Him.

Other religious leaders have presented a program of spiritual disciplines and said, "This is the way," but Jesus said, "I am the way." Others have presented a body of teaching and said, "This is the truth," but Jesus said, "I am the truth." Others have said, "Do this and you will have life." Jesus said, "I am the life" (John 14:6).

The world is filled with many claims, and it is not always easy to tell truth from error. So how are we to assess the claims of Jesus? He comes alongside and tells us that He can bring us to the Father and when, like the taxi driver, He invites us to "get in," we face a decision: Are we ready to stake our destiny on Him?

This decision involves an act of trust, and since the issue at stake is your eternal destiny, it is not a decision you will want to make lightly. The Gospels were written to help you make that decision.

WHY SHOULD I BELIEVE?

"These are written that you may believe." (JOHN 20:31)

Over the years I have met many people who have been given an inadequate answer to the question, "Why should I believe?" Some have been taught that they should believe because the church says so. The problem with this answer is that it leaves very little room for honest questions.

The result is that many people choose either to turn away from the invitation to believe or else "sign off" on certain beliefs, without those beliefs really becoming personal. "I believe what the church teaches: I'm not sure it makes a whole lot of sense, but who am I to question the church?" That hardly leads you to the kind of personal trust that Jesus invites you to place in Him.

The same thing can happen in family life where zealous parents drum Christian teaching into their children, who feel that honest questions are regarded as a sign of unbelief or rebellion. That kind of pressure to believe can lead to the conclusion of the little boy who was asked what faith was and answered, "Faith is believing what you know isn't true."

The story is told of a preacher who left his notes on the pulpit after a Sunday morning service. One of the board members took the opportunity to look through the pages. They were beautifully printed, and in the margins there were some notes to help with presentation. About half way through there were some strong red lines in the margin, and beside them the words, "Argument weak here; shout louder."

The church has not been free from blame in this regard. But when you open the New Testament, you enter a different world. The apostles were not authoritarian preachers who leaned out of their pulpits and shouted loudly, "Believe, believe!" They were compassionate pastors, who laid out the evidence of what they had seen and heard of Jesus Christ so that people could look at it honestly and come to a verdict.

Trying to Get the Feeling

I wish that I had a dollar for every time someone told me that they believe because they feel it. This is repeated so often; yet some spend years waiting for this feeling to happen to them.

If the church in the past has fallen into the error of trying to build faith on the bullying tactics of authoritarianism, then the church today is in much greater danger of building faith on the manipulative tactics of sentimentalism. The church in the modern world is increasingly under pressure to use techniques that induce temporary states of feeling.

The problem for many is that they have experienced warm feelings in worship, but that is all they have experienced. When they are faced with great darkness, or they are challenged with the cost of following Christ, the warm feelings fade, and there is no rock on which their faith can rest.

This is surely why the apostle Paul said that he had "renounced secret and shameful ways" and refused to have anything to do with deception or distortions of the Word of God (2 Corinthians 4:2).

God created you with a mind, a heart, and a will, and He wants to possess all of them. He seeks a relationship of integrity with His people in which a person's mind is convinced, heart filled, and will committed.

It's like falling in love: When you discover that special person and you know he or she is the one, your mind says so, your heart says so, and your will says so. The order may vary, but you are looking for three green lights, and if one of them is missing, there's usually a problem.

This is where God wants to bring us. Some people are intuitive. God gains the attention of their hearts before He gains the conviction of their minds. Feeling precedes understanding. There is nothing wrong with that so long as the understanding is eventually engaged.

Others are more cerebral. They need to come to a settled conviction before the heart is opened. The heart cannot embrace what the mind will not believe. Others are activists. They want to do something and are quick to step forward and become involved. The order is not important. What matters is that the whole person becomes involved.

This is why God gives us the evidence on which faith is based in the Gospels. The Gospels present the case for Christ. They are evidence that demands a verdict.

YOU ARE THE JURY

Imagine that you are in a court of law. You are part of the jury, and the apostle John wants to present you with certain evidence. When he is finished presenting his evidence, he will be looking for you to give a verdict.

He is not like a bully attorney, trying to intimidate you. Nor is he a tearjerker, trying to gain your sympathy. He is presenting the evidence of what he has seen and heard as a direct witness over the three years he has been with Jesus. All he asks is that we hear the evidence without prejudice.

And that's our problem. When a jury is sworn in, the key question is whether there are any ways in which they may be prejudiced with regard to the particular case that is going to be tried. You may be a very good member of the jury in one trial, but you may be highly prejudiced when it comes to another.

Many people have issues that prejudice their hearing of the evidence about Jesus. Our culture is highly prejudiced against the possibility that any one person could be the Savior of the world. Then there is prejudice in our hearts because we know that if we come to the verdict that Jesus is the Christ, it will have a major impact on the direction of our lives. So many want to be excused from the jury. "I can't try this case," they say. "Sorry!"

If you are not in heaven on the last day, it will not be because God has failed to provide you with evidence or opportunity. Recall John's words about his gospel: "These are written that you may believe."

"JESUS IS THE CHRIST"

"These are written that you may believe that Jesus is the Christ." *(V.20, EMPHASIS ADDED)*

If you were asked to summarize the core of the Christian faith in one sentence, what would you say? John boils the essence of the faith down to just four words: *"Jesus is the Christ."*

It is obviously important for us to know what the name *Christ* means. We know that our Lord was given the birth name of Jesus, so why do we call Him Jesus *Christ?*

Our English word *Christ* comes from the Greek word *Christos*, which means Messiah, or "Anointed One." "Christ" is a title referring to One promised in the Old Testament who would be anointed by God. A quick review of the people who were anointed in the Old Testament will help us to understand its significance.

Throughout the Bible story, God engages in three activities. He reveals Himself so that we may know Him, He reconciles us to Himself so that we come to Him, and He rules the world so that His purposes may be fulfilled.

In the Old Testament, certain people were "anointed" as a sign that God would use them in one of these activities. They were prophets, priests, and kings.

The prophets were anointed for God's work of revealing. God spoke to them directly so that they could speak the Word of God to the people. Prophets were "anointed" for this task. At the end of Elijah's life, he was told to go and "anoint Elisha" to be a prophet after him (1 Kings 19:16). Isaiah said the Spirit of the Lord had "anointed" him to preach good news to the poor (Isaiah 61:1).

The priests were anointed for God's work of reconciling. While the prophets spoke on behalf of God to men, the priests spoke on behalf of men to God. They had the unenviable task of offering sacrifices on behalf of the people.

The ceremony for anointing the high priest is described in Exodus 29. Aaron was dressed in the high priest's clothing and brought before the people. Moses poured oil over his head until it ran down over his beard (Psalm 133:2). It must have been a spectacular occasion. Nobody could be in any doubt that God had chosen this man and anointed him for the ministry of high priest.

Different expectations developed regarding this Messiah, or Anointed One.

The kings were anointed for God's work of ruling. Samuel anointed David as king of Israel by pouring oil over his head. When he did this, "the Spirit of the LORD came upon David in power" (1 Samuel 16:13).

In the Old Testament, "God's anointed one" could be a prophet who spoke God's word, a priest who offered sacrifices, or a king who subdued the people's enemies, but as the Old Testament story progressed, there was a growing expectation that God would one day send an anointed one par excellence into the world.

Since God's anointed one could be a prophet, priest, or king, it is easy to understand how different expectations developed regarding this Messiah, or Anointed One. Some thought He would be a prophet; they were looking for God to send a new teacher of righteousness. Others were looking for a priest who would bring a reformation of worship. Still others, like Judas Iscariot, were convinced that the Messiah would be a freedom fighter who would lead a political uprising and deliver the people from the oppression of the Roman Empire.

Jesus Christ is God's Anointed One par excellence.

Throughout the Old Testament story, God raised up prophets, priests, and kings. There was always new truth to be revealed, new sacrifices for sin to be made, and new enemies to be faced. God's people were continually in need of God's anointed, but increasingly, they looked for "*The* anointed," the One *who had been promised.*

Then God did something absolutely staggering. He anointed His own Son to fulfill not one, but all of the Old Testament offices. The Father said to the Son, "You go and be their Prophet. You go and be their High Priest. You go and be their King."

Jesus Christ is God's Anointed One par excellence, and John lays out the evidence to show us that Jesus is indeed the Deliverer, promised by God since the beginning of time, who will reveal the truth, reconcile men and women to God, and defeat our greatest enemy.

Jesus Christ has given us the definitive revelation of God. He is God with us, and in Him the Father has made Himself known. In laying down His life, Jesus has made the final sacrifice that will cover the sins of all who will come to Him. Jesus has also overcome our greatest enemy and broken his stranglehold over the human race through His death and resurrection.

John sets out the evidence that Jesus is the Christ. He points to Christ the prophet, who knew the hidden truth about a Samaritan woman. She said to him, "I know that Messiah . . . is coming. When he comes, he will explain everything to us." Jesus said to her, "I who speak to you am he" (John 4:25–26).

"'We have found the Messiah' (that is, the Christ)."

John tells us about the death of Jesus. At the beginning of the gospel, John the Baptist identified Jesus as "the Lamb of God, who takes away the sin of the world!" (John 1:29). When John said this, one of His disciples, Andrew, began to follow Jesus. He told his brother Peter, "'We have found the Messiah' (that is, the Christ)" (v. 41).

John goes on to explain how Christ would take away the sins of the world. Jesus spoke of laying down His life. That's the language of sacrifice. When Jesus died, John records His triumphant words, "It is finished" (19:30), indicating the sacrifice was complete and reconciliation between God and man was accomplished.

John also gives us the evidence that Christ is the King who delivers us from our enemies. One day Jesus came to the tomb of a friend who had died four days earlier. He said, "I am the resurrection and the life" and asked the dead man's sister Martha if she believed this. "Yes, Lord," she said, "I believe that you are the Christ, the Son of God, who was to come into the world" (11:27).

Jesus asked for the stone to be rolled back and then demonstrated His authority over death by calling the dead man to come out. This King has authority over greater enemies than the Romans. He can deliver men and women from the tyranny of death and hell.

The reason that all these things were written was so "that you may [know] that Jesus is the Christ" (20:31). Jesus is *the Prophet* who speaks the Word of God, He is *the Priest* who offers the sacrifice acceptable to God, and He is *the King* who routs the enemies of God. He is God's Anointed One. Jesus is the Christ.

When we know who Jesus is, we will understand what it means to have faith in Him. Jesus Christ is Prophet, Priest, and King. So believing in Him means that we trust what He says as Prophet and take His Word as the standard of truth by which all else is measured. It means that we trust Him as Priest to bring us into the presence of God. It means that we each submit ourselves to Him as King, to live under His authority and rule.

THE OUTCOME OF FAITH: LIFE IN HIS NAME

> *These are written that you may believe that Jesus is the Christ, the Son of God, and that by believing* you may have life in his name. *(V. 31, EMPHASIS ADDED)*

Faith is not an end in itself. John tells us that "by believing [we] have life in his name." *Life* is one of the great themes of John's gospel, and it is important that we understand what John is talking about.

As you read this book, you are, by definition, alive. But Jesus spoke to people about another kind of life that He could give to them. He said that He had come so that men and women might have "life . . . to the full" (10:10). What did He mean by that?

Once again, the big picture of the Bible story will help us to understand. Jesus was speaking about the life Adam and Eve enjoyed in the garden. There they enjoyed a life free from the frustrations of age and the fear of death. They knew a wonderful partnership together, in which they pursued meaningful work, in beautiful surroundings. But most of all, they enjoyed the presence and companionship of God who came down and made Himself visible to them so that they could know Him. That was life to the full, and they lost it all when they made their disastrous choice to know about evil.

They were driven out of the garden, and afterward Adam must have known that he was living half a life. His children never experienced what their father and mother had known. All they knew was life in this fallen world, with its disease, danger, disasters, and death. Adam must have told them about the life he had known, but it would have been difficult for his children even to imagine.

> Christ came . . . so that you [might have] what is beyond your imagination.

When I was at high school, I taught myself to write in Braille because I had two friends who were blind. One had been blind from birth, and the other had become blind through an accident. Their experience was very different. One knew what the colors were and he knew what he was missing. You could describe things to him more easily. The other had no notion of color, except what he produced in his own imagination.

That is the great difference between Adam and us. Adam had been in Paradise. He knew what it was to walk with God. He knew what life could be without the knowledge of evil. He knew that he was living half a life.

Our problem is that we have never seen what he saw. We have never experienced what he enjoyed. We find it difficult to imagine what it would be like to be free from evil and to enjoy the visible presence of God.

Christ came into the world so that you should have the opportunity of entering into what is beyond your imagination. God wants you to enjoy the life Adam knew and lost, the life that his descendants have never seen or known.

Jesus offers to take you into this everlasting life. God has anointed Him for the task. He is the Christ. The Gospels present the evidence, showing how He fulfills the role of God's anointed Prophet, Priest, and King, and God invites you, through the Scriptures, to come to a verdict of faith. That's why John wrote his gospel: "that you may believe that Jesus is the Christ, the Son of God, and that by believing you may have life in his name" (20:31).

SOMETHING MAGNIFICENT

Do you see the glory of this?

A few weeks ago, Karen and I had the opportunity of hearing the Chicago Symphony Orchestra with Frank Peter Zimmerman, their guest soloist. They were playing Tchaikovsky, and it was magnificent.

The soloist played as if his bow would set his violin on fire. At the end, the audience rose in a standing ovation. It was irresistible. The applause went on and on as the artist came back to the stage and in the end, when it would not subside, he raised his violin and treated us to an encore. That brought the house down.

Then we went out for the intermission, our spirits raised high, the audience buzzing with delight. In the foyer an older man was talking with great animation to a younger woman whom I guessed might be his daughter. He seemed very upset. As they walked by us, I heard him say, "I've been coming here for thirty years, and I have never seen that before." He was referring to the encore. "I don't like it," he said. "I can't see any reason for it!"

We have been in the presence of something truly magnificent.

I had to restrain myself. Here was a man who had been in the presence of something magnificent, which had lifted hundreds of other people around him, and he saw nothing out of the ordinary. It was staggering.

What was wrong with the man?

As we have followed the Bible story through the Gospels, we have been in the presence of something truly magnificent. We have seen the breathtaking sweep of God's plan in which the Son of God took our flesh, faced our enemy, laid down His life as a sacrifice, rose from the dead, and ascended into heaven—all accomplished so that we may be brought into everlasting life through faith in His name.

Nothing is more tragic than for someone to be confronted with the claims of Christ and the offer of the gospel and to go away as if he or she had not heard anything out of the ordinary.

UNLOCKED

The name *Christ* means Messiah, or Anointed One. In the Old Testament, God anointed prophets, priests, and kings to advance His purposes in the world. They pointed forward to One who would fulfill what they could only illustrate. God had promised that there would be an Anointed One par excellence, who would speak the Word of God, offer the sacrifice acceptable to God, and rout the enemies of God.

The Gospels give us the evidence that Jesus is the Christ and show us how He uniquely fulfills the ancient roles of Prophet, Priest, and King. The centerpiece of God's purpose for history is that God Himself took human flesh and entered the world as a man in the person of Jesus. It is through Jesus Christ that all the promises of God are fulfilled.

The New Testament declares that Jesus is the Christ and gives us the evidence for this claim so that we may come to faith in Him.

PAUSE FOR PRAYER

Gracious Father,

I thank You today for the magnificence and the glory of the gospel. I want to affirm my faith that Jesus is the Christ. Thank You that in all my difficulties, struggles, inconsistencies, and problems, my entering into "life to the full" does not depend on me getting everything right but on Christ taking me there.

I lift my heart in praise and adoration to bless You for anointing Your Son to be my Christ, my Savior, and my Lord. Amen.

19

Power

ACTS 2

What makes a

church alive?

19 Power

ACTS 2

DISCOVER

the significance of Pentecost for today.

LEARN

why the disciples spoke in tongues.

WORSHIP

as you see how God can use you in the work of His kingdom.

THE chairman reported that the church roll now stood at 120 members. They had not been able to obtain a building, so they were still meeting in a second-floor room that they had been able to rent in the city. There had been a lot of discussion about how they should fill a leadership position that had become vacant, but besides that, not a lot had been happening.

The task of reaching their community seemed to be beyond them. There was very little money, very few people, a lot of fear, and outside of their meeting place, a culture that had very little room for their message.

I don't know if you have ever experienced a church like that, but that is pretty much how it was in the only church in existence at the beginning of the book of Acts. When Christ ascended to heaven, there were only about 120 believers in Jerusalem (Acts 1:15). They believed that Christ died for their sins and rose again, but they had focused essentially on themselves and their own internal organization. Nothing that was happening among them would make any difference to the world outside the doors of the church.

But Christ had spoken about an event that would change all that. In a few days, He had said, they would be "baptized with the Holy Spirit" (Acts 1:5). Then, He said, "You will receive power when the Holy Spirit comes on you; and you will be my witnesses in Jerusalem, and in all Judea and Samaria, and to the ends of the earth" (v. 8).

They did not have to wait long. Just ten days after Jesus ascended into heaven and fifty days after the resurrection, there was a festival called Pentecost. It was a celebration of the beginning of harvest and of the occasion when God came down to Mount Sinai and gave the Law to Moses. Jerusalem was crammed with visitors from many countries. Luke tells us that people had come "from every nation under heaven" (2:5).

On the Day of Pentecost, the Holy Spirit was poured out on the first Christian believers. After that, things were never the same.

A Sound Like the Wind

> *When the day of Pentecost came, they were all together in one place. Suddenly a sound like the blowing of a violent wind came from heaven and filled the whole house where they were sitting.* (vv. 1–2)

In many ancient languages, there is one word that can mean *wind* or *breath* or *Spirit*.[1] In Hebrew, that word is *ruach*. It is one of those words that sounds like what it means. If you pronounce *ruach* correctly, it sounds like the rushing of the wind.

If you think about it, the sound of the wind is pretty much the same as the sound of breath, only it is much louder and it lasts longer. In the ancient world, they thought the wind was like breath on a large scale, so they used the same word for both.

Now, whenever you find something unusual in the Bible, it is usually helpful to ask, "Where have we come across something like this before?" And if we ask, "Where have we come across the sound of wind or breath before?" there are two obvious answers.

The first is at the very beginning of the Bible story, where we read about God breathing life into Adam. God shaped a lifeless corpse from the dust of the ground. It just lay there. Then God breathed into this skeletal frame. God gave Adam the kiss of life, and the first man became a living being.

Then, after the Resurrection, Jesus "breathed on [the disciples] and said, 'Receive the Holy Spirit'" (John 20:22). Jesus was explaining what would happen on the Day of Pentecost. He was saying to His disciples, "This is what it will be like: I am going to ascend to heaven, but when I do, I will breathe my life into you from above." Then He took a deep breath and blew it out toward them. It sounded like the rushing of the wind.

So when the disciples heard a sound like the rushing wind a few weeks later, they would immediately associate it with the sound of Jesus breathing on them, and recognize that this was the fulfillment of what Jesus had promised.

There is a wonderful parallel between God breathing life into Adam, and Christ breathing life into the church. In Genesis 2, there was a body without life. God breathed into that body, and Adam became a living being. In Acts 2, there is another body. The church is the body of Christ, but at the beginning of the book of Acts, it was also lifeless. Like the body of Adam, it was organized but dead. It remained behind closed doors, and there was nothing about it that would have an impact on the surrounding world.

But now the ascended Christ blows His breath, wind, or Spirit (remember, it's all the same word) on them. This was not a little breath. It was the sound of a gale-force wind. God blew life into these people.

Think about an Olympic sprinter, taking in great gulps of air that pulsate through his chest as oxygen fills his lungs and energizes his body. That's what happened at Pentecost. God breathed new life into them, and they were never again the same.

Of course, the Spirit of God had been at work in the lives of the disciples before. Jesus had sent them out in ministry. They would not have been able to do what they did without the power of the Spirit. The Holy Spirit came on many individuals in the Old Testament, anointing them for specific tasks, and the disciples' experience before Pentecost would have been similar. But this was something entirely new. The Spirit of God was not only with them, but in them.

GREAT BALLS OF FIRE

They saw what seemed to be tongues of fire that separated and came to rest on each of them. (v. 3)

Try to imagine yourself among these 120 people when this happened. What they saw at first must have looked absolutely terrifying. A great ball or a pillar of fire was coming right toward them. As the fireball came nearer, it divided into individual flames, or "tongues of fire," so that a flame from this fire came to rest on every person in the room. The astonishing thing was that none of them was burned.

Once again, the best way to understand this is to ask where in the Bible we have seen something like it before. Where have we come across a fire that rested on something but did not burn it up? The answer: in the story of Moses and the burning bush. "The angel of the LORD appeared to him in flames of fire from within a bush. Moses saw that though the bush was on fire it did not burn up" (Exodus 3:2). Then God said to Moses, "I am who I am," and Moses realized that he was in the immediate presence of God.

As noted earlier (chapter 5 of volume 1), the fire did not depend on the bush for fuel. It was a self-sustaining fire. Fire normally depends on the fuel that it consumes. When the fuel is burned up, the fire goes out. But this fire did not depend on the bush to sustain it, and that's why the bush didn't burn up.

The fire in which God made His presence known was self-sustaining and it never went out. God has life in Himself. He depends on nothing and needs no one. When He revealed Himself to Moses, He chose to make Himself known through a fire that rested on a bush but did not consume it. Now, on the Day of Pentecost, God gave the same sign of His immediate presence with the first disciples. It must have been awesome.

When God appeared to Moses, he was a believing man whose life was going nowhere. He had built a successful life in Egypt and then, after some trouble, left the country and settled down into a kind of semiretirement in the desert. His life was counting for little or nothing in advancing the purposes of God in the world.

God came to him in the fire to give him a new commission. "Moses, I have something for you to do. I have heard the cries of suffering people and I am sending you to Pharaoh." So God called this man out of his aimless retirement and gave him a ministry that turned out to be for the glory of God.

Before the Day of Pentecost, the church was like Moses in the desert. It consisted of a group of believing people who enjoyed their prayer meetings and spent a great deal of time discussing how to elect their leaders. But nothing was happening through them to advance God's purpose in the world. Then God's fire came down.

Try and imagine the picture with me. You look up and see the fire above you slowly descending over the middle of the room. You realize what is happening: God's presence is coming among His people. You are filled with a sense of awe. The God who appeared to Moses is making His presence known again, and you are there in the room.

God [commissions] *every* believer to advance His purpose in the world.

You remember that when the fire came to Moses, he was commissioned to advance God's purpose. So you wonder whom the fire will rest on now. Your first thoughts are, *It will be Peter, or perhaps James and John. Maybe it will be all three of them.*

You look up as the ball of fire hovers over the room, and then to your absolute astonishment, it separates into tongues of flame, more flames than you can count at that moment, and as the flames separate they seem to be falling toward many in the room. You look up with awe as you realize that one of the flames is coming toward you. You look around at the others in the room, and a flame of fire rests on every one of them.

God is commissioning *every* believer to advance His purpose in the world. The presence and power of Almighty God rests on you.

In the Old Testament, we saw prophets, priests, and kings anointed by God for ministry. The focus was on a few people who held special positions. But in the New Testament, it is completely different. God's fire falls not only on Peter, James, and John, but also on the unnamed believers, who did not aspire to leadership positions, but who loved Jesus and wanted to follow Him. God's Spirit rested on them, and every one had a part to play in advancing God's purpose for the world.

They Spoke in Other Tongues

All of them were filled with the Holy Spirit and began to speak in other tongues as the Spirit enabled them. (v. 4)

A third remarkable event followed on this extraordinary day. Suddenly and spontaneously, 120 believers found that they were able to speak in languages they had never learned.

Again, the best way to understand this is to ask where we have seen something like it before. Where in the Bible have we seen a group of people who suddenly began to speak in languages they had never learned?

That is exactly what happened at the Tower of Babel (Genesis 11; discussed in volume 1, chapter 4). Early in the Bible story, as man's rebellion against God was gaining momentum, people decided to build a city with a tower in the area of Shinar. They wanted to provide their own security and proclaim their own greatness in a city where there would be no place for God.

It was another example of man grasping at the throne of God. He did not want to worship God or believe in God, but rather to worship himself and believe in himself.

So God came down and broke the momentum of man's godless kingdom by introducing the confusion of multiple languages for the first time into the human race (Genesis 11:1–9).

It must have been very strange. One morning, as you arrive on the building site, the colleague you have been working with for weeks begins talking to you, and you can't understand him. When you take your break for lunch, you find that the whole workforce is in confusion as people babble all kinds of incomprehensible sounds.

Eventually you find someone else who talks your language. You immediately identify together. "I am so glad to find somebody else who talks sense," you say. "All the rest of these folks have gone nuts!"

God used the gift of language to . . . advance . . . Christ's kingdom.

All over the building site, little groups of people are gathering together, bound together by the identity of a common language. They are all coming to the same conclusion: It's time to leave the madhouse and make a new life with people whose language they can understand. So they scatter to the north, south, east, and west. These little groups of people understood each other but they could not understand anybody else.

The Day of Pentecost was exactly the opposite. People from every nation under heaven had gathered in Jerusalem (Acts 2:5), and when the Spirit of God came, the apostles found themselves spontaneously speaking in languages they had never learned, so that all the people could hear and understand the good news of Jesus Christ in their own language.

At Babel, the tongues were a judgment from God that led to confusion and people being scattered. At Pentecost, the tongues were a blessing from God that led to understanding and people being gathered together.

At Babel, God used the curse of language to slow up the advance of man's city. At Pentecost, God used the gift of language to speed up the advance of Christ's kingdom.

To Every Tribe and Nation

Shortly after the disaster at the Tower of Babel, God gave a wonderful promise to Abraham. "I will bless you . . . and all peoples on earth will be blessed through you" (Genesis 12:2–3). God's judgment on the nations at Babel was not His final word. He determined that His blessing would come through Abraham to all the scattered peoples and language groups of the world.

On the Day of Pentecost, God's wind blew, and His fire fell on 120 children of Abraham. God was filling these people with new life, and anointing them for ministry. These people found themselves speaking in languages they had never learned because God's purpose was to communicate the good news of Jesus to people from every language group on the face of the earth.

On the same day, God had gathered a vast crowd from every nation under heaven. When the crowds in the city heard the sound of the wind (Acts 2:6), they headed in the direction it had come from to see what was going on. When they arrived, they found the 120 believers declaring the great things God had done in different languages.

If you had been a visitor to Jerusalem that day, you would have looked for someone who spoke your language. That's exactly what happened. Small groups gathered around each of the believers and heard the great things God had done in their own language. It was Babel in reverse.

God had determined that people from every nation and language group would hear the good news of Jesus Christ. Language would be no barrier to the gospel. Jesus had said that when the Spirit came, the disciples would be His witnesses in Jerusalem, Judea, Samaria, and to the ends of the earth. In an extraordinary way, that began on the first day.

Eventually, Peter called the crowd to order. Some people had suggested that the believers were drunk. It was time to give an explanation. Peter spoke about Jesus, telling the people how He had been crucified just over seven weeks before. But God had raised Him from the dead. He was exalted at the right hand of the Father, and He had now poured out the Holy Spirit on His people. That was the explanation of what the crowd were seeing and hearing.

They understood from the beginning that this good news was for people from every nation.

Peter's point was not lost on the crowd. If Jesus was indeed the One God had promised from the beginning of time, and the people had killed Him, what were they to do?

These people clearly believed what Peter had said about Jesus, so he told them the next step:

> *"Repent and be baptized, every one of you, in the name of Jesus Christ for the forgiveness of your sins. And you will receive the gift of the Holy Spirit. The promise is for you and your children and for all who are far off—for all whom the Lord our God will call."* (vv. 38–39)

Three thousand people responded to Peter's invitation. They understood from the beginning that this good news was for people from every nation. In the next few days, these children of Abraham would return to their homes and take the good news of Jesus to people whose language they already knew.

Just as the 120 had communicated the good news to the groups that gathered around them on the Day of Pentecost, so now the three thousand returned to their homes and began to communicate the good news of Jesus to the cities and nations from which they had come.

God took a church that was like a lifeless corpse and breathed new life into it. God's presence came and rested on all His people, as He commissioned them to advance His purpose in the world. On the Day of Pentecost, a missionary church was born. People from many cultures came to faith in Christ and then went back to their homes to spread the gospel among their own people, so that folk from every language and culture would discover the blessing of the gospel.

What Has All This Got to Do with Us?

As we have studied the Bible, we have seen several occasions when God's presence was made known in a visible way. We call these occasions theophanies, and they are always of great importance. In a theophany, God does for some people in a visible way what He does for all His people in an invisible way.

For example, when the Lord brought Eve to Adam, He was doing in a visual way for that first couple what He does for every couple joined together in marriage. When Karen and I were married, our college professor joined our hands and pronounced that we were one. We didn't see God joining us together: We didn't need to. God did that once visibly for Adam and Eve so that we could understand what He does secretly and invisibly at every wedding.

It seems to me that this is how we should apply the remarkable events on the Day of Pentecost. God is teaching us through what He did once in a visible way, what He always wants to do in an invisible way among His people.

God breathes new life into His people. He does not want His church to be an inward-looking organization that functions at a merely human level, but a living body filled with the life of God.

God anoints not just a few leaders but every one of His people for ministry. The presence and the power of almighty God rest upon every believer in the Lord Jesus Christ.

And God's great purpose is that His blessing will flow through His people to all the nations of the earth. Every Christian and every church has a part to play in that purpose. For some people that will mean going to another culture to learn another language, so that the good news of Jesus may be known. For others, God's call may be to find our voice in the language God has already given us.

God puts groups of people around every believer so that he or she can communicate the good news of Jesus in their language. Maybe you can speak the language of high-school students or of children. God has wired you in a way that makes it possible for you to communicate with a certain group of people. Find out who they are, get among them, and tell them about Jesus.

In looking at the Day of Pentecost, let's not get lost in the signs or drama of the story. On several occasions, people have told me how much they enjoyed a story I told sometime previously. More than once, they have said, "I'm afraid I can't remember the point you were trying to make, but it was a great story!" That's always a bit discouraging. The miraculous events on the Day of Pentecost carry the same danger. It's easy to become so interested in the power of God's visual aids—the wind, the fire, and the tongues—that we miss the point that He is teaching us through them. Visual aids are a wonderful way of communicating, but the problem is that people can easily become so interested in the illustration that they forget the point it was given to make.

The events of Pentecost demonstrate these truths about God: He wants to breathe new life into His church; He wants to anoint and commission every believer; and He wants to mobilize the church to take the good news of Jesus Christ to the ends of the earth so that God's blessing may come to all nations. That's what Pentecost is all about.

UNLOCKED

The life of the church depends entirely on the presence and work of the Holy Spirit. When God breathed into the lifeless corpse of Adam at the creation, Adam became a living being. In the same way it is God's Spirit who brings spiritual life to the church.

The Holy Spirit equips and empowers all believers for service and ministry. In the Old Testament, God gifted and used some people for particular ministries, but in the New Testament, the Holy Spirit lives in and works through all believers.

The church has been commissioned to proclaim the good news of Jesus Christ to the nations. The Holy Spirit equips and sends out believers to communicate across cultural and linguistic barriers so that God's people will be drawn from every tribe, language, nation, and people on the face of the earth.

PAUSE FOR PRAYER

Heavenly Father,

Thank You for the gift of the Holy Spirit to all of Your children. Breathe Your life into me and fill me with Your Spirit. Equip me for all that You are calling me to do. Open my eyes to see the people You have placed around me, and give me courage and boldness to speak about You in a way that they can understand. Use me to advance Your purpose, and to bring Your blessing to others.

I pray for Your church. May we know Your life of Your Spirit among us and play our part together in bringing the good news of Jesus to the world. I pray this in Jesus' name. Amen.

Note

1. Leon Morris, *Spirit of the Living God* (London: InterVarsity, 1960), 16. Morris noted that "One of the difficulties that confronts translators from almost any ancient language is that the words for 'spirit,' 'breath,' and 'wind' are identical."

20

Gentiles

ACTS 9

How has God's

blessing come to

the nations?

20 Gentiles

ACTS 9

DISCOVER
the unique place of the Jewish people in God's plan for the nations.

LEARN
the origin of the name "Christian."

WORSHIP
because God is bringing people from every culture to faith in Jesus Christ.

AS we approach the end of this third volume of *Unlocking the Bible Story*, it is time to look back and see where we've come. After sin entered the world, God promised that He would send a Deliverer. More specifically, He appeared to Abraham and said, "I will bless you . . . and all peoples on earth will be blessed through you" (Genesis 12:2–3).

The blessing God gave to Abraham continued on his descendants, and God promised that His blessing would come through them to all the nations on the face of the earth.

In volumes 1 and 2, we followed the story of Abraham's descendants through the Old Testament. It is the story of what God did among the Jewish people. We discovered laws for the Jews, a land for the Jews, and blessings for the Jews.

Now, in this third volume, we have followed the story of the Gospels and again have discovered that the New Testament is also a very Jewish book. Jesus Christ was born a Jew. God took human flesh from a Jewish woman. Christ said that He had come to the lost sheep of Israel. His ministry began in a synagogue, where He read the Old Testament Scriptures. He rarely ventured outside Israel.

After His death and resurrection, Christ commissioned eleven disciples. All of them were Jewish. Jesus did not choose a single Gentile.

On the Day of Pentecost, a great crowd was gathered in Jerusalem. They were all either Jewish or they were converts to Judaism (Acts 2:5). When the Holy Spirit was poured out, three thousand of them came to faith in Christ. When those Jews traveled back to their homes, they began to speak about Jesus, and as others came to Christ, they met for instruction, encouragement, and worship in the synagogues.

There are 1,094 pages in my Bible, and the story of Pentecost is recorded on page 962. With only 132 pages left in the Bible story, those of us who are not Jewish might be forgiven for asking, "Is there anything here for us?"

God's blessing broadens out . . . to all nations.

Up to this point the whole story has been about God's blessing to Israel. We have seen the fulfillment of God's promise to Abraham, but we have not seen much evidence of God's promise to bless all nations *through* Abraham.

There have been some signs: The story of Ruth the Moabitess being included in the line of David, or Jonah going to the people of Nineveh, or Jesus talking with the Samaritan woman. But beyond that, there is little evidence of the blessing of God reaching beyond the Jewish people. We are now 90 percent of the way through the Bible story, and the river of God's grace is still flowing between narrow banks.

But now we come to a major turning point in the Bible story. The book of Acts tells us how the river of God's blessing broadens out so that God's promise to bring His blessing through the Jewish people to all nations on earth is wonderfully fulfilled.

As the number of disciples grew in Jerusalem, the Jews who had believed in Jesus faced growing opposition. The apostles were flogged and imprisoned. Then one of the young leaders among the believers was stoned to death. His name was Stephen.

While this violence was going on, a rather sinister character was standing in the background, holding the coats of those who threw the stones. His name was Saul of Tarsus. He was determined to stamp out these Jewish communities of believers in Jesus. "Saul began to destroy the church. Going from house to house, he dragged off men and women and put them in prison" (Acts 8:3).

THE ROAD TO DAMASCUS

The death of Stephen sparked a wave of persecution against believers, and many of them were scattered. But Saul was not content that the believing communities should be broken up. He sought authorization to arrest these Jewish believers in other cities and bring them back to Jerusalem. The first city that he targeted for his roundup was Damascus.

It was on the road to Damascus that the risen Lord Jesus Christ intercepted Saul's life.

> *As he neared Damascus on his journey, suddenly a light from heaven flashed around him. He fell to the ground and heard a voice say to him, "Saul, Saul, why do you persecute me?"*
>
> *"Who are you, Lord?" Saul asked.*
>
> *"I am Jesus, whom you are persecuting," he replied. "Now get up and go into the city, and you will be told what you must do."* (ACTS 9:3–6)

This angry man was completely stopped in his tracks. The whole direction of his life turned around, and the greatest enemy of the church became its greatest evangelist. We know him better as the apostle Paul.

THE RIVER BURSTS ITS BANKS

> *"This man is my chosen instrument to carry my name before the Gentiles and their kings and before the people of Israel."* (V. 15)

Christ had a new commission for Paul. This Jewish believer was to bring the name of Christ to both Jews and Gentiles. Paul wrote about this commission in a letter to believers in Rome. He said, "I am not ashamed of the gospel, because it is the power of God for the salvation of everyone who believes: first for the Jew, then for the Gentile" (Romans 1:16).

The rest of the book of Acts tells us about the flow of this widening river of God's blessing across cultural barriers. At first the believers who were scattered by the persecution told the message of Jesus only to other Jews. But in Antioch, some of them began to share the good news with Greeks as well (Acts 11:19–20).

The church in Antioch was breaking new ground by crossing cultural barriers with the gospel. When news of this got back to leaders of the church at Jerusalem, they sent a man called Barnabas to check out what was going on.

Barnabas, in turn co-opted Saul (Paul), and the two of them stayed in Antioch and became teachers of the large and growing multicultural community of believers there (Acts 11:22–26).

What's in a Name?

It was there in Antioch that the disciples were first called "Christians" (Acts 11:26). It was a nickname. That's all.

Don't get hung up on the name Christian, especially if you are Jewish. For many Jewish people, and indeed for many in the Muslim world, the word "Christian" represents a Western monolithic structure. Don't let the word "Christian" be a barrier to you hearing or communicating the good news of Jesus Christ.

Remember that in the earliest times in the book of Acts, the name "Christian" was unknown. Jewish believers in Jesus told their Gentile friends the good news. The Gentile believers joined their Jewish friends as they worshiped Jesus.

Then some folks in Antioch gave them the nickname "Christian." It simply means "followers of Christ."

The gospel crosses cultural barriers. It belongs first to the Jews, and it came through them to the Gentiles. It is the fulfillment of God's promise to bless Abraham and then to bless the nations of the earth through him.

As Jews and Gentiles came to faith in Jesus, they discovered that the old barriers between them were broken down and that they were truly one as they worshiped together.

The church in Antioch became a bridgehead for taking the gospel further across the Roman Empire. The church commissioned Saul and Barnabas—their two most gifted leaders—to undertake a missionary journey. They traveled widely, preaching the good news to Jews and Gentiles. Wherever they went, their practice was to preach in the synagogues. God was at work, and many Jews and Gentiles professed faith in Jesus.

Unity in a Cross-cultural Community

Eventually the cultural issue came to a head. There were no problems as long as only a few Gentiles professed faith in Jesus, but soon, the trickle became a flood, and some of the leaders in Jerusalem became alarmed.

The problem was that the Gentiles who professed faith in Jesus were not being circumcised and embracing Judaism. They were simply professing their faith in Jesus and being baptized.

The Jewish believers had no problem with welcoming Gentiles. Even in the Old Testament, God's people had opened their arms to outsiders. The question was whether a Gentile could be accepted as a follower of Jesus without embracing Judaism first. Some were of the opinion that the way to Christ was open to anybody who wanted to come, but that those who came must be circumcised.

Acts tells us that "Some men came down from Judea to Antioch and were teaching the brothers: 'Unless you are circumcised, according to the custom taught by Moses, *you cannot be saved*'" (15:1, emphasis added).

These visitors were telling the young Christians at Antioch that faith in Christ was not enough for them to be saved. Something else had to be added. But as soon as you say that, you have undermined the gospel.

The first believers were now at a crossroads. The issue went to the core of their message, and the gospel itself was at stake. Had Jesus done everything that was needed to save those who would come to Him, or were other "rites of passage" necessary? Was it necessary for Gentile believers to embrace the traditions of Judaism as they came to Christ, or was it possible for Gentiles to come from their varying traditions directly to faith in Jesus Christ?

The issue was of great importance. The first believers had to decide whether God was giving the gospel to the world so that the world would be brought to Judaism, or whether God had given the gospel to the Jews so that the Jews could bring the gospel to the world.

It is not surprising that this led to a "sharp dispute" (v. 2). But the believers handled it wisely. Paul and Barnabas were appointed by the believers at Antioch to go to Jerusalem and meet with the apostles and elders there.

The issue was discussed honestly and openly in Jerusalem and the result was clear and decisive. The Jewish believers understood that Jesus Christ, their Savior, had opened the way for people from every background to come to God, and they determined not to put anything in the way.

> The Council of Jerusalem was a decisive . . . moment in the Bible story.

That was the principle. At the same time, they wrote a pastoral letter making two points. First, those who wanted to be accepted as believers must make a decisive break with sin; patterns of sexual immorality that were notorious among the Gentiles must stop.

Second, those who wanted to be accepted as believers were asked to show sensitivity toward others in the body of Christ. In particular, where there were Jewish believers, the Gentiles were asked to refrain from food that their Jewish brothers and sisters would not eat. That was not a condition of the gospel; it was an expression of love. If Jews and Gentiles were to share fellowship together, they would have to restrain their liberty out of love for others.

The Council of Jerusalem was a decisive and wonderful moment in the Bible story. It affirmed the heart of the gospel, protected the unity of the believers, and opened the door for Paul's mission to both Jews and Gentiles which is the focus of the rest of the book of Acts.

THE PRIVILEGE OF JEWISH PEOPLE

Paul's commission was to carry the name of Jesus before the Gentiles and the people of Israel (9:15). This Jewish man was commissioned by Christ to bring the gospel to his own people.

Paul grasped this part of his commission with great passion. He wrote about the great privileges of the Jewish people and his deep longing that his own people would believe in Jesus.

> *I have great sorrow and unceasing anguish in my heart. For I could wish that I myself were cursed and cut off from Christ for the sake of my brothers, those of my own race, the people of Israel.* (ROMANS 9:2–4)

Paul listed the great privileges that God has given to the Jewish people. "Theirs," he wrote, "is the adoption as sons" (v. 4). In the Old Testament, God called Israel His son (Exodus 4:23). God has not given that privilege to any other national group: certainly not the Scots; and not the Americans either. God has blessed many nations, but there is only one nation that God has chosen to be the means of His blessing to the world and that is the Jewish nation.

Paul continued: "Theirs [are] the divine glory, the covenants, the receiving of the law, the temple worship and the promises" (v. 4). Who else has known the presence of God with them in a pillar of cloud by day and a pillar of fire by night? To which other people has the cloud of God's glory come down?

If you are Jewish, . . . value your heritage. God has blessed you.

Then Paul listed the highest privilege. "Theirs are the patriarchs, and from them is traced the human ancestry of Christ, who is God over all, forever praised! Amen" (v. 5).

Gentile believers should never forget the great debt of gratitude we owe to the Jewish people. God chose to bless them first, and then to bless the Gentiles through them. Gentile believers should have a deep love for the Jewish people. God has chosen them and placed His love on them.

Some of us need to exercise much greater respect and sensitivity toward Jewish people and to recognize that through the centuries, the Christian church has created many barriers that have made it difficult for Jewish people to see Jesus.

If you are Jewish, then I encourage you to value your heritage. God has blessed you. The Bible story is all about God's blessing on Abraham and his descendants. It is through your people that God's blessing in Jesus Christ has come to the world. Treasure what God has given you. You are highly privileged.

Privileged People Need Jesus

So why does Paul say that he is in great sorrow and unceasing anguish over his own people? It is possible to be in a position of great privilege, and yet to miss out on the greatest thing God wants to give you. "With all the rich heritage of God's blessing through the years," Paul was saying, "my heart would break, because my own people have missed the greatest blessing of God which is in Jesus."

The apostle Paul spoke from his own experience. He had thrown everything he had into the pursuit of an exemplary life. He had a great education, and would have held a distinguished teaching position and earned a high salary. But when Christ intercepted his life, he discovered that whatever else he had going for him seemed to fade in importance compared to the surpassing value of knowing Jesus as His Savior and Lord (Philippians 3:8).

He discovered that privilege doesn't save anybody, and so he longed that his own people who had been so richly blessed by God should come to know Jesus.

Although I am not Jewish, I look at my own life and feel highly privileged with a stable home, a good education, and open doors of opportunity. Perhaps you feel the same. Remember that privileged people need Jesus. Perhaps you can identify with Bill in a poem I wrote about growing up surrounded by privilege.

The first time Bill had come to church he looked a bonnie lad;
His mum and dad had dressed him up in the best things that they had.
The pastor said a prayer for Bill, who smiled his little charms,
But Bill knew nothing of it as he lay there in their arms.

The prayers for Bill continued in the years that lay ahead.
In Sunday school they taught him from the Bible that he read,
And as he grew our Bill began to thrive in all the sports,
At basketball and baseball and on the tennis courts.

With confidence now growing, Bill soon did graduate,
And seeking independence went to college out of state,
His mother told him sternly, "Keep from drugs and keep from beer,
And don't waste too much time with girls; remember your career."

Back home some folks still prayed for Bill, but with a heavy heart,
For though he was successful and always did his part,
It seemed something was missing in his now well-ordered life,
With his brood of little children, two-car garage, and his wife.

Bill brought his kids to church, just as when he was a lad,
And he dressed them up real bonnie in the best things that they had,
And the pastor said a prayer for them as they smiled with all their charms;
But they knew nothing of it as they lay there in his arms.

As years advanced, Bill prospered, and life was not the same,
He really was quite generous with the money he did gain.
On Boards, and on the sports fields, in church, and on the track,
Bill made his contribution and gave a great deal back.

Then one day Bill's life ended, and on that very day,
His eyes were truly opened as he heard the Savior say,
"I poured My blessings on you, as anyone could see,
But the reason that I gave them was to turn your heart to Me."

Christ came to give His life for all who in Him put their trust,
Those who are unrighteous, and those who think they're just.
Lay hold of Christ as Savior and call upon His name,
For those who are so privileged, need Him just the same.

DESPERATE PEOPLE CAN COME TO JESUS

Christ also commissioned Paul to carry His name to the Gentiles, and Paul wrote about their desperate spiritual condition.

> *Remember that formerly you who are Gentiles by birth . . . were separate from Christ, excluded from citizenship in Israel and foreigners to the covenants of the promise, without hope and without God in the world.* (EPHESIANS 2:11–12)

That's just about as far from God as you could get.

The desperate position of the Gentiles was illustrated by the way that the Jewish temple was set up. There were distinct areas marked off for different classes of people. The most distant area on the outside perimeter was called the "court of the Gentiles." Then there was a separate court for women and a court for the priests. At the center was the Most Holy Place, where God's presence was made known, but only the high priest could go there and only once a year.

GAME, SET, AND MATCH

The structure of the temple makes me think about the tennis championships at Wimbledon. When we lived in London, I enjoyed going there. At the time, you could get into the grounds late in the afternoon for five pounds (about $8.00). But that only gave you access to the outer courts. Usually that meant watching players few people had heard of. Like most other people, I wanted to get onto the center court, but for that you needed a different ticket, and they were extremely hard to find.

I succeeded in getting onto the center court on a few occasions, but I never once managed to get into the locker rooms! They are restricted to a very select group of people.

That's how it was in the Jewish temple. There were different levels of access, and Paul reminded the Gentile believers that they were about as far away from God as it was possible to get. They were out on the perimeter. "But now," he wrote, "in Christ Jesus you who once were far away have been brought near through the blood of Christ" (Ephesians 2:13).

When Jesus died on the cross, the curtain in front of the Most Holy Place was torn in two from top to bottom. It was as if God reached down from heaven and ripped it apart.

That was wonderful, but if that was all that happened, it would only benefit the Jews. It would be like announcing to those on Wimbledon's center court that they could visit the locker rooms. That would be marvelous for the privileged few who were already on Center Court, but it would only heighten the frustrations of those who were outside.

It was as if God took a bulldozer . . . creating a path . . . into the Most Holy Place.

If God had done nothing more than tear the curtain, it would still leave the Gentiles outside. But Paul reminded the Gentiles that Christ has done more than tear the curtain. "For he himself is our peace, who has made the two one and has *destroyed the barrier*, the dividing wall of hostility" (Ephesians 2:14, emphasis added).

Christ has brought Jews and Gentiles together by destroying the dividing wall between us. Paul is talking here about the wall that separated the court of the Gentiles from the court of the Jews. So it's not just that the curtain has been torn apart so that the Jews who were already near to God's presence could get in. The dividing walls further out were also demolished so that those who were far off could also come all the way into the presence of God.

Think of a series of concentric walls. When Christ died on the cross, it was as if God took a bulldozer and plowed through all the walls, creating a path from the furthest horizon right into the Most Holy Place at the center. All the walls came down. All the divisions of privilege and race and gender came down, and equal access to God was opened up to all through Jesus Christ.

It's not just the privileged Jew who may come and receive the mercy of God in Jesus Christ, but also the desperate Gentile. The person who is as far from God as it is possible to be may come. Christ has opened the way.

The Great Invitation

Paul was commissioned to take the name of Christ to the most privileged people in the world and to tell them that they *must* come. The Jews need Jesus. But he was also commissioned to take the name of Christ to the most desperate people in the world, and tell them that they *may* come. The way is open for the Gentiles to come to God through Jesus too.

Perhaps you feel about as far from God as anyone could be, and you wonder how God could ever be interested in you again.

Picture that bulldozer demolishing one wall after another and creating a path between you and the presence of God. The rubble is piled high on either side of the opened pathway. That's what Jesus Christ has done for you. There is grace and forgiveness for the most desperate person in the world.

Paul described the background of some of the early Gentile believers in Corinth. Some were male prostitutes, some thieves, others drunkards or sexually immoral. But when they came to Christ, they were washed and they were accepted into the fellowship of believers.

Paul was commissioned to take that good news to Jews and Gentiles. As he did, God raised up communities of believers where the privileged worshiped alongside those who had been desperate, and discovered that they were one as they walked on the same path opened up by Jesus Christ. They discovered that "There is neither Jew nor Greek, slave nor free, male nor female, for you are all one in Christ Jesus" (Galatians 3:28).

The stream of God's blessing had burst out of its narrow banks. God's blessing on Abraham's descendants began to flow through them to all nations. The most privileged and the most desperate found themselves worshiping together as one at the feet of Jesus.

Your life will intersect at some point with thousands of people. Some will be very privileged. They need Jesus. Others will be very desperate. They can come to Jesus. We must tell the privileged not to presume and tell the desperate not to despair. Our mission, like Paul's, is to carry the name of Jesus to the privileged and the desperate, and invite them to come to Him.

UNLOCKED

God has fulfilled His ancient promise to Abraham and his descendants. The gospel came to the Jews first, and through them to the nations of the world. The book of Acts traces the story of this widening stream of God's mercy and shows us how the gospel came to the most privileged and the most desperate people in the world.

The first believers in Jesus were all Jewish, but these Jewish believers realized that God was calling them to bring the good news to their Gentile neighbors and friends. As Jews and Gentiles came to faith in Jesus, they were reconciled to each other and stood together in pursuing God's great commission to take the good news of the Gospel to the ends of the earth.

PAUSE FOR PRAYER

Almighty Father,

Thank You that You have fulfilled Your promise to Abraham and that Your blessing has come to the whole world in Jesus Christ. Thank You for breaking down the walls that divide us from one another and from You, and for making it possible for people from every race and culture to come to You through faith in Your Son, Jesus.

May Your blessing be poured out upon the Jewish people in a special way in this generation. May many Jews come to faith in their Savior, Jesus Christ. May Your church reach across many cultural barriers so that the gospel may come to all peoples. May Your Church demonstrate unity in Jesus Christ that crosses all barriers and divisions.

I ask all this for the glory of Jesus Christ and pray in His name. Amen.

☐ **January 1**
Genesis 1:1–2:25
Matthew 1:1–2:12
Psalm 1:1-6
Proverbs 1:1-6

☐ **January 2**
Genesis 3:1–4:26
Matthew 2:13–3:6
Psalm 2:1-12
Proverbs 1:7-9

☐ **January 3**
Genesis 5:1–7:24
Matthew 3:7–4:11
Psalm 3:1-8
Proverbs 1:10-19

☐ **January 4**
Genesis 8:1–10:32
Matthew 4:12-25
Psalm 4:1-8
Proverbs 1:20-23

☐ **January 5**
Genesis 11:1–13:4
Matthew 5:1-26
Psalm 5:1-12
Proverbs 1:24-28

☐ **January 6**
Genesis 13:5–15:21
Matthew 5:27-48
Psalm 6:1-10
Proverbs 1:29-33

☐ **January 7**
Genesis 16:1–18:15
Matthew 6:1-24
Psalm 7:1-17
Proverbs 2:1-5

☐ **January 8**
Genesis 18:16–19:38
Matthew 6:25–7:14
Psalm 8:1-9
Proverbs 2:6-15

☐ **January 9**
Genesis 20:1–22:24
Matthew 7:15-29
Psalm 9:1-12
Proverbs 2:16-22

☐ **January 10**
Genesis 23:1–24:51
Matthew 8:1-17
Psalm 9:13-20
Proverbs 3:1-6

☐ **January 11**
Genesis 24:52–26:16
Matthew 8:18-34
Psalm 10:1-15
Proverbs 3:7-8

☐ **January 12**
Genesis 26:17–27:46
Matthew 9:1-17
Psalm 10:16-18
Proverbs 3:9-10

☐ **January 13**
Genesis 28:1–29:35
Matthew 9:18-38
Psalm 11:1-7
Proverbs 3:11-12

☐ **January 14**
Genesis 30:1–31:16
Matthew 10:1-23
Psalm 12:1-8
Proverbs 3:13-15

☐ **January 15**
Genesis 31:17–32:12
Matthew 10:24–11:6
Psalm 13:1-6
Proverbs 3:16-18

☐ **January 16**
Genesis 32:13–34:31
Matthew 11:7-30
Psalm 14:1-7
Proverbs 3:19-20

☐ **January 17**
Genesis 35:1–36:43
Matthew 12:1-21
Psalm 15:1-5
Proverbs 3:21-26

☐ **January 18**
Genesis 37:1–38:30
Matthew 12:22-45
Psalm 16:1-11
Proverbs 3:27-32

☐ **January 19**
Genesis 39:1–41:16
Matthew 12:46–13:23
Psalm 17:1-15
Proverbs 3:33-35

☐ **January 20**
Genesis 41:17–42:17
Matthew 13:24-46
Psalm 18:1-15
Proverbs 4:1-6

☐ **January 21**
Genesis 42:18–43:34
Matthew 13:47–14:12
Psalm 18:16-36
Proverbs 4:7-10

☐ **January 22**
Genesis 44:1–45:28
Matthew 14:13-36
Psalm 18:37-50
Proverbs 4:11-13

☐ **January 23**
Genesis 46:1–47:31
Matthew 15:1-28
Psalm 19:1-14
Proverbs 4:14-19

☐ **January 24**
Genesis 48:1–49:33
Matthew 15:29–16:12
Psalm 20:1-9
Proverbs 4:20-27

☐ **January 25**
Genesis 50:1—Exodus 2:10
Matthew 16:13–17:9
Psalm 21:1-13
Proverbs 5:1-6

☐ **January 26**
Exodus 2:11–3:22
Matthew 17:10-27
Psalm 22:1-18
Proverbs 5:7-14

☐ **January 27**
Exodus 4:1–5:21
Matthew 18:1-22
Psalm 22:19-31
Proverbs 5:15-21

☐ **January 28**
Exodus 5:22–7:25
Matthew 18:23–19:12
Psalm 23:1-6
Proverbs 5:22-23

☐ **January 29**
Exodus 8:1–9:35
Matthew 19:13-30
Psalm 24:1-10
Proverbs 6:1-5

☐ **January 30**
Exodus 10:1–12:13
Matthew 20:1-28
Psalm 25:1-15
Proverbs 6:6-11

☐ **January 31**
Exodus 12:14–13:16
Matthew 20:29–21:22
Psalm 25:16-22
Proverbs 6:12-15

☐ **February 1**
Exodus 13:17–15:18
Matthew 21:23-46
Psalm 26:1-12
Proverbs 6:16-19

☐ **February 2**
Exodus 15:19–17:7
Matthew 22:1-33
Psalm 27:1-6
Proverbs 6:20-26

☐ **February 3**
Exodus 17:8–19:15
Matthew 22:34–23:12
Psalm 27:7-14
Proverbs 6:27-35

☐ **February 4**
Exodus 19:16–21:21
Matthew 23:13-39
Psalm 28:1-9
Proverbs 7:1-5

☐ **February 5**
Exodus 21:22–23:13
Matthew 24:1-28
Psalm 29:1-11
Proverbs 7:6-23

☐ **February 6**
Exodus 23:14–25:40
Matthew 24:29-51
Psalm 30:1-12
Proverbs 7:24-27

☐ **February 7**
Exodus 26:1–27:21
Matthew 25:1-30
Psalm 31:1-8
Proverbs 8:1-11

☐ **February 8**
Exodus 28:1-43
Matthew 25:31–26:13
Psalm 31:9-18
Proverbs 8:12-13

☐ **February 9**
Exodus 29:1–30:10
Matthew 26:14-46
Psalm 31:19-24
Proverbs 8:14-26

☐ **February 10**
Exodus 30:11–31:18
Matthew 26:47-68
Psalm 32:1-11
Proverbs 8:27-32

☐ **February 11**
Exodus 32:1–33:23
Matthew 26:69–27:14
Psalm 33:1-11
Proverbs 8:33-36

☐ **February 12**
Exodus 34:1–35:9
Matthew 27:15-31
Psalm 33:12-22
Proverbs 9:1-6

☐ **February 13**
Exodus 35:10–36:38
Matthew 27:32-66
Psalm 34:1-10
Proverbs 9:7-8

☐ **February 14**
Exodus 37:1–38:31
Matthew 28:1-20
Psalm 34:11-22
Proverbs 9:9-10

☐ **February 15**
Exodus 39:1–40:38
Mark 1:1-28
Psalm 35:1-16
Proverbs 9:11-12

☐ **February 16**
Leviticus 1:1–3:17
Mark 1:29–2:12
Psalm 35:17-28
Proverbs 9:13-18

☐ **February 17**
Leviticus 4:1–5:19
Mark 2:13–3:6
Psalm 36:1-12
Proverbs 10:1-2

☐ **February 18**
Leviticus 6:1–7:27
Mark 3:7-30
Psalm 37:1-11
Proverbs 10:3-4

☐ **February 19**
Leviticus 7:28–9:6
Mark 3:31–4:25
Psalm 37:12-29
Proverbs 10:5

☐ **February 20**
Leviticus 9:7–10:20
Mark 4:26–5:20
Psalm 37:30-40
Proverbs 10:6-7

☐ **February 21**
Leviticus 11:1–12:8
Mark 5:21-43
Psalm 38:1-22
Proverbs 10:8-9

☐ **February 22**
Leviticus 13:1-59
Mark 6:1-29
Psalm 39:1-13
Proverbs 10:10

☐ **February 23**
Leviticus 14:1-57
Mark 6:30-56
Psalm 40:1-10
Proverbs 10:11-12

☐ **February 24**
Leviticus 15:1–16:28
Mark 7:1-23
Psalm 40:11-17
Proverbs 10:13-14

☐ **February 25**
Leviticus 16:29–18:30
Mark 7:24–8:10
Psalm 41:1-13
Proverbs 10:15-16

☐ **February 26**
Leviticus 19:1–20:21
Mark 8:11-38
Psalm 42:1-11
Proverbs 10:17

☐ **February 27**
Leviticus 20:22–22:16
Mark 9:1-29
Psalm 43:1-5
Proverbs 10:18

☐ **February 28**
Leviticus 22:17–23:44
Mark 9:30–10:12
Psalm 44:1-8
Proverbs 10:19

☐ **March 1**
Leviticus 24:1–25:46
Mark 10:13-31
Psalm 44:9-26
Proverbs 10:20-21

☐ **March 2**
Leviticus 25:47–27:13
Mark 10:32-52
Psalm 45:1-17
Proverbs 10:22

☐ **March 3**
Leviticus 27:14—Numbers 1:54
Mark 11:1-25
Psalm 46:1-11
Proverbs 10:23

☐ **March 4**
Numbers 2:1–3:51
Mark 11:27–12:17
Psalm 47:1-9
Proverbs 10:24-25

☐ **March 5**
Numbers 4:1–5:31
Mark 12:18-37
Psalm 48:1-14
Proverbs 10:26

☐ **March 6**
Numbers 6:1–7:89
Mark 12:38–13:13
Psalm 49:1-20
Proverbs 10:27-28

☐ **March 7**
Numbers 8:1–9:23
Mark 13:14-37
Psalm 50:1-23
Proverbs 10:29-30

☐ **March 8**
Numbers 10:1–11:23
Mark 14:1-21
Psalm 51:1-19
Proverbs 10:31-32

☐ **March 9**
Numbers 11:24–13:33
Mark 14:22-52
Psalm 52:1-9
Proverbs 11:1-3

☐ **March 10**
Numbers 14:1–15:16
Mark 14:53-72
Psalm 53:1-6
Proverbs 11:4

☐ **March 11**
Numbers 15:17–16:40
Mark 15:1-47
Psalm 54:1-7
Proverbs 11:5-6

☐ March 12
Numbers 16:41–18:32
Mark 16:1-20
Psalm 55:1-23
Proverbs 11:7

☐ March 13
Numbers 19:1–20:29
Luke 1:1-25
Psalm 56:1-13
Proverbs 11:8

☐ March 14
Numbers 21:1–22:20
Luke 1:26-56
Psalm 57:1-11
Proverbs 11:9-11

☐ March 15
Numbers 22:21–23:30
Luke 1:57-80
Psalm 58:1-11
Proverbs 11:12-13

☐ March 16
Numbers 24:1–25:18
Luke 2:1-35
Psalm 59:1-17
Proverbs 11:14

☐ March 17
Numbers 26:1-51
Luke 2:36-52
Psalm 60:1-12
Proverbs 11:15

☐ March 18
Numbers 26:52–28:15
Luke 3:1-22
Psalm 61:1-8
Proverbs 11:16-17

☐ March 19
Numbers 28:16–29:40
Luke 3:23-38
Psalm 62:1-12
Proverbs 11:18-19

☐ March 20
Numbers 30:1–31:54
Luke 4:1-30
Psalm 63:1-11
Proverbs 11:20-21

☐ March 21
Numbers 32:1–33:39
Luke 4:31–5:11
Psalm 64:1-10
Proverbs 11:22

☐ March 22
Numbers 33:40–35:34
Luke 5:12-28
Psalm 65:1-13
Proverbs 11:23

☐ March 23
Numbers 36:1—Deuteronomy 1:46
Luke 5:29–6:11
Psalm 66:1-20
Proverbs 11:24-26

☐ March 24
Deuteronomy 2:1–3:29
Luke 6:12-38
Psalm 67:1-7
Proverbs 11:27

☐ March 25
Deuteronomy 4:1-49
Luke 6:39–7:10
Psalm 68:1-18
Proverbs 11:28

☐ March 26
Deuteronomy 5:1–6:25
Luke 7:11-35
Psalm 68:19-35
Proverbs 11:29-31

☐ March 27
Deuteronomy 7:1–8:20
Luke 7:36–8:3
Psalm 69:1-18
Proverbs 12:1

☐ March 28
Deuteronomy 9:1–10:22
Luke 8:4-21
Psalm 69:19-36
Proverbs 12:2-3

☐ March 29
Deuteronomy 11:1–12:32
Luke 8:22-39
Psalm 70:1-5
Proverbs 12:4

☐ March 30
Deuteronomy 13:1–15:23
Luke 8:40–9:6
Psalm 71:1-24
Proverbs 12:5-7

☐ March 31
Deuteronomy 16:1–17:20
Luke 9:7-27
Psalm 72:1-20
Proverbs 12:8-9

☐ April 1
Deuteronomy 18:1–20:20
Luke 9:28-50
Psalm 73:1-28
Proverbs 12:10

☐ April 2
Deuteronomy 21:1–22:30
Luke 9:51–10:12
Psalm 74:1-23
Proverbs 12:11

☐ April 3
Deuteronomy 23:1–25:19
Luke 10:13-37
Psalm 75:1-10
Proverbs 12:12-14

☐ April 4
Deuteronomy 26:1–27:26
Luke 10:38–11:13
Psalm 76:1-12
Proverbs 12:15-17

☐ April 5
Deuteronomy 28:1-68
Luke 11:14-36
Psalm 77:1-20
Proverbs 12:18

☐ April 6
Deuteronomy 29:1–30:20
Luke 11:37–12:7
Psalm 78:1-31
Proverbs 12:19-20

☐ April 7
Deuteronomy 31:1–32:27
Luke 12:8-34
Psalm 78:32-55
Proverbs 12:21-23

☐ April 8
Deuteronomy 32:28-52
Luke 12:35-59
Psalm 78:56-64
Proverbs 12:24

☐ **April 9**
Deuteronomy 33:1-29
Luke 13:1-21
Psalm 78:65-72
Proverbs 12:25

☐ **April 10**
Deuteronomy 34:1—Joshua 2:24
Luke 13:22–14:6
Psalm 79:1-13
Proverbs 12:26

☐ **April 11**
Joshua 3:1–4:24
Luke 14:7-35
Psalm 80:1-19
Proverbs 12:27-28

☐ **April 12**
Joshua 5:1–7:15
Luke 15:1-32
Psalm 81:1-16
Proverbs 13:1

☐ **April 13**
Joshua 7:16–9:2
Luke 16:1-18
Psalm 82:1-8
Proverbs 13:2-3

☐ **April 14**
Joshua 9:3–10:43
Luke 16:19–17:10
Psalm 83:1-18
Proverbs 13:4

☐ **April 15**
Joshua 11:1–12:24
Luke 17:11-37
Psalm 84:1-12
Proverbs 13:5-6

☐ **April 16**
Joshua 13:1–14:15
Luke 18:1-17
Psalm 85:1-13
Proverbs 13:7-8

☐ **April 17**
Joshua 15:1-63
Luke 18:18-43
Psalm 86:1-17
Proverbs 13:9-10

☐ **April 18**
Joshua 16:1–18:28
Luke 19:1-27
Psalm 87:1-7
Proverbs 13:11

☐ **April 19**
Joshua 19:1–20:9
Luke 19:28-48
Psalm 88:1-18
Proverbs 13:12-14

☐ **April 20**
Joshua 21:1–22:20
Luke 20:1-26
Psalm 89:1-13
Proverbs 13:15-16

☐ **April 21**
Joshua 22:21–23:16
Luke 20:27-47
Psalm 89:14-37
Proverbs 13:17-19

☐ **April 22**
Joshua 24:1-33
Luke 21:1-28
Psalm 89:38-52
Proverbs 13:20-23

☐ **April 23**
Judges 1:1–2:9
Luke 21:29–22:13
Psalm 90:1–91:16
Proverbs 13:24-25

☐ **April 24**
Judges 2:10–3:31
Luke 22:14-34
Psalm 92:1–93:5
Proverbs 14:1-2

☐ **April 25**
Judges 4:1–5:31
Luke 22:35-53
Psalm 94:1-23
Proverbs 14:3-4

☐ **April 26**
Judges 6:1-40
Luke 22:54–23:12
Psalm 95:1–96:13
Proverbs 14:5-6

☐ **April 27**
Judges 7:1–8:17
Luke 23:13-43
Psalm 97:1–98:9
Proverbs 14:7-8

☐ **April 28**
Judges 8:18–9:21
Luke 23:44–24:12
Psalm 99:1-9
Proverbs 14:9-10

☐ **April 29**
Judges 9:22–10:18
Luke 24:13-53
Psalm 100:1-5
Proverbs 14:11-12

☐ **April 30**
Judges 11:1–12:15
John 1:1-28
Psalm 101:1-8
Proverbs 14:13-14

☐ **May 1**
Judges 13:1–14:20
John 1:29-51
Psalm 102:1-28
Proverbs 14:15-16

☐ **May 2**
Judges 15:1–16:31
John 2:1-25
Psalm 103:1-22
Proverbs 14:17-19

☐ **May 3**
Judges 17:1–18:31
John 3:1-21
Psalm 104:1-23
Proverbs 14:20-21

☐ **May 4**
Judges 19:1–20:48
John 3:22–4:3
Psalm 104:24-35
Proverbs 14:22-24

☐ **May 5**
Judges 21:1—Ruth 1:22
John 4:4-42
Psalm 105:1-15
Proverbs 14:25

☐ **May 6**
Ruth 2:1–4:22
John 4:43-54
Psalm 105:16-36
Proverbs 14:26-27

☐ **May 7**
1 Samuel 1:1–2:21
John 5:1-23
Psalm 105:37-45
Proverbs 14:28-29

☐ **May 8**
1 Samuel 2:22–4:22
John 5:24-47
Psalm 106:1-12
Proverbs 14:30-31

☐ **May 9**
1 Samuel 5:1–7:17
John 6:1-21
Psalm 106:13-31
Proverbs 14:32-33

☐ **May 10**
1 Samuel 8:1–9:27
John 6:22-42
Psalm 106:32-48
Proverbs 14:34-35

☐ **May 11**
1 Samuel 10:1–11:15
John 6:43-71
Psalm 107:1-43
Proverbs 15:1-3

☐ **May 12**
1 Samuel 12:1–13:23
John 7:1-30
Psalm 108:1-13
Proverbs 15:4

☐ **May 13**
1 Samuel 14:1-52
John 7:31-53
Psalm 109:1-31
Proverbs 15:5-7

☐ **May 14**
1 Samuel 15:1–16:23
John 8:1-20
Psalm 110:1-7
Proverbs 15:8-10

☐ **May 15**
1 Samuel 17:1–18:4
John 8:21-30
Psalm 111:1-10
Proverbs 15:11

☐ **May 16**
1 Samuel 18:5–19:24
John 8:31-59
Psalm 112:1-10
Proverbs 15:12-14

☐ **May 17**
1 Samuel 20:1–21:15
John 9:1-41
Psalm 113:1–114:8
Proverbs 15:15-17

☐ **May 18**
1 Samuel 22:1–23:29
John 10:1-21
Psalm 115:1-18
Proverbs 15:18-19

☐ **May 19**
1 Samuel 24:1–25:44
John 10:22-42
Psalm 116:1-19
Proverbs 15:20-21

☐ **May 20**
1 Samuel 26:1–28:25
John 11:1-54
Psalm 117:1-2
Proverbs 15:22-23

☐ **May 21**
1 Samuel 29:1–31:13
John 11:55–12:19
Psalm 118:1-18
Proverbs 15:24-26

☐ **May 22**
2 Samuel 1:1–2:11
John 12:20-50
Psalm 118:19-29
Proverbs 15:27-28

☐ **May 23**
2 Samuel 2:12–3:39
John 13:1-30
Psalm 119:1-16
Proverbs 15:29-30

☐ **May 24**
2 Samuel 4:1–6:23
John 13:31–14:14
Psalm 119:17-32
Proverbs 15:31-32

☐ **May 25**
2 Samuel 7:1–8:18
John 14:15-31
Psalm 119:33-48
Proverbs 15:33

☐ **May 26**
2 Samuel 9:1–11:27
John 15:1-27
Psalm 119:49-64
Proverbs 16:1-3

☐ **May 27**
2 Samuel 12:1-31
John 16:1-33
Psalm 119:65-80
Proverbs 16:4-5

☐ **May 28**
2 Samuel 13:1-39
John 17:1-26
Psalm 119:81-96
Proverbs 16:6-7

☐ **May 29**
2 Samuel 14:1–15:22
John 18:1-24
Psalm 119:97-112
Proverbs 16:8-9

☐ **May 30**
2 Samuel 15:23–16:23
John 18:25–19:22
Psalm 119:113-128
Proverbs 16:10-11

☐ **May 31**
2 Samuel 17:1-29
John 19:23-42
Psalm 119:129-152
Proverbs 16:12-13

☐ **June 1**
2 Samuel 18:1–19:10
John 20:1-31
Psalm 119:153-176
Proverbs 16:14-15

☐ **June 2**
2 Samuel 19:11–20:13
John 21:1-25
Psalm 120:1-7
Proverbs 16:16-17

☐ **June 3**
2 Samuel 20:14–21:22
Acts 1:1-26
Psalm 121:1-8
Proverbs 16:18

☐ **June 4**
2 Samuel 22:1–23:23
Acts 2:1-47
Psalm 122:1-9
Proverbs 16:19-20

☐ **June 5**
2 Samuel 23:24–24:25
Acts 3:1-26
Psalm 123:1-4
Proverbs 16:21-23

☐ **June 6**
1 Kings 1:1-53
Acts 4:1-37
Psalm 124:1-8
Proverbs 16:24

☐ **June 7**
1 Kings 2:1–3:2
Acts 5:1-42
Psalm 125:1-5
Proverbs 16:25

☐ **June 8**
1 Kings 3:3–4:34
Acts 6:1-15
Psalm 126:1-6
Proverbs 16:26-27

☐ **June 9**
1 Kings 5:1–6:38
Acts 7:1-29
Psalm 127:1-5
Proverbs 16:28-30

☐ **June 10**
1 Kings 7:1-51
Acts 7:30-50
Psalm 128:1-6
Proverbs 16:31-33

☐ **June 11**
1 Kings 8:1-66
Acts 7:51–8:13
Psalm 129:1-8
Proverbs 17:1

☐ **June 12**
1 Kings 9:1–10:29
Acts 8:14-40
Psalm 130:1-8
Proverbs 17:2-3

☐ **June 13**
1 Kings 11:1–12:19
Acts 9:1-25
Psalm 131:1-3
Proverbs 17:4-5

☐ **June 14**
1 Kings 12:20–13:34
Acts 9:26-43
Psalm 132:1-18
Proverbs 17:6

☐ **June 15**
1 Kings 14:1–15:24
Acts 10:1-23
Psalm 133:1-3
Proverbs 17:7-8

☐ **June 16**
1 Kings 15:25–17:24
Acts 10:24-48
Psalm 134:1-3
Proverbs 17:9-11

☐ **June 17**
1 Kings 18:1-46
Acts 11:1-30
Psalm 135:1-21
Proverbs 17:12-13

☐ **June 18**
1 Kings 19:1-21
Acts 12:1-23
Psalm 136:1-26
Proverbs 17:14-15

☐ **June 19**
1 Kings 20:1–21:29
Acts 12:24–13:15
Psalm 137:1-9
Proverbs 17:16

☐ **June 20**
1 Kings 22:1-53
Acts 13:16-41
Psalm 138:1-8
Proverbs 17:17-18

☐ **June 21**
2 Kings 1:1–2:25
Acts 13:42–14:7
Psalm 139:1-24
Proverbs 17:19-21

☐ **June 22**
2 Kings 3:1–4:17
Acts 14:8-28
Psalm 140:1-13
Proverbs 17:22

☐ **June 23**
2 Kings 4:18–5:27
Acts 15:1-35
Psalm 141:1-10
Proverbs 17:23

☐ **June 24**
2 Kings 6:1–7:20
Acts 15:36–16:15
Psalm 142:1-7
Proverbs 17:24-25

☐ **June 25**
2 Kings 8:1–9:13
Acts 16:16-40
Psalm 143:1-12
Proverbs 17:26

☐ **June 26**
2 Kings 9:14–10:31
Acts 17:1-34
Psalm 144:1-15
Proverbs 17:27-28

☐ **June 27**
2 Kings 10:32–12:21
Acts 18:1-22
Psalm 145:1-21
Proverbs 18:1

☐ **June 28**
2 Kings 13:1–14:29
Acts 18:23–19:12
Psalm 146:1-10
Proverbs 18:2-3

☐ **June 29**
2 Kings 15:1–16:20
Acts 19:13-41
Psalm 147:1-20
Proverbs 18:4-5

☐ **June 30**
2 Kings 17:1–18:12
Acts 20:1-38
Psalm 148:1-14
Proverbs 18:6-7

☐ **July 1**
2 Kings 18:13–19:37
Acts 21:1-17
Psalm 149:1-9
Proverbs 18:8

☐ **July 2**
2 Kings 20:1–22:2
Acts 21:18-36
Psalm 150:1-6
Proverbs 18:9-10

☐ **July 3**
2 Kings 22:3–23:30
Acts 21:37–22:16
Psalm 1:1-6
Proverbs 18:11-12

☐ **July 4**
2 Kings 23:31–25:30
Acts 22:17–23:10
Psalm 2:1-12
Proverbs 18:13

☐ **July 5**
1 Chronicles 1:1–2:17
Acts 23:11-35
Psalm 3:1-8
Proverbs 18:14-15

☐ **July 6**
1 Chronicles 2:18–4:4
Acts 24:1-27
Psalm 4:1-8
Proverbs 18:16-18

☐ **July 7**
1 Chronicles 4:5–5:17
Acts 25:1-27
Psalm 5:1-12
Proverbs 18:19

☐ **July 8**
1 Chronicles 5:18–6:81
Acts 26:1-32
Psalm 6:1-10
Proverbs 18:20-21

☐ **July 9**
1 Chronicles 7:1–8:40
Acts 27:1-20
Psalm 7:1-17
Proverbs 18:22

☐ **July 10**
1 Chronicles 9:1–10:14
Acts 27:21-44
Psalm 8:1-9
Proverbs 18:23-24

☐ **July 11**
1 Chronicles 11:1–12:18
Acts 28:1-31
Psalm 9:1-12
Proverbs 19:1-3

☐ **July 12**
1 Chronicles 12:19–14:17
Romans 1:1-17
Psalm 9:13-20
Proverbs 19:4-5

☐ **July 13**
1 Chronicles 15:1–16:36
Romans 1:18-32
Psalm 10:1-15
Proverbs 19:6-7

☐ **July 14**
1 Chronicles 16:37–18:17
Romans 2:1-24
Psalm 10:16-18
Proverbs 19:8-9

☐ **July 15**
1 Chronicles 19:1–21:30
Romans 2:25–3:8
Psalm 11:1-7
Proverbs 19:10-12

☐ **July 16**
1 Chronicles 22:1–23:32
Romans 3:9-31
Psalm 12:1-8
Proverbs 19:13-14

☐ **July 17**
1 Chronicles 24:1–26:11
Romans 4:1-12
Psalm 13:1-6
Proverbs 19:15-16

☐ **July 18**
1 Chronicles 26:12–27:34
Romans 4:13–5:5
Psalm 14:1-7
Proverbs 19:17

☐ **July 19**
1 Chronicles 28:1–29:30
Romans 5:6-21
Psalm 15:1-5
Proverbs 19:18-19

☐ **July 20**
2 Chronicles 1:1–3:17
Romans 6:1-23
Psalm 16:1-11
Proverbs 19:20-21

☐ **July 21**
2 Chronicles 4:1–6:11
Romans 7:1-13
Psalm 17:1-15
Proverbs 19:22-23

☐ **July 22**
2 Chronicles 6:12–8:10
Romans 7:14–8:8
Psalm 18:1-15
Proverbs 19:24-25

☐ **July 23**
2 Chronicles 8:11–10:19
Romans 8:9-25
Psalm 18:16-36
Proverbs 19:26

☐ **July 24**
2 Chronicles 11:1–13:22
Romans 8:26-39
Psalm 18:37-50
Proverbs 19:27-29

☐ **July 25**
2 Chronicles 14:1–16:14
Romans 9:1-24
Psalm 19:1-14
Proverbs 20:1

☐ **July 26**
2 Chronicles 17:1–18:34
Romans 9:25–10:13
Psalm 20:1-9
Proverbs 20:2-3

☐ **July 27**
2 Chronicles 19:1–20:37
Romans 10:14–11:12
Psalm 21:1-13
Proverbs 20:4-6

☐ **July 28**
2 Chronicles 21:1–23:21
Romans 11:13-36
Psalm 22:1-18
Proverbs 20:7

☐ **July 29**
2 Chronicles 24:1–25:28
Romans 12:1-21
Psalm 22:19-31
Proverbs 20:8-10

☐ **July 30**
2 Chronicles 26:1–28:27
Romans 13:1-14
Psalm 23:1-6
Proverbs 20:11

☐ **July 31**
2 Chronicles 29:1-36
Romans 14:1-23
Psalm 24:1-10
Proverbs 20:12

☐ **August 1**
2 Chronicles 30:1–31:21
Romans 15:1-22
Psalm 25:1-15
Proverbs 20:13-15

☐ **August 2**
2 Chronicles 32:1–33:13
Romans 15:23–16:9
Psalm 25:16-22
Proverbs 20:16-18

☐ **August 3**
2 Chronicles 33:14–34:33
Romans 16:10-27
Psalm 26:1-12
Proverbs 20:19

☐ **August 4**
2 Chronicles 35:1–36:23
1 Corinthians 1:1-17
Psalm 27:1-6
Proverbs 20:20-21

☐ **August 5**
Ezra 1:1–2:70
1 Corinthians 1:18–2:5
Psalm 27:7-14
Proverbs 20:22-23

☐ **August 6**
Ezra 3:1–4:24
1 Corinthians 2:6–3:4
Psalm 28:1-9
Proverbs 20:24-25

☐ **August 7**
Ezra 5:1–6:22
1 Corinthians 3:5-23
Psalm 29:1-11
Proverbs 20:26-27

☐ **August 8**
Ezra 7:1–8:20
1 Corinthians 4:1-21
Psalm 30:1-12
Proverbs 20:28-30

☐ **August 9**
Ezra 8:21–9:15
1 Corinthians 5:1-13
Psalm 31:1-8
Proverbs 21:1-2

☐ **August 10**
Ezra 10:1-44
1 Corinthians 6:1-20
Psalm 31:9-18
Proverbs 21:3

☐ **August 11**
Nehemiah 1:1–3:14
1 Corinthians 7:1-24
Psalm 31:19-24
Proverbs 21:4

☐ **August 12**
Nehemiah 3:15–5:13
1 Corinthians 7:25-40
Psalm 32:1-11
Proverbs 21:5-7

☐ **August 13**
Nehemiah 5:14–7:60
1 Corinthians 8:1-13
Psalm 33:1-11
Proverbs 21:8-10

☐ **August 14**
Nehemiah 7:61–9:21
1 Corinthians 9:1-18
Psalm 33:12-22
Proverbs 21:11-12

☐ **August 15**
Nehemiah 9:22–10:39
1 Corinthians 9:19–10:13
Psalm 34:1-10
Proverbs 21:13

☐ **August 16**
Nehemiah 11:1–12:26
1 Corinthians 10:14-33
Psalm 34:11-22
Proverbs 21:14-16

☐ **August 17**
Nehemiah 12:27–13:31
1 Corinthians 11:1-16
Psalm 35:1-16
Proverbs 21:17-18

☐ **August 18**
Esther 1:1–3:15
1 Corinthians 11:17-34
Psalm 35:17-28
Proverbs 21:19-20

☐ **August 19**
Esther 4:1–7:10
1 Corinthians 12:1-26
Psalm 36:1-12
Proverbs 21:21-22

☐ **August 20**
Esther 8:1–10:3
1 Corinthians 12:27–13:13
Psalm 37:1-11
Proverbs 21:23-24

☐ **August 21**
Job 1:1–3:26
1 Corinthians 14:1-17
Psalm 37:12-29
Proverbs 21:25-26

☐ **August 22**
Job 4:1–7:21
1 Corinthians 14:18-40
Psalm 37:30-40
Proverbs 21:27

☐ **August 23**
Job 8:1–11:20
1 Corinthians 15:1-28
Psalm 38:1-22
Proverbs 21:28-29

☐ **August 24**
Job 12:1–15:35
1 Corinthians 15:29-58
Psalm 39:1-13
Proverbs 21:30-31

☐ **August 25**
Job 16:1–19:29
1 Corinthians 16:1-24
Psalm 40:1-10
Proverbs 22:1

☐ **August 26**
Job 20:1–22:30
2 Corinthians 1:1-11
Psalm 40:11-17
Proverbs 22:2-4

☐ **August 27**
Job 23:1–27:23
2 Corinthians 1:12–2:11
Psalm 41:1-13
Proverbs 22:5-6

☐ **August 28**
Job 28:1–30:31
2 Corinthians 2:12-17
Psalm 42:1-11
Proverbs 22:7

☐ **August 29**
Job 31:1–33:33
2 Corinthians 3:1-18
Psalm 43:1-5
Proverbs 22:8-9

☐ **August 30**
Job 34:1–36:33
2 Corinthians 4:1-12
Psalm 44:1-8
Proverbs 22:10-12

☐ **August 31**
Job 37:1–39:30
2 Corinthians 4:13–5:10
Psalm 44:9-26
Proverbs 22:13

☐ **September 1**
Job 40:1–42:17
2 Corinthians 5:11-21
Psalm 45:1-17
Proverbs 22:14

☐ **September 2**
Ecclesiastes 1:1–3:22
2 Corinthians 6:1-13
Psalm 46:1-11
Proverbs 22:15

☐ **September 3**
Ecclesiastes 4:1–6:12
2 Corinthians 6:14–7:7
Psalm 47:1-9
Proverbs 22:16

☐ **September 4**
Ecclesiastes 7:1–9:18
2 Corinthians 7:8-16
Psalm 48:1-14
Proverbs 22:17-19

☐ **September 5**
Ecclesiastes 10:1–12:14
2 Corinthians 8:1-15
Psalm 49:1-20
Proverbs 22:20-21

☐ **September 6**
Song of Songs 1:1–4:16
2 Corinthians 8:16-24
Psalm 50:1-23
Proverbs 22:22-23

☐ **September 7**
Song of Songs 5:1–8:14
2 Corinthians 9:1-15
Psalm 51:1-19
Proverbs 22:24-25

☐ **September 8**
Isaiah 1:1–2:22
2 Corinthians 10:1-18
Psalm 52:1-9
Proverbs 22:26-27

☐ **September 9**
Isaiah 3:1–5:30
2 Corinthians 11:1-15
Psalm 53:1-6
Proverbs 22:28-29

☐ **September 10**
Isaiah 6:1–7:25
2 Corinthians 11:16-33
Psalm 54:1-7
Proverbs 23:1-3

☐ **September 11**
Isaiah 8:1–9:21
2 Corinthians 12:1-10
Psalm 55:1-23
Proverbs 23:4-5

☐ **September 12**
Isaiah 10:1–11:16
2 Corinthians 12:11-21
Psalm 56:1-13
Proverbs 23:6-8

☐ **September 13**
Isaiah 12:1–14:32
2 Corinthians 13:1-13
Psalm 57:1-11
Proverbs 23:9-11

☐ **September 14**
Isaiah 15:1–18:7
Galatians 1:1-24
Psalm 58:1-11
Proverbs 23:12

☐ **September 15**
Isaiah 19:1–21:17
Galatians 2:1-16
Psalm 59:1-17
Proverbs 23:13-14

☐ **September 16**
Isaiah 22:1–24:23
Galatians 2:17–3:9
Psalm 60:1-12
Proverbs 23:15-16

☐ **September 17**
Isaiah 25:1–28:13
Galatians 3:10-22
Psalm 61:1-8
Proverbs 23:17-18

☐ **September 18**
Isaiah 28:14–30:11
Galatians 3:23–4:31
Psalm 62:1-12
Proverbs 23:19-21

☐ **September 19**
Isaiah 30:12–33:9
Galatians 5:1-12
Psalm 63:1-11
Proverbs 23:22

☐ **September 20**
Isaiah 33:10–36:22
Galatians 5:13-26
Psalm 64:1-10
Proverbs 23:23

☐ **September 21**
Isaiah 37:1–38:22
Galatians 6:1-18
Psalm 65:1-13
Proverbs 23:24

☐ **September 22**
Isaiah 39:1–41:16
Ephesians 1:1-23
Psalm 66:1-20
Proverbs 23:25-28

☐ **September 23**
Isaiah 41:17–43:13
Ephesians 2:1-22
Psalm 67:1-7
Proverbs 23:29-35

☐ **September 24**
Isaiah 43:14–45:10
Ephesians 3:1-21
Psalm 68:1-18
Proverbs 24:1-2

☐ **September 25**
Isaiah 45:11–48:11
Ephesians 4:1-16
Psalm 68:19-35
Proverbs 24:3-4

☐ **September 26**
Isaiah 48:12–50:11
Ephesians 4:17-32
Psalm 69:1-18
Proverbs 24:5-6

☐ **September 27**
Isaiah 51:1–53:12
Ephesians 5:1-33
Psalm 69:19-36
Proverbs 24:7

☐ **September 28**
Isaiah 54:1–57:14
Ephesians 6:1-24
Psalm 70:1-5
Proverbs 24:8

☐ **September 29**
Isaiah 57:15–59:21
Philippians 1:1-26
Psalm 71:1-24
Proverbs 24:9-10

☐ **September 30**
Isaiah 60:1–62:5
Philippians 1:27–2:18
Psalm 72:1-20
Proverbs 24:11-12

☐ **October 1**
Isaiah 62:6–65:25
Philippians 2:19–3:3
Psalm 73:1-28
Proverbs 24:13-14

☐ **October 2**
Isaiah 66:1-24
Philippians 3:4-21
Psalm 74:1-23
Proverbs 24:15-16

☐ **October 3**
Jeremiah 1:1–2:30
Philippians 4:1-23
Psalm 75:1-10
Proverbs 24:17-20

☐ **October 4**
Jeremiah 2:31–4:18
Colossians 1:1-17
Psalm 76:1-12
Proverbs 24:21-22

☐ **October 5**
Jeremiah 4:19–6:15
Colossians 1:18–2:7
Psalm 77:1-20
Proverbs 24:23-25

☐ **October 6**
Jeremiah 6:16–8:7
Colossians 2:8-23
Psalm 78:1-31
Proverbs 24:26

☐ **October 7**
Jeremiah 8:8–9:26
Colossians 3:1-17
Psalm 78:32-55
Proverbs 24:27

☐ October 8
Jeremiah 10:1–11:23
Colossians 3:18–4:18
Psalm 78:56-72
Proverbs 24:28-29

☐ October 9
Jeremiah 12:1–14:10
1 Thessalonians 1:1–2:8
Psalm 79:1-13
Proverbs 24:30-34

☐ October 10
Jeremiah 14:11–16:15
1 Thessalonians 2:9–3:13
Psalm 80:1-19
Proverbs 25:1-5

☐ October 11
Jeremiah 16:16–18:23
1 Thessalonians 4:1–5:3
Psalm 81:1-16
Proverbs 25:6-8

☐ October 12
Jeremiah 19:1–21:14
1 Thessalonians 5:4-28
Psalm 82:1-8
Proverbs 25:9-10

☐ October 13
Jeremiah 22:1–23:20
2 Thessalonians 1:1-12
Psalm 83:1-18
Proverbs 25:11-14

☐ October 14
Jeremiah 23:21–25:38
2 Thessalonians 2:1-17
Psalm 84:1-12
Proverbs 25:15

☐ October 15
Jeremiah 26:1–27:22
2 Thessalonians 3:1-18
Psalm 85:1-13
Proverbs 25:16

☐ October 16
Jeremiah 28:1–29:32
1 Timothy 1:1-20
Psalm 86:1-17
Proverbs 25:17

☐ October 17
Jeremiah 30:1–31:26
1 Timothy 2:1-15
Psalm 87:1-7
Proverbs 25:18-19

☐ October 18
Jeremiah 31:27–32:44
1 Timothy 3:1-16
Psalm 88:1-18
Proverbs 25:20-22

☐ October 19
Jeremiah 33:1–34:22
1 Timothy 4:1-16
Psalm 89:1-13
Proverbs 25:23-24

☐ October 20
Jeremiah 35:1–36:32
1 Timothy 5:1-25
Psalm 89:14-37
Proverbs 25:25-27

☐ October 21
Jeremiah 37:1–38:28
1 Timothy 6:1-21
Psalm 89:38-52
Proverbs 25:28

☐ October 22
Jeremiah 39:1–41:18
2 Timothy 1:1-18
Psalm 90:1–91:16
Proverbs 26:1-2

☐ October 23
Jeremiah 42:1–44:23
2 Timothy 2:1-21
Psalm 92:1–93:5
Proverbs 26:3-5

☐ October 24
Jeremiah 44:24–47:7
2 Timothy 2:22–3:17
Psalm 94:1-23
Proverbs 26:6-8

☐ October 25
Jeremiah 48:1–49:22
2 Timothy 4:1-22
Psalm 95:1–96:13
Proverbs 26:9-12

☐ October 26
Jeremiah 49:23–50:46
Titus 1:1-16
Psalm 97:1–98:9
Proverbs 26:13-16

☐ October 27
Jeremiah 51:1-53
Titus 2:1-15
Psalm 99:1-9
Proverbs 26:17

☐ October 28
Jeremiah 51:54–52:34
Titus 3:1-15
Psalm 100:1-5
Proverbs 26:18-19

☐ October 29
Lamentations 1:1–2:19
Philippians 1:1-25
Psalm 101:1-8
Proverbs 26:20

☐ October 30
Lamentations 2:20–3:66
Hebrews 1:1-14
Psalm 102:1-28
Proverbs 26:21-22

☐ October 31
Lamentations 4:1–5:22
Hebrews 2:1-18
Psalm 103:1-22
Proverbs 26:23

☐ November 1
Ezekiel 1:1–3:15
Hebrews 3:1-19
Psalm 104:1-23
Proverbs 26:24-26

☐ November 2
Ezekiel 3:16–6:14
Hebrews 4:1-16
Psalm 104:24-35
Proverbs 26:27

☐ November 3
Ezekiel 7:1–9:11
Hebrews 5:1-14
Psalm 105:1-15
Proverbs 26:28

☐ November 4
Ezekiel 10:1–11:25
Hebrews 6:1-20
Psalm 105:16-36
Proverbs 27:1-2

☐ **November 5**
Ezekiel 12:1–14:11
Hebrews 7:1-17
Psalm 105:37-45
Proverbs 27:3

☐ **November 6**
Ezekiel 14:12–16:41
Hebrews 7:18-28
Psalm 106:1-12
Proverbs 27:4-6

☐ **November 7**
Ezekiel 16:42–17:24
Hebrews 8:1-13
Psalm 106:13-31
Proverbs 27:7-9

☐ **November 8**
Ezekiel 18:1–19:14
Hebrews 9:1-10
Psalm 106:32-48
Proverbs 27:10

☐ **November 9**
Ezekiel 20:1-49
Hebrews 9:11-28
Psalm 107:1-43
Proverbs 27:11

☐ **November 10**
Ezekiel 21:1–22:31
Hebrews 10:1-17
Psalm 108:1-13
Proverbs 27:12

☐ **November 11**
Ezekiel 23:1-49
Hebrews 10:18-39
Psalm 109:1-31
Proverbs 27:13

☐ **November 12**
Ezekiel 24:1–26:21
Hebrews 11:1-16
Psalm 110:1-7
Proverbs 27:14

☐ **November 13**
Ezekiel 27:1–28:26
Hebrews 11:17-31
Psalm 111:1-10
Proverbs 27:15-16

☐ **November 14**
Ezekiel 29:1–30:26
Hebrews 11:32–12:13
Psalm 112:1-10
Proverbs 27:17

☐ **November 15**
Ezekiel 31:1–32:32
Hebrews 12:14-29
Psalm 113:1–114:8
Proverbs 27:18-20

☐ **November 16**
Ezekiel 33:1–34:31
Hebrews 13:1-25
Psalm 115:1-18
Proverbs 27:21-22

☐ **November 17**
Ezekiel 35:1–36:38
James 1:1-18
Psalm 116:1-19
Proverbs 27:23-27

☐ **November 18**
Ezekiel 37:1–38:23
James 1:19–2:17
Psalm 117:1-2
Proverbs 28:1

□ **November 19**
Ezekiel 39:1–40:27
James 2:18–3:18
Psalm 118:1-18
Proverbs 28:2

□ **November 20**
Ezekiel 40:28–41:26
James 4:1-17
Psalm 118:19-29
Proverbs 28:3-5

□ **November 21**
Ezekiel 42:1–43:27
James 5:1-20
Psalm 119:1-16
Proverbs 28:6-7

□ **November 22**
Ezekiel 44:1–45:12
1 Peter 1:1-12
Psalm 119:17-32
Proverbs 28:8-10

□ **November 23**
Ezekiel 45:13–46:24
1 Peter 1:13–2:10
Psalm 119:33-48
Proverbs 28:11

□ **November 24**
Ezekiel 47:1–48:35
1 Peter 2:11–3:7
Psalm 119:49-64
Proverbs 28:12-13

□ **November 25**
Daniel 1:1–2:23
1 Peter 3:8–4:6
Psalm 119:65-80
Proverbs 28:14

□ **November 26**
Daniel 2:24–3:30
1 Peter 4:7–5:14
Psalm 119:81-96
Proverbs 28:15-16

□ **November 27**
Daniel 4:1-37
2 Peter 1:1-21
Psalm 119:97-112
Proverbs 28:17-18

□ **November 28**
Daniel 5:1-31
2 Peter 2:1-22
Psalm 119:113-128
Proverbs 28:19-20

□ **November 29**
Daniel 6:1-28
2 Peter 3:1-18
Psalm 119:129-152
Proverbs 28:21-22

□ **November 30**
Daniel 7:1-28
1 John 1:1-10
Psalm 119:153-176
Proverbs 28:23-24

□ **December 1**
Daniel 8:1-27
1 John 2:1-17
Psalm 120:1-7
Proverbs 28:25-26

□ **December 2**
Daniel 9:1–11:1
1 John 2:18–3:6
Psalm 121:1-8
Proverbs 28:27-28

☐ **December 3**
Daniel 11:2-35
1 John 3:7-24
Psalm 122:1-9
Proverbs 29:1

☐ **December 4**
Daniel 11:36–12:13
1 John 4:1-21
Psalm 123:1-4
Proverbs 29:2-4

☐ **December 5**
Hosea 1:1–3:5
1 John 5:1-21
Psalm 124:1-8
Proverbs 29:5-8

☐ **December 6**
Hosea 4:1–5:15
2 John 1:1-13
Psalm 125:1-5
Proverbs 29:9-11

☐ **December 7**
Hosea 6:1–9:17
3 John 1:1-15
Psalm 126:1-6
Proverbs 29:12-14

☐ **December 8**
Hosea 10:1–14:9
Jude 1:1-25
Psalm 127:1-5
Proverbs 29:15-17

☐ **December 9**
Joel 1:1–3:21
Revelation 1:1-20
Psalm 128:1-6
Proverbs 29:18

☐ **December 10**
Amos 1:1–3:15
Revelation 2:1-17
Psalm 129:1-8
Proverbs 29:19-20

☐ **December 11**
Amos 4:1–6:14
Revelation 2:18–3:6
Psalm 130:1-8
Proverbs 29:21-22

☐ **December 12**
Amos 7:1–9:15
Revelation 3:7-22
Psalm 131:1-3
Proverbs 29:23

☐ **December 13**
Obadiah 1:1-21
Revelation 4:1-11
Psalm 132:1-18
Proverbs 29:24-25

☐ **December 14**
Jonah 1:1–4:11
Revelation 5:1-14
Psalm 133:1-3
Proverbs 29:26-27

☐ **December 15**
Micah 1:1–4:13
Revelation 6:1-17
Psalm 134:1-3
Proverbs 30:1-4

☐ **December 16**
Micah 5:1–7:20
Revelation 7:1-17
Psalm 135:1-21
Proverbs 30:5-6

☐ **December 17**
Nahum 1:1–3:19
Revelation 8:1-13
Psalm 136:1-26
Proverbs 30:7-9

☐ **December 18**
Habakkuk 1:1–3:19
Revelation 9:1-21
Psalm 137:1-9
Proverbs 30:10

☐ **December 19**
Zephaniah 1:1–3:20
Revelation 10:1-11
Psalm 138:1-8
Proverbs 30:11-14

☐ **December 20**
Haggai 1:1–2:23
Revelation 11:1-19
Psalm 139:1-24
Proverbs 30:15-16

☐ **December 21**
Zechariah 1:1-21
Revelation 12:1-17
Psalm 140:1-13
Proverbs 30:17

☐ **December 22**
Zechariah 2:1–3:10
Revelation 13:1-18
Psalm 141:1-10
Proverbs 30:18-20

☐ **December 23**
Zechariah 4:1–5:11
Revelation 14:1-20
Psalm 142:1-7
Proverbs 30:21-23

☐ **December 24**
Zechariah 6:1–7:14
Revelation 15:1-8
Psalm 143:1-12
Proverbs 30:24-28

☐ **December 25**
Zechariah 8:1-23
Revelation 16:1-21
Psalm 144:1-15
Proverbs 30:29-31

☐ **December 26**
Zechariah 9:1-17
Revelation 17:1-18
Psalm 145:1-21
Proverbs 30:32

☐ **December 27**
Zechariah 10:1–11:17
Revelation 18:1-24
Psalm 146:1-10
Proverbs 30:33

☐ **December 28**
Zechariah 12:1–13:9
Revelation 19:1-21
Psalm 147:1-20
Proverbs 31:1-7

☐ **December 29**
Zechariah 14:1-21
Revelation 20:1-15
Psalm 148:1-14
Proverbs 31:8-9

☐ **December 30**
Malachi 1:1–2:17
Revelation 21:1-27
Psalm 149:1-9
Proverbs 31:10-24

□ **December 31**
Malachi 3:1–4:6
Revelation 22:1-21
Psalm 150:1-6
Proverbs 31:25-31